For people who live in communities transformed by powerful outside forces, narrative accounts of culture contact and change create identity through the idiom of shared history. How may we understand the potent social, emotional and political meanings of such accounts for those who tell them? How and why do some narratives acquire a kind of mythic status as they are told and retold in a variety of contexts and genres?

Identity through history takes up these questions in an ethnography of identity formation on the island of Santa Isabel in the Solomon Islands. The people of Santa Isabel are heirs to one of the great stories of socio-religious transformation in the Pacific Islands region. Victimized by raiding headhunters in the nineteenth century, the entire population embraced Christianity around the turn of the century. This epic storyline is repeated often in narratives of conversion creating images of a shared past that enliven and personify understandings of self and community.

But just as history is never finished, neither is identity. It is continually refashioned as people make cultural meaning out of shifting social and political circumstances. Geoffrey White offers an approach to the cultural dynamics of self-construction that is at once synchronic and diachronic. He examines local histories as discourses of contemporary identity, while locating emergent identities within the longer perspective of one hundred years of colonial experience. The approach makes innovative use of recent work in psychological and historical anthropology to illuminate concepts of person and history that emerge in peoples' ongoing attempts to define and direct their lives.

Cambridge Studies in Social and Cultural Anthropology
Editors: Ernest Gellner, Jack Goody, Stephen Gudeman,
Michael Herzfeld, Jonathan Parry

83
Identity through history

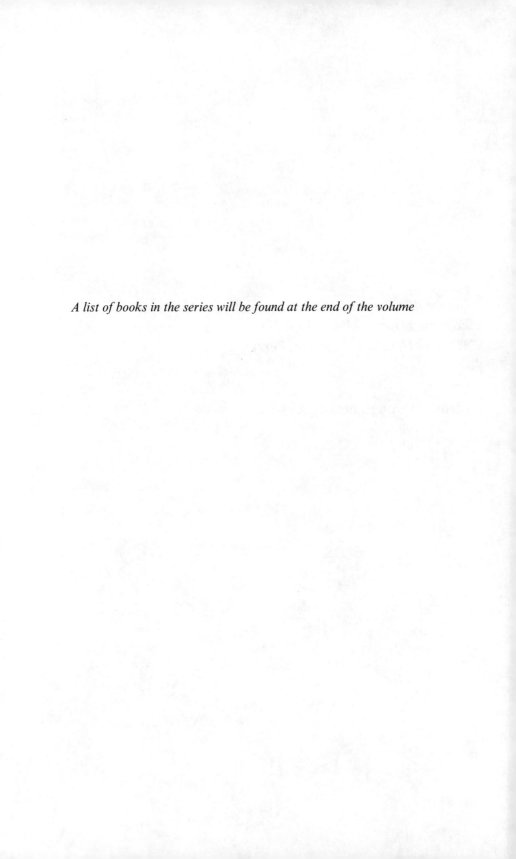

A list of books in the series will be found at the end of the volume

IDENTITY THROUGH HISTORY

Living stories in a Solomon Islands society

GEOFFREY M. WHITE
Institute of Culture and Communication
East–West Center, Honolulu, Hawaii

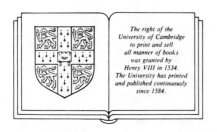

CAMBRIDGE UNIVERSITY PRESS
Cambridge
New York   Port Chester
Melbourne   Sydney

Published by the Press Syndicate of the University of Cambridge
The Pitt Building, Trumpington Street, Cambridge CB2 1RP
40 West 20th Street, New York, NY 10011-4211, USA
10 Stamford Road, Oakleigh, Melbourne 3166, Australia

First published 1991

Printed in Great Britain at the University Press, Cambridge

A catalogue record for this book is available from the British Library

Library of Congress cataloguing in publication data

White, Geoffrey M. (Geoffrey Miles), 1949–
    Identity through history: living stories in a Solomon Islands
society / Geoffrey M. White.
        p.   cm. – (Cambridge studies in social and cultural
anthropology : 83)
    Includes bibliographical references and index.
    ISBN 0 521 40172 0
    1. Ethnology – Solomon Islands – Santa Isabel Island. 2. Ethnicity –
Solomon Islands – Santa Isabel Island. 3. Missions – Solomon
Islands – Santa Isabel Island – History. 4. Oral tradition – Solomon
Islands – Santa Isabel Island. 5. Santa Isabel Island (Solomon
Islands) – Religious life and customs. 6. Santa Isabel Island
(Solomon Islands) – History. I. Title. II. Series.
GN671.S6W45   1992
306'.099593 – dc20   90-25590   CIP

ISBN 0 521 40172 0 hardback

For Nancy and Michael

Contents

Illustrations

Preface

Books are journeys. But unlike more ordinary forms of travel, points of departure and arrival are often not so easily fixed. One starting place for the present work can be located in December 1974 when I first went to the Solomon Islands to undertake research on the island of Santa Isabel for a doctoral degree in cultural anthropology. After spending a year and a half in the Solomons, I returned to write up my work in a dissertation titled "Big Men and Church Men: social images in Santa Isabel, Solomon Islands" (1978, University of California, San Diego). Despite many unexpected turns and twists, I managed in the dissertation to carry through with my initial plan to examine shared images of important or prestigious people, suggesting that such images are a kind of focal point for changes taking place in society.

However, with the benefit of hindsight and subsequent periods of research on Santa Isabel (in 1984, 1987 and 1988), I became increasingly dissatisfied with that work. One reason for the dissatisfaction was the sense that I had somehow not done justice to the wonderful stories that people tell about their society and about the past, especially as personified in ancestors and other historic figures. This book is an attempt to give those stories their due, while still probing for the cultural threads that hold history and identity together. In taking this tack, it has become resoundingly clear that it is in large measure through such stories, both small and large, personal and collective, that Santa Isabel people do much of the "identity work" which I had started out to investigate in the first place.

Placing narrative texts and practices at the centerpiece of this study, rather than at the margins as a source of statements about "oral history" or "precontact culture," serves to highlight the constructed character of culture and identity as constantly remade in the course of everyday life. To reiterate what has become a familiar refrain in contemporary anthropology, culture and identity are neither homogenous nor static, but emerge in social contexts where multiple realities contend for a hearing. The questions which guide this study, then, are not to find "the culture" or to give a definitive portrait of Santa Isabel identity, but rather to explore those processes – both conceptual and social – that make identity and history out of experience.

Of course, this book is itself a story – a kind of story of stories – that ultimately conspires with its subject to produce a coherent (and authoritative) narrative of cultural history. There is a certain inevitability about this. Focusing upon stories that are repeated often adds yet further repetition, expanding their field of circulation. And, translating and publishing oral narratives in written form not only extends their range of circulation (now finding a place on dusty shelves in foreign libraries), but adds to their local prestige and fixity. It is here that interpretive caution is urged. While I am deliberately focusing upon dominant forms of collective representation in Santa Isabel, this volume is inevitably shaped by my own identity, by the historical moment in which I have done fieldwork, by the nature of my relations with people discussed, and by the obvious limits of my knowledge of local language and culture.

First of all, this text both benefits and suffers from being written by an outsider to Isabel society. Since I first began work there in 1975, several Santa Isabel writers have produced their own published commentaries about local culture and history – commentaries that figure significantly in the pages to follow (e.g., Lagusu 1986; Naramana 1987; Vilasa 1986; Zeva 1983; and cf. Bogesi 1948). These writings are an important development in local modes of self-representation (heralding new practices which, combined with the advent of audio and video recording for similar purposes, are affecting the nature of modern identity-making). In many ways these local works are complementary to the present volume, with descriptive and documentary aims that differ from this book's more analytic and comparative objectives. Nonetheless, the work presented here has benefited greatly from information and perspectives garnered from the work of authors who are part of Isabel society and who draw upon a wealth of local knowledge and intuition. In the spirit of reciprocity, I hope that this volume will provide a resource for these scholars and others interested in examining their own society and history from new perspectives.

Secondly, I have no doubt that a female ethnographer would spend more time talking with women than I have, would uncover and emphasize dimensions of Isabel society that are missed or only glimpsed here. I am acutely aware of this limitation, and only hope that some of the gaps and distortions in this study will emerge with enough clarity to stimulate further research on issues related to gender and women's lives in Santa Isabel.

As a final qualifying note, a word about islands. It is all too easy to produce images of "culture" or "community" as bounded units, especially when writing about island societies where geography offers spatial boundaries that frequently do become a basis for group definition. In one sense, this is a book about Santa Isabel society. But most of the cultural material derives from only one of four language groups (Cheke Holo or A'ara) that inhabit the island, and, within that area, from one specific subregion (Maringe). I have hedged on this issue in the title for this volume by referring to "a Solomon Islands society," but even such a singular notion as that tends to reify the fluid nature of cultural identity. One of the arguments made in this book is that a sense of island identity, of Isabelness, is historically emergent and subject to the forces that interconnect Santa Isabel villages with wider arenas of meaning and power. The geocultural focus of this book may be visualized as a series of permeable concentric circles, with the center focused on a few villages in the Maringe area of Santa Isabel, and people, ideas and material flowing back and forth through island, national and international spheres of activity. The significance of this traffic for the subject of this book – making identity through history – can hardly be overemphasized. With a new satellite dish just introduced into the island's provincial center providing telephone and facsimile service to villagers who can afford them, and with numerous entrepreneurs now running village video showings, the emergence of new histories and new identities is assured.

Acknowledgments

This study is based on fieldwork on the island of Santa Isabel in the Solomon Islands begun during sixteen months in 1975 and 1976, and continued during shorter two-month visits in 1984, 1987 and 1988. During most of the first period of fieldwork my wife, Nancy Montgomery, shared the experience and assisted immeasurably with the tasks of living and learning. At that time we lived in the village of Vavarenitu on the eastern side of the Maringe coast. We focused our work in the villages within daily walking distance of Vavarenitu, but also traveled occasionally by boat or canoe to other parts of the island. During subsequent visits I (and, on one occasion, we – including son Michael) have resided primarily in Buala village, at the center of the Maringe area. There is simply no way adequately to thank our friends and acquaintances in those areas who have consistently welcomed us into their homes and villages, showing kindness through our on-again off-again associations.

Although it is difficult to single out individuals, Eric and Vivian Anderson, Fr. Dudley Bale, Fr. John Bale, Willie Betu, Eric and Edith Ehamana, Florence Gasetei, Griffin and Grace Hebala, Nathaniel Hebala, Kamnis Kame, Henry Kelimana, David Kera, Francis Kokhonigita, George Kolton, Timothy Lehemae, Josepa Lokutadi, Lionel Longa, Dennis Lulei, Bafet Luvu, David Nagadi, Richard Naramana, Bishop Ellison Pogo, Hugo Pulomana, Patteson Radukana, Charles Thegna Pado, Thomas Tugamana, retired Bishop Dudley Tuti, Forest Voko and Brown Zalamana have all given special support.

The study would not have been possible without the help of several organizations at key points. Fieldwork in 1975–6 was supported by a Foreign Area Fellowship from the Social Science Research Council and a grant from the Wenner Gren Foundation for Anthropological Research. Subsequent research has been supported by the Wenner Gren Foundation in 1984 and the National Endowment for the Humanities in 1987 and 1988 (RO-21385). Their assistance is gratefully acknowledged.

Many people have provided guidance and assistance making it possible to meet the demands and opportunities of fieldwork. Lawrence Foanaota at the National Museum has been a valued friend and continuing source of advice, as has Joseph Wale at the University of the South Pacific Center. During her period at the Solomon Islands Museum, Anna Craven was both a hospitable host and a unique source of practical help. Brian Hackman generously shared his knowledge, word-lists and notes on the sound patterns of Isabel languages; and my work in the National Library of Australia was facilitated by a stay with Ian and Lala Frazer in Canberra. Lastly, I am indebted to Harold Scheffler and Roger Keesing for steering me toward Santa Isabel and the Maringe area in the first place.

Intellectual debts accumulated in the planning and execution of this study amount to a genealogy too complex to enumerate adequately. I have gained valuable historical information through conversation and correspondence with David Akin, the Rev. Richard Fallowes, David Hilliard, Kim Jackson and Hugh Laracy, among others. Numerous members of the Department of Anthropology at the University of California, San Diego provided ideas, advice and inspiration during the initial stages of this work, especially Roy D'Andrade, Fred Bailey, Donald Tuzin, and Theodore Schwartz, who first introduced me to Melanesia and the rites fieldwork.

My thinking and writing during recent years has profited enormously from continuing conversations with a number of colleagues, including Vilsoni Hereniko, Dorothy Holland, Edwin Hutchins, Karen Ito, Catherine Lutz, Peggy Miller, Naomi Quinn, Donald Rubinstein, George Saunders and Karen Watson-Gegeo. I would particularly like to thank John Kirkpatrick as well as David Gegeo, Lamont Lindstrom and Bradd Shore for critical readings that led to substantial improvements in this book. Finally, I thank my wife Nancy who has been a contributor and partner in this journey from the beginning.

Orthography

The language with which this study is concerned is spoken in both the Maringe and Hograno regions of Santa Isabel. The name of the language is a matter of some variation. Whereas it is most often referred to as "Maringe language" or "Hograno language" in these regions, names for the language as a whole include "A'ara" and "Cheke Holo" (literally, "bush language"). Following local preferences, the latter usage is adopted in this volume.

In a recently completed dictionary of Cheke Holo, I outline two different orthographies: one that is most commonly in use by Cheke Holo speakers today, and another that does not call for diacritic marks so that it can be more easily rendered on a typewriter (White, Kokhonigita and Pulomana 1988: xi). It is the latter form that I use here, with the exception of personal names for which local spellings are retained. I do not make any strong claims of phonemic exhaustiveness for the orthography outlined below.

Perhaps the most difficult aspect of the language's sounds for an English speaker is its extensive use of aspirated/unaspirated distinctions. The English consonants /l/, /r/, /m/, /n/, /p/, /t/ and /k/ all have both aspirated and unaspirated realizations, as do the velar affricate "ɣ" (written /gh/), the velar nasal "ŋ" (written /ng/) and the nasal palatal as in the Italian "campagna" (written /gn/). Aspiration is indicated by an "h," either following (/ph/, /kh/, /th/) or preceding (/hl/, /hr/, /hm/, /hn/, /hgh/, /hng/, /hgn/) the relevant consonant. The phonemic repertoire also includes /h/, /b/, /v/, /d/, /f/, /s/, /ch/ and a glottal stop /'/. The palatal sounds /j/ and /z/ appear to be in free variation, with /z/ being replaced by /j/ in the idiolects of younger speakers. There are five vowels: /i/ as in "eat," /e/ as in "egg," /a/ as in the first a of "banana," /o/ as in "open" and /u/ as in "new."

1

Introduction

Soga, before he converted to the Christian religion, offered a human sacrifice to his god, cutting off a child's head, and with his warriors drank the blood of the child to make his conversion to Christianity and renounce his allegiance to his god.

Excerpt from program to install a paramount chief, Sepi village, July 8, 1975

In July of 1975 people from all parts of the island of Santa Isabel congregated in Sepi village for a ceremony to install a paramount chief and celebrate the independence of the Church of Melanesia. The status of paramount chief, which had lain dormant for two decades, was revived in a masterful ritual performance that saw the Bishop of Santa Isabel, Dudley Tuti, "anointed" as paramount chief. To observers accustomed to separating indigenous custom from Christianity, there would appear to be considerable irony in the melding of the two agendas: installing a paramount chief, symbol of local tradition, at the same time as marking the independence of the church – the institution that has had the most to do with transforming indigenous practices. However, for the actors involved, the Sepi ceremony was anything but ironic. For them the ceremony was but the latest, if most dramatic, attempt to realize models of identity and history that intertwine elements of "custom" (*kastom* in local Pidgin) and Christianity that run deep in Santa Isabel social experience.

The Sepi ceremony was ritual performance on a grand scale. Most of the island's adult population participated in the planning, and about two thousand joined in the celebrations that lasted two days. In practical, political terms, however, the events at Sepi had little immediate effect. A paramount chief was installed, but the man given that title, Bishop Dudley Tuti, was already a kind of de facto paramount chief who wielded island-wide influence as the dominant spiritual leader and spokesman for community development. Furthermore the ritual installation effected no change in the government apparatus of the time that consisted of elected officials giving only rhetorical recognition to the role of "chiefs" in the colonial state. Why, then, the enthusiasm for an event that would seem to be largely symbolic in effect? The answers to this question lie partly in the significance of the "paramount chief" for cultural self-understanding, and partly in the longer process of colonial history that has given the idea both meaning and force through time.

By framing the Sepi ceremony with allusions to the conversion of the first paramount chief, Soga, the organizers located the occasion within a historical perspective extending one hundred years into the past. One of the remarkable aspects of the status of paramount chief on Santa Isabel is that it is avowedly an invented tradition, a product of colonial and missionary experience. But far from detracting from its value, the mission origins of the paramount chief give the status much of its significance as a symbol that enlivens and combines just those meanings that originate in the conjunction of *kastom* and Christianity. By engaging in a ritual performance that revives a "traditional" status by harking back to its mission origins, the participants in the Sepi ceremony remind us that traditions and the social identities that embody them do not consist of discrete essences or dichoto-mous oppositions such as pagan/Christian or indigenous/Western, but are always relational, creative and emergent (cf. Clifford 1988: 10).

Whereas the resurgence of self-conscious notions of tradition or *kastom* throughout island Melanesia is often framed in terms of exclusionary oppositions and struggles for power (see Keesing and Tonkinson 1982), cases such as Santa Isabel exemplify attempts to fashion identities that combine oppositional themes in novel syncretic formulations. The contem-porary Pacific is full of such syncretic or "creolized" forms – forms that challenge simplistic or dichotomous notions of tradition and modernity. As Pacific Islanders in all parts of the region grapple with exogenous forces of colonialism and world capitalism, symbols of the indigenous, of tradition, have emerged as a central idiom of self-definition and political action (Linnekin 1990). Inevitably, the proliferation of self-conscious images of the pre-Western past in the speeches of national politicians, in art festivals and in church ceremonies has evoked commentaries of inauthenticity from observers who balk at the juxtaposition of Christian hymns and custom songs in national ceremonies or at chiefly statuses created for modern purposes (e.g., Babadzan 1988). However, these apparent ironies are more a problem for the observer than for people involved. Debates about these issues are producing a greater awareness of the inherently creative and processual quality of culture, challenging our implicit separation of unchanging "tradition" from changing "history" (Handler and Linnekin 1983; Hanson 1989; Jolly 1990; Toren 1989; and cf. Wagner 1975). What seems clear from this interpretive wrangle is that anyone interested in the study of cultural traditions must pay close attention to the processes through which local understandings of tradition and history are con-structed and valorized. A finer appreciation of the ways in which the past is conceptualized and put to use in people's lives is showing that questions about what aspects of culture are "indigenous" or "authentic" do not tell us much about either culture or social process. As stated by Jolly, ". . . let us look more carefully and comparatively at the encoding of past–present relations in the variety of symbolic constituents of tradition. Then our questions might cease to be those of persistence versus invention, or whether tradition is genuine or spurious" (1990: 19).

Students of ethnic and cultural identity have often suggested that self-conscious constructions of identity emerge under conditions of contrast and opposition; that only with an awareness of difference do reflexive understandings of culture become externalized and objectified. For example, one of the postulates put forward in a collection of essays on "reinventing traditional culture" in Melanesia is that the experience of colonialism induces people to view collective identity in more self-conscious ways than ever before, with indigenous traditions that were once taken for granted becoming objects of reflection and evaluation (Keesing and Tonkinson 1982). It seems clear that the colonial encounter challenged local forms of meaning and power to a degree never experienced before. But to what extent externalizations of local culture in the colonial context are qualitatively different from precolonial constructions remains an open question, especially in a region as acutely aware of microcultural differences as Melanesia (Jolly 1990; Linnekin and Poyer 1990). To answer such questions we must examine the contexts and practices in which self-conscious understandings of tradition are formulated in relation to broader social, political and personal concerns. As illustrated by the Santa Isabel paramount chief ceremony, one of the most potent modes of externalizing understandings of culture and difference is historical reflection – often used to recall moments of contact and change that link a modern or "new" present with a traditional or "old" past (Thomas 1991).

Person, self and history
The 1975 installation of a paramount chief was a somewhat larger and more dramatic version of the storytelling and ritual practices that villagers commonly employ to recall the past. Histories told and remembered by those who inherit them are discourses of identity; just as identity is inevitably a discourse of history. Recent anthropological studies, especially in the Pacific, have drawn attention to the pervasive *use* of history within local frameworks of meaning and action (e.g., Biersack 1991; Borofsky 1987; Carrier n.d.; Parmentier 1987). Moving away from earlier views of oral history or ethnohistory which saw local recollections as distorted representations that could be useful only if cleansed of biases and inaccuracies, these approaches look to historical narration precisely because it is

ideological. Parmentier, who acknowledges the place of actors' intentions in historical ethnography, puts the matter succinctly: ". . . the historical study of other cultures is always the study of historicizing activities within those cultures" (1987: 7).

With a growing number of ethnographies that are explicitly historical (e.g., Gewertz 1983) and histories that are culturally informed (e.g., Dening 1980; Hanlon 1988), there is increasing interest in the problems of representing transformative processes in culture on the one hand, and assessing the role of cultural meaning in history on the other. One of the most influential statements to emerge from this nexus of culture and history is the work of Marshall Sahlins, based on careful analyses of early Hawaiian, Maori and Fijian contact history (e.g., 1985). Sahlins has sought to identify semiotic structures that give meaning to events, at the same time as the structures are themselves transformed by time and circumstance. Framed in this way, a central problematic becomes the reconciliation of cultural "structure" and historical "event," so that culture can be put in motion, and history can be reinvested with local significance. But formulating the problem in this way tends to reify culture by locating meaning in abstract relational structures that must then be reconnected with the politicized and emotionalized world of experience. In this book I am also concerned with finding threads of cultural continuity and discontinuity through time, but rather than seek these in textual histories, I look toward the meaning-making activities of people who live and remember a past that leads unerringly to the present.

The theoretical formulations that emerge from Sahlins' structural history are driven in large measure by the nature of his data: observations from afar of historic, even heroic, figures whose actions and motives must be divined from documentary sources long since removed from the contexts in which interested actors seek to negotiate matters of feeling and power. While Sahlins says that historically significant signs take on meaning according to their "instrumental value to the acting subject" (1985: 150) (as well as from their relations with other signs), he does not pursue the implications of this formulation. Without contemporary islanders included in the analysis, the possibilities for exploring cultural understandings from the vantage point of reflexive selves are distinctly limited. In this book, where the historical events of interest continue to be remembered and negotiated by those involved (or their descendants), culturally constituted histories express the social concerns and motives of local actors. Particularly in small island communities where individual and collective identities are so tightly bound, historical discourse locates both self and community within a nexus of relations between past and present, self and other.

In a recent commentary on "the ease with which it is argued that people represent 'society' to themselves," Strathern (1988: 9) argues that ethnographic accounts of Pacific cultures frequently impute global modes of self-reflection that falsely homogenize and systematize the inherently diverse and emergent quality of social process. This critique leads to the questions "What *do* people represent to themselves?" and "For what purposes, and in what contexts do self-conscious formulations of identity emerge?" For, as Strathern notes, it cannot be assumed in this kind of cross-cultural endeavor that "their" contexts and "our" contexts are so easily mapped. In this volume I focus particularly on practices of collective self-representation, and ask how certain forms of understanding obtain intersubjective meaning and force. "What are the cognitive, social and political processes that make certain types of discourse meaningful and compelling as representations of collective identity?"

One of the broad themes to emerge from historical ethnographies in Pacific societies is that people in small villages inevitably orient to, and struggle with, powerful encapsulating forces of colonialism and modernity. Typical of the broad shift in ethnographic writing during the 1970s and 80s toward themes of colonialism and resistance (Bruner 1986), recent studies in the Pacific have focused upon "the resources Pacific islanders have for the active and creative reproduction of their social identities in face of the enormous material and meaning-making power of an expanding 'world system'" (Lederman 1986: 3). One of the major resources islanders have in these efforts is history-making. Island peoples everywhere are producing narratives of colonization and acculturation that forcefully shape the social realities of contemporary life.

Stories about the past are an important, universal vehicle for self-definition (see Gergen 1990; Miller et al. 1990). Whether we call them "social history," "life history" or "personal stories," retrospective narratives create the present through idioms of remembrance. It may seem odd to lump together social history and personal stories, given our predilections for regarding the former as collective, societal and distant, and the latter as individual, psychological and immediate, but the differences are more a product of our (Western) concepts of the person than any given quality of social reality.

Despite the view articulated by symbolic interactionists that self-understanding emerges from *dialectic* processes of "internalization" and "externalization" (Berger and Luckmann 1967; Mead 1934), most theorizing has tended to split these processes and to turn the study of the self into a study of "what gets internalized" in individuals (cf. Kondo 1990). What gets lost, however, is the obverse process of externalization whereby cultural meanings are socially constructed and valorized. Charles Taylor notes the loss of "common meaning" as one of the silences in social theory maintained by these dichotomizing tendencies in our language:

Common meanings, as well as intersubjective ones, fall through the net of mainstream social science. They can find no place in its categories. For they are not simply a converging set of subjective reactions, but part of the common world. What the ontology of mainstream social science lacks is a notion of meaning as not just for an individual subject; of a subject who can be a "we" as well as an "I." The exclusion of this possibility, of the communal, comes once again from the baleful influence of the epistemological tradition for which all knowledge is reconstructed from the impressions imprinted on the individual subject. *(Taylor 1979: 52; cited in Shore 1991: 10–11)*

Anyone who has been in Pacific villages has become accustomed to hearing people speak in the voice of the communal "we," whether inclusively toward comembers or exclusively toward listening "others." Rather than assume that these usages simply indicate a plurality of individual "I"s, we might ask what they say about forms of subjectivity and experience. These pronominal forms find parallels in a great many representational practices that center agency and identity in collectivities and relations rather than (or in addition to) individuals. And, conversely, other historical practices turn individual actions into metonyms of communal experience. In the tightly interwoven and constantly public arenas of village life where persons are conceptualized as enmeshed in interdependent relations of all sorts (Read 1955; Leenhardt 1979; Shore 1982; Kirkpatrick 1983; White and Kirkpatrick 1985), social and moral thought frequently de-emphasize the individual as the primary locus of experience.

One of the most effective means for reproducing communal selfhood is historical narration. The approach taken here seeks to avoid reducing historical discourse to either the sociological abstraction of Durkheimian collective representations or the psychological reduction of inner selves. Much of the sociological research on collective identities has proceeded on the basis of assumptions about ethnicity that bundle together such "primordial sentiments" of shared ancestry, language and religion (cf. Linnekin and Poyer 1990). However, presuming the existence of ethnic groups or uniform folk concepts of ethnicity has diverted attention away from the contexts and processes that actually produce shared identifications during the course of everyday social life. In studying a case of somewhat ambiguous, emergent "ethnicity," Karen Blu concludes:

Collective identities that can be seen as irreducible tangles of concepts, emotions, and motivations can be found in many areas of the world, but it is far from clear that all of what have been labeled "ethnic groups" have the same kind of identity. Some or even much of what has been designated in the literature as ethnicity might better be considered as varieties of politicized self-identification.   *(1980: 234)*

The history of Christianization and colonization in Santa Isabel has seen the emergence of new collective identifications at the level of the island as a whole. Notions of a shared island-wide identity shaped by Anglican Christianity and government institutions have emerged in counterpoint with the island's linguistic and regional microtraditions. While it is tempting to draw parallels between these developments and attempts globally to build national identities that contend with prior ethnic affiliations, the mix of creolized identities in Santa Isabel is not well represented by rigid distinctions between primordial ethnic identifications and the more inclusive forms of an incipient state. Rather, the recent history of Santa Isabel offers an opportunity to explore the emergence of syncretic political forms that interpenetrate and compete with the standard orthodoxies of Western style democratic government. Whether these novel forms succeed or not, they emanate from, and find legitimacy in, local discourses of tradition and history.

Conversion narrative

Historical narrative is widespread in the daily life of Santa Isabel villages, and is particularly prominent during occasions of feasting and celebration when people engage in exchange practices that define social and political relations. Such occasions always involve speeches, songs and/or dramatic performances that recall past events constitutive of relations among participants. The most prominent and frequently repeated topics in these local histories are moments of first contact with missionaries and subsequent conversion to Christianity. Although World War II and national independence are also significant junctures in temporal consciousness, the events of Christian conversion are uniquely important in the organization of sociohistorical memory. Indications of this salience are to be found in the many regional variants of conversion stories throughout the island, and in their repeated performance on ceremonial occasions. When I first began to work in Santa Isabel, I had not anticipated the significance of these mythic histories. It was only in digesting the stories that were repeatedly volunteered for recording, and in observing numerous re-enactments of mission history, that I began to realize their importance.

For societies whose recent history is one of accommodation with colonial institutions of mission and government, stories of past encounters with "outsiders" reproduce understandings of community structured by oppositions of "inside" and "outside." In the process of producing images of community, narratives of early Christian contact and transformation also use oppositions of "old" and "new" to revitalize contemporary Christian identity. In doing so, such narratives do more than represent a calculus of identity types; they also constitute moral parables.

As an example of the overtly moral tones of some historical narration, consider the following excerpt from an essay written by a Santa Isabel schoolboy. At my request, a class of junior high school children (standard seven) in Santa Isabel wrote essays on the topic "What was life like in Santa Isabel before the church came?" Allowing for the fact that simply posing a question in this way tends to elicit highly stereotypic answers, most of the essays formulated their image of the past by inverting ideals of the present. An excerpt from the beginning of one essay written by a sixteen-year-old boy is typical of many responses (my translation):

Beginning in the past, our ancestors, our fathers and mothers did not understand the love (*nahma*) that we know today. And they didn't know about the togetherness (*fofodu*) of the present time either. They did know about killing people, about eating people and about fighting . . . But life in the past was extremely difficult. People did not live in happiness (*gleale'a*) or love. Nor did they sleep calmly (*blakno*). If they were traveling or sleeping, they could not forget their clubs, their axes or their spears. They would always prepare so that if they went and saw another group they could attack them . . .

This excerpt crystallizes the manner in which images of past and present define one another in historical narrative. By beginning his essay with the remark that his ancestors "did not understand the love that we know today," the author makes explicit what is often left unstated: characterizations of the past presume a culturally constituted present. In this instance, the ethos of pre-Christian life is portrayed in terms of contemporary understandings about persons, emotions and actions associated with Christian identity. The past life is imaged in terms of violent activities (killing and cannibalism) and personal experiences that are the antithesis of Christian "love" and "togetherness." The essay is notable for its use of negation: the narrator's pre-Christian ancestors are characterized as living without "love," "togetherness" or "happiness." No shadings of ambiguity or syncretism here: the features of past and present are sharply drawn through a series of contrastive oppositions. In its overdrawn simplicity the boy's portrait echoes the rhetoric of early missionary writings throughout the Pacific that consistently phrased their project in terms of polarized images of "light" and "dark," "kindness" and "cruelty," "knowledge" and "ignorance."

Indeed, missionary writers also found in Santa Isabel a story of transformation that was easily appropriated to narratives of missionary progress. At the time missionaries first began to work on the island in the latter part of the nineteenth century, most of the population had been victimized by headhunting raids emanating from the western Solomons where enterprising groups had armed themselves with new weapons acquired in a thriving trade with Europeans (Jackson 1975; White 1979). The resulting killing and disruption depopulated some regions and forced many Isabel people off their land. As one missionary writer described pre-Christian life on the island:

Fifty years ago Santa Isabel in the Solomon Islands must have been anything but a pleasant place of residence. Head hunters came down from New Georgia and Roviana, or the chiefs raided among themselves. No man could have felt his head securely fixed, and the only tolerably safe dwelling places were the forts on the hills and the houses in the trees. *(Wilson 1935: 6)*

This author's characterization of unrestrained violence and fear is the ground against which the figure of Christianity was often drawn in mission accounts, much like the schoolboy's account of a past in which people "could not forget their clubs, their axes or their spears." The parallel suggests that missionary discourse has shaped local understandings of the past. For evidence of this one could point to the widespread use of missionary metaphors of "light" and "dark" to refer to "heathens" and Christians ("heathens" as *bongihehe* or, literally, "dark mind" and Christianity as *Khilo'au*, "call out of darkness"), as evident in the uniforms of the Melanesian Brothers, an evangelical group of young Solomon Islands Anglicans formed in 1925 who wear black shirts and shorts with a white sash and black waistcloth symbolizing "the light of Christ, shining in the midst of the heathen" (Whiteman 1983: 238). But the hegemony of mission rhetoric is by no means complete. When used within the contexts of local social and religious practice, terms that originate in missionary language are assimilated to local frameworks of meaning and modes of understanding.

The overriding feature of locally produced histories that distinguishes them from European mission history is that they are reflexive – about people's own ancestors and communities. In this sense, they are also about the self. In the school essay, like the many stories and songs that portray mission history, historical figures are often extensions of the self. When the boy begins his statement by referring to "our ancestors, our fathers and mothers," he links himself to the past (and the narrative that represents it) through bonds of descent, land and "custom." Present and past, self and other are joined in mutually defining relations. Even where the relations are posed in an idiom of opposition or difference, they presuppose a sense of self-continuity through time. Where the subjects of recollection are connected to the narrator, the significance of historical narrative as self-commentary is inescapable.

The moral dimension of the schoolboy's portrait emerges in the emotional language used to characterize the past as a certain kind of *ethos* – a way of being or feeling. Evocative words such as *nahma* ("love"), *fofodu* ("togetherness"), *gleale'a* ("happiness") and *blakno* ("calm") portray an imagined past in terms that resonate with personal experience in the present. Taking note of such resonances, this book explores the emotional as well as political uses of stories of common history – stories which are about change, but which also bring potent subplots of continuity to bear on the creation of identity. Particularly when considered in their contexts of performance, one may see the capacity of narrated histories to construct identity in more complex, textured and layered terms than the abstract and polarized images of mission journals or school essays.

Chiefs

It may seem unusual for a work on a Melanesian society to talk about "chiefs" rather than "big-men," the hallmark of Melanesian styles of political leadership distinguished by personalized, achieved forms of power. My preference for the usage of "chief" (commonly used by local speakers of English and Melanesian Pidgin) is an attempt to sidestep the problematic typology of chiefs *versus* big-men, and to give local conceptions of chiefship their full due. "Chiefs" in Santa Isabel have long occupied center stage in the dramas of colonial history. Given their prominence in this respect, conceptions of chiefs have been crucial sites for contending ideas about identity and power. The latest instance of island-wide (paramount) chiefship offers an important opportunity to learn firsthand about processes of identity-making as they unfold.

As ideal types, "chiefs" and "big-men" (Sahlins 1963) have been useful reference points for comparative discussion of legitimacy and power in Oceania. But the greatest liability of this typology has been the underlying evolutionary model that sees chiefdoms growing out of big-man polities as societies in eastern Oceania achieved greater forms of political and economic integration (see Douglas 1979). Rather than freeze descriptions of leadership in Santa Isabel in terms of political types, it is preferable to view local leaders as working to create and legitimate forms of power and influence within the constraints of material and symbolic resources (cf. Allen 1984).

The colonial history of Santa Isabel is characterized by the rapid aggregation of scattered populations into Christian villages and the rise of Christian chiefs and catechists with unprecedented political influence. This story of consolidation presents its own microcosm of political evolution that has seen the transformation of local descent-based polities into larger and more inclusive forms of social integration, even anticipating the more expansive institutions of a modern nation state. However, rather than appropriate these events to a narrative of "modernization" that sees small-scale personalistic forms subsumed by large-scale bureaucratic ones, we might examine the dialectic relations between indigenous realities and the institutions of church and state. Seen in this light, the apparent hegemony of introduced, exogenous forms dissolves in their confrontation with local meanings.

Ideas about chiefs, past and present, are not just abstractions, they are put to use by people seeking cultural solutions to problems and contradictions in the colonial (and neocolonial) milieu. Often reduced to singular issues of power, these problems are framed locally in terms of a wide range of concerns relevant to people's personal and social well-being. These concerns pertain particularly to the nature of interpersonal relations – relations that are crucial for the reputation and legitimacy of aspiring leaders. It is ironic that, in a region noted for the significance of personal reputation and style in creating and sustaining leadership status, only recently have local conceptions of person been given much attention in anthropological writing (Read's 1955 study is a noted early exception). Hau'ofa (1975: 286) noted the silence in his comments that

> . . . after decades of anthropological field research in Melanesia we have come up only with pictures of people who fight, compete, trade, pay bride-prices, engage in rituals, invent cargo cults, copulate and sorcerise each other. There is hardly anything in our literature to indicate whether these people have any such sentiments as love, kindness, consideration, altruism and so on . . . We know little about their systems of morality, specifically their ideas of the good and the bad, and their philosophies; though we sometimes get around to these, wearing dark glasses, through our fascination with cargo cults.

Chiefs are themselves a personification of morality – moralities that are frequently articulated through idioms of person, custom and history. Rather than take it for granted that we know what local talk of "chiefs" is all about (e.g., that they are a reification of "custom" or a reflection of colonial categories), we should investigate the processes that produce prevailing conceptions of chiefly leadership.

The power and prominence of chiefs in many parts of the Solomon Islands have been read as indices of the health of indigenous traditions. As the colonizing forces of mission and government were seen to erode or supplant the roles of chiefs, their diminished authority and influence personified larger narratives of cultural decline. So, for example, in the western Solomons the cessation of headhunting and the expansion of the Methodist mission were bemoaned by some through expressions of regret about the loss of prestige among well-known chiefs (Hocart 1922). And, in Malaita, where a British district officer and his entire patrol were massacred while collecting taxes in 1928, conflict between colonial regime and local polities took the form of struggles for power between competing big-men (Keesing and Corris 1980). But the narrative of colonization runs somewhat differently in Santa Isabel. With its pre-Christian history of victimization, relations between local communities and mission and government originated in a rhetoric of cooperation that saw new forms of expanded chiefship emerge. Never fixed or static, the cultural significance of chiefship has continued to shift and transform throughout colonial history as relations with colonial centers have oscillated between periods of alliance and confrontation.

The course of colonial history in Santa Isabel is marked by several island-wide movements aimed at sociopolitical transformation. Beginning with wholesale conversion to Christianity, followed by efforts to resist the intrusion of a colonial government, then the tumultuous events of World War II and postwar moves for autonomy, and most recently national independence, these historical junctures have each evoked organized attempts at reforming relations between local communities and forces of colonization. Throughout this episodic history, chiefs and other local leaders have been both agents and objects of discourses of change.

Just as social movements worldwide proceed by constructing more satisfying models of self and community that define and guide efforts at transforming the social world (Wallace 1956), so Christianization in Santa Isabel was accomplished through the propagation of stories and models of a new identity personified by "Christian chiefs" (*funei Khilo'au*) and "Christian persons" (*naikno Khilo'au*) living in a "new life" (*nakahra majaghani*). As is common in missionary rhetoric everywhere, the language of identity transformation is embedded in narratives of change that locate the self in trajectories of renewal (cf. Stromberg 1990). (Compare Rosaldo's comment (1980: 46) on the effects of conversion on Ilongot subjectivity: "New Christians appeared to feel that they were riding the wave of the future, and the poignant nostalgia of many others indicated that for them the world was grayer.") Now, in the 1980s and 90s, nearly one hundred years after the epoch of first conversion, new "born-again" evangelical ideologies are contending with the established Anglican order using some of the same rhetorical language that first characterized the arrival of Christianity.

Approaches and methods

At one time the tensions implied by the oxymoronic phrase "participant observation" were regarded as a particular strength of anthropological method – a source of insight to be derived from the experience of the fieldworker who moves back and forth between postures of involvement ("participation") and more dispassionate reflection ("observation"). But the last two decades have seen this mainstay of ethnography come in for a consistent drubbing from both inside and outside the field. First the interpretive turn in the social sciences drew attention to the cognitive and social limitations of "observation" and its problematic relation to the things that people actually think they are up to. Then increasing awareness of the politics of fieldwork has thoroughly recast the nature of "participation" as always shaped by the peculiar dialogics of research and "otherness." And yet, even as the phrase has been made problematic by postmodern critiques, "participant observation" somehow continues to capture the dilemmas and opportunities inherent in cultural research. If nothing else, awareness of these problems has produced some concerted rethinking about the sorts of methodologies appropriate to the naturalistic study of human experience.

Perhaps the most generally accepted dictum of interpretive anthropology has been the directive to fieldworkers to pay attention to meaning-making activities, to the semiotic and social processes that produce cultural understanding. Similar emphases have emerged in most of the human sciences in the form of elevated interest in representational practices, as in the rediscovery of Vygotski's work in developmental psychology (e.g., Wertsch 1985) or in the interest in narrativity in history and political science (H. White 1990; Jameson 1981). Within anthropology, many of the responses (and challenges) to the interpretive directive converge in their interest in "discourse." But the proliferation of discourse-centered approaches belies persistent differences in aims and methods. Consider, for example, the differences between research focusing on cognitive models (e.g., Holland and Quinn 1987), on communicative practices (e.g., Bauman 1986; Bourdieu 1977; Sherzer 1988) and, after Foucault, on discursive processes that sustain relations of power (e.g., Lindstrom 1990).

While each of these orientations offers insights, our subdisciplinary preferences for carving up social reality in these ways also hold distinct liabilities for understanding the ways historical discourse shapes social reality. Stories that are told and retold, especially those that become the subject of ritualized retelling, are likely to be at the same time culturally meaningful, emotionally powerful and politically effective (Miller et al. 1990). Narratives of shared experience and history do not simply represent identities and emotions. They constitute them. The relationship between the cognitive-emotional process through which a story is understood and the performative activity through which it is socially constituted reflects the dialectic of internalization and externalization that is the creative cauldron of culture (Berger and Luckmann 1967). Especially in communities where people profess a sense of common identity and subjectivity, that sense is often produced in jointly constructed stories about the past.

How and why are stories about the collective past produced? What may be learned by attending to their presumptions, purposes, and performances? The problems of searching out historicizing activities in island societies are well voiced by Francis Hezel in comments on his efforts to document local Micronesian versions of church history: "In Yap church history was danced; in Truk it was sung in a number of hymns, each composed by a separate island group; and in Pohnpei it was dramatized in a series of humorous tableaux . . . Each of the island groups had its history, presented in an art form that best suited its genius, and I had my monographs" (Hezel 1988: 103). Most of the performative genres mentioned by Hezel, especially singing and acting, are part of the repertoire of historical practices in Santa Isabel. The reproduction of distinct histories of Christian origins in different locales and in different communicative forms offers numerous strategies for comparative analysis. My approach is to identify convergences that suggest the operation of cultural understandings, while at the same time examining the sociopolitical processes that turn remembrance into history.

I examine a number of communicative genres, including ordinary conversation, storytelling, speechmaking and dramatic performance, used to represent history. Focusing upon the representation of persons and events in a variety of narratives exposes the multiplicity of meanings and valences that surround key identities. For example, as Levy (1973: 217) and others have noted, Pacific perceptions of ancestors and their pre-Western ways may be fraught with ambivalence, encompassing both ridicule of primitivism and respect for a lost vitality and power. The shifting social meanings of such ambivalent perceptions can best be read in performative contexts where metacommunicative commentaries frame their evaluative significance for specific audiences. Thus, for example, the caricature of heathen ancestors in stories with tropes of exaggeration and humor expresses a degree of self-conscious ambivalence that might otherwise be stripped away in less contextualized representations.

Throughout this work I make use of the notion of "cultural model" (Quinn and Holland 1987: 25) to refer to cognitively organized processes of understanding (or "schemas") that may be inferred from recurrent forms of talk and interaction. Such schemas are important because they give meaning to social action at the same time as they themselves are shaped by socially organized activities. The interplay of social and cognitive processes is especially apparent in historical discourse where identity models obtain a degree of cognitive and political fixity to the degree that they are externalized in narratives of a shared past. Much like the Navaho images of the "Whiteman" discussed by Basso (1979: 4), identities such as the "Christian person" or the "chief" are of particular interest because they are embedded in moral narratives that powerfully shape self-understanding and social reality.

At various points this book orders its presentation according to conventions of chronological progression, but not so as to separate a historical past from an ethnographic present. Rather, the exposition intertwines history and ethnography in order to seek out points of mutual relation between events and models, histories and selves.

Beginning with a narrative about my own introduction to Santa Isabel and the kinds of stories evoked by my arrival, chapters 2, 3 and 4 introduce the constructs of descent, land and chiefly leadership that orient self-understanding on the island. It is in relation to these orientations, and the activities that produce them, that historical narratives do much of their "identity work."

Chapters 5 and 6 examine the most prominent juncture in Santa Isabel history and historiography: conversion to Christianity. After first discussing the period of nineteenth-century raiding and killing that provides the background for narratives of conversion, chapter 6 focuses upon the process of conversion itself as it swept up whole communities in the moral idiom of "new lives."

Chapters 7 and 8 take up local narratives of conversion, beginning with a dramatic performance used regularly by one village to commemorate its Christian origins. Chapter 8 takes a somewhat different tack by examining several distinct accounts of a single, legendary encounter between the missionary Henry Welchman and the renowned chief Figrima. The juxtaposition of different accounts of the "same" events, including the missionary's own diary, is used to examine the significance of conversion histories as creative, cultural constructions.

Chapters 9 and 10 conjoin ethnography and history by turning attention to the process of colonial history as it has been constituted in discourses of chiefly identity and power. Interpretation of a series of local responses to the colonial intrusion is aimed at articulating the shifting historical contexts of past attempts at collective self-definition. Chapter 10 brings this history up to date by focusing upon the ceremony to install the paramount chief and its uses of the past. This penultimate chapter examines the power of "old" stories to produce a new yet distinctly familiar moment in island history.

I *Orienting*

2

First encounters

When I first flew into the capital town of Honiara I knew no one in Santa Isabel or, for that matter, in the entire country (at that time still a British colony). My only contacts had been through correspondence with the British Permanent Secretary responsible for research approvals. Yet, with very little effort on my part, within a month I was situated in an Isabel village and busily engaged in work I had come to do. The relative ease of entrée, and the events which followed, say a great deal about the posture of Isabel people vis-à-vis the wider world.

As often happens in such situations, I was taken in tow almost immediately by my first acquaintance from the island. The above-mentioned British official introduced me to a young man, Eric Ehamana, from the area of Maringe where I was intending to work.[1] Eric promptly suggested that I settle in his part of Maringe. And, since he and his family were about to go out to the island on holiday, he suggested that I accompany them.

The island

About three weeks after first touching down in the Solomon Islands, the Ehamana family and I boarded a small inter-island vessel, the *Ligomo*, for the journey to Santa Isabel. As Honiara faded to a small patch on the side of the massive green expanse that is Guadalcanal, we settled in for an all-day voyage to a village on the southernmost end of the island where we would spend the night before going on up to the coast the next day to the government district center at Buala (see map 1). Typical of the many small cargo vessels that have plied the waters of the Solomon Islands for decades, the *Ligomo* was designed to ship copra from Santa Isabel to Honiara markets and then carry commercial goods ("cargo") back to Isabel villages. About forty feet in length, the only accommodation for passengers was the space on top of the main cargo hold and other parts of the deck area. For most villagers, for whom air travel is out of reach (either geographically or

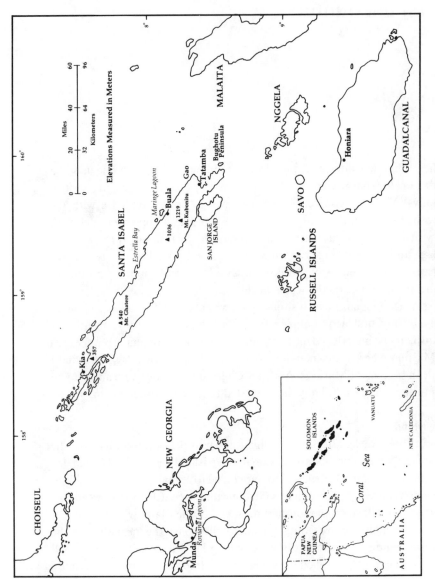

Map 1 Santa Isabel and the western Solomon Islands

economically), this is the primary means for making the increasingly frequent trips between the worlds of rural village and port town (Honiara).

My memory of the voyage is largely sensorial – of a glassy calm sea and the *Ligomo* rolling through the ocean swell with the low drone of its diesel engine in the background. Our slow but steady progress was an appropriate reminder of the wide expanse of sea that dominates the Solomons archipelago. As we neared the islands of Savo and Nggela (which could be seen from the outset) Santa Isabel became visible on the horizon. First to appear were the low forested hills of the Bughotu peninsula – our destination for the night. It was nearly dark by the time we anchored at the village of Sigana and disembarked for an overnight in the village resthouse.

The next morning we worked our way slowly up the coast. For a new visitor such as myself, the effect of gazing upon the island of Santa Isabel from offshore may be hypnotic. The dominant impression is one of tropical serenity, punctuated by the cries of cockatoos and colorful parrots flying in the treetops. Even though Honiara was itself a quiet town in 1975, it suddenly seemed a hub of urban activity in contrast with an island the size of Santa Isabel (120 miles long, 20 miles across) with no roads and a coastline dominated by forest, coconut trees, and occasional small villages.

As we chugged along the southeastern coast, the island became progressively more mountainous, ascending to some 1,220 meters just inland from Buala (see map 2). The low hills and ridges covered with rain forest and lush tropical vegetation gave way to precipitous ridges rising sharply from the coast, cut in regular places by deep valleys winding back into the island's interior and its cloud-shrouded mountains. The rivers which flow out of these valleys are fed by heavy rains, up to 200 inches annually in parts of Maringe. The seasonal rains turn mere streams into rushing torrents during the months from January through March when the shift in prevailing winds from southeast to northwest brings more stormy weather.

The wet and warm climate of the island (it is located eight degrees south of the equator) sustains abundant plant and animal life, with the forest and ocean offering many supplements to villagers' staple diet of garden crops. Opossum, flying fox and wild pig are among the larger forms of wildlife; and all are hunted regularly. Freshwater eels and crayfish are delicacies caught in inland streams. For its part, the ocean supplies a wide variety of fish and reef creatures, including sea urchins, bêches-de-mer and shellfish.

From our vantage point on board the *Ligomo*, we could also observe the signs of subsistence gardening and agricultural activity. In some areas, a patchwork of garden plots in various stages of production covered the hillsides. Root crops such as sweet potato, taro, yams and manioc are the mainstay of the Isabel diet; and the tasks of clearing, burning, planting, weeding and harvesting gardens dominate the rhythms of everyday life. It is

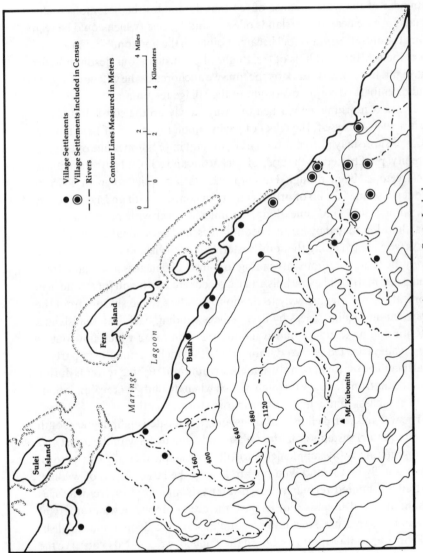

Map 2 Maringe area, Santa Isabel

in the fertile hills and valleys that villagers work their gardens. Almost all of the level arable land along the coast is devoted to coconut plantations and the production of copra, the island's major cash crop. Orderly rows of coconut palms are testimony to an industry that began with European planters but is increasingly localized.

The *Ligomo* provided a good view not only of the island's ecology, but also of its demographic patterns. Most villages today are located along the coast, either on the shoreline itself or immediately inland on the first tier of hills and ridges. The primary reason for this is that coastal location allows easy access to the routes of trade and transportation that link Isabel villages with the world beyond. As if to illustrate, the *Ligomo* stopped at numerous villages along the way just long enough to load up the ship's boat with cargo and passengers, row them ashore, and return.

Even though we were cruising along the most populated stretch of coastline, the island in 1975 was sparsely settled – less than 10,000 people spread across the 120-mile length of the island.[2] The sparse population, however, belied the distance we traveled in terms of linguistic diversity. Between our departure point in Bughotu and our subsequent arrival in Buala, thirty-five miles up the coast, we would traverse the regions of three distinct language groups (of four spoken on the island): Bughotu spoken by almost one-fourth of the island's population; Gao by a diminishing six percent; and Cheke Holo by over half of the population (see White et al. 1988: vii). Furthermore, we had crossed a major linguistic divide, separating two language families located in the central and western parts of the Solomons archipelago. The Bughotu language is similar to languages spoken in Nggela, Guadalcanal and Malaita; whereas Cheke Holo, Gao and the fourth Isabel language, Zabana or Kia, are more closely associated with languages in the western Solomons.

Not long before reaching Buala, we stopped offshore from Eric Ehamana's area, Hofi, where I intended to settle in a few days. For the moment, however, I was proceeding on to Buala to make the acquaintance of several local leaders before returning to Hofi. A driving tropical rain descended on the *Ligomo* just as we were off-loading passengers and cargo, obscuring the only structures visible along the shore – a canoe house and copra drier. A small group of people who had gathered at the landing to await the *Ligomo* could be seen taking shelter from the rain as they awaited the parties coming ashore, including the Ehamanas.

After leaving the Ehamanas and others at Hofi, we continued on to our final destination, Buala. Both village and government center, Buala is situated at the foot of the island's most imposing mountain range, and at the edge of an expansive lagoon, the Maringe Lagoon. The full extent of the lagoon became visible as the *Ligomo* rounded its southernmost edge.

Looking toward the island, village settlements seemed almost continuous along the shoreline. Here population density is more than a relative term. The *Ligomo*'s slow progress toward Buala midway along the lagoon shoreline offered ample opportunity for surveying these settlements and wondering about village life.

As we drew near the wharf, a cluster of people awaited the arriving ship with its weekly load of passengers and cargo from Honiara. Since I had written in advance to two of the main Isabel leaders in Buala (Nathaniel Hebala, a prominent Maringe leader, and Dudley Tuti, the Anglican Bishop of Santa Isabel), I knew that I was expected. And, indeed, one of the two people who greeted me stepping off the *Ligomo* was Nathaniel Hebala. The other was the clerk to the Isabel council, a young man from another island posted there in government service. Both of these people were well used to looking after visitors and helped considerably to smooth over my transition to Isabel life, especially during the next three days in Buala.

"We talk a lot about culture"

As the process of "development" has increasingly affected Santa Isabel, Buala has been its epicenter. In 1975 the tangible evidence for this was the cluster of buildings made out of concrete, sideboard and iron: hospital, council building (also housing the bank and post-office), agricultural office and houses for government officials, particularly the council clerk and

Plate 1 Author talks with (left to right) James Sao, Charles Pado and Nathaniel Hebala

doctor (when one could be found to take up residence). Although I was eager to get out to Hofi and the type of village setting I envisioned for my project, I later realized that some of the conversations and activities encountered during those first days in Buala offered glimpses of transformative processes that are at work in all corners of the island.

The day after my arrival I sat in on a meeting of local church and village leaders called to discuss plans to develop local businesses. "Big-men" from the Maringe area gathered for the meeting at the neighboring settlement of Jejevo, headquarters of the Church of Melanesia and site of a junior-secondary school and houses for the bishop and other officials. The meeting took place in one of the classrooms and, because several participants were from outside Maringe, most of the discussion was conducted in Solomons Pidgin.

The meeting had been called to address confusions about relations between government-sponsored cooperative stores and the locally initiated Isabel Development Company (IDC). It generated the sort of self-reflective discourse that is characteristic of many such discussions of "development" around the island. Three men were seated at a table at the front of the room: Bishop Dudley Tuti, the manager of IDC and the government agricultural officer assigned to Santa Isabel (and hence representing the government's cooperative society plan). The bishop, who over the past few years had taken an active role in promoting the IDC as a new public company, chaired the meeting and held the attention of the audience throughout. A number of speakers framed their discussion of the controversy in terms of more fundamental issues involving relations between church, government and local communities (or "the people"). At one point Bishop Tuti drew a diagram on the board depicting three sectors – "church," "council" (government) and "business" – and connected them to both "people" and "development." As will become more apparent in subsequent chapters, his choice of labels here reflects structures and tensions that re-emerge continually in the island's colonial history.

Tuti began the afternoon session by drawing another diagram, this time adding the word "chief" to the trilogy of "church," "council" and "business." The "chief," he stated, was the link to the people, to holding meetings and getting people to "cooperate." If I was somewhat surprised to hear such deliberate talk about the roles of chiefs, I was even more so as Tuti began to talk of "culture," using the English word to address issues of tradition and change. In a combination of Pidgin and English, he asserted: "We talk a lot about culture. Culture has to change. Some of it prevents us from going forward; and some encourages us to go forward. It's up to us to decide what to abolish or get rid of." At the time this struck me as the faintly familiar rhetoric of culture as an object of interest among colonial agents attending to the ambivalent place of "tradition" in modernization. But the significance of this resonance should not be taken as transparent. The appropriation of overt talk of culture does not imply that Western forms have exerted a complete hegemony over indigenous thought. This manner of externalizing culture as an object of discussion and manipulation has probably always been a dimension of local political discourse, although not necessarily with English terms and categories.

The topic of "culture" led Tuti to acknowledge my presence (the only white person) in the room. Even though we had not yet met, he had received my letter stating my intent to study language and culture. (It is even possible that the letter had influenced his choice of terms on this occasion.) As he raised the problem of the "fit" between Isabel "custom" (Pidgin: *kastom*) and modern, Western-style "development," he motioned toward me and indicated that this is something I might be able to help with. In this instance, as in others during the months to come, general notions about the importance of recording and preserving traditional culture (*kastom*) provided an easily understood rationale for my presence as observer and learner of local ways.

Contrary to the image of rural island life as uneventful, village time is punctuated by a constant round of meetings and ceremonial events, each providing a focal point for conversation and directive activity. Within a week, then, I would sit in on three major meetings: the meeting of entrepreneurs, a land "inquiry" held in the village of Vavarenitu where I would settle and a session of the government council in Buala. Although differing in purpose and scope, each of these events concerned itself in some way with problems of contemporary society that evoked self-conscious constructions of tradition and modernity. Like the Jejevo meeting, each of the other events fostered reflections about *kastom* and its relation to wider contexts of central, colonial government and the world system beyond.

Councilors and chiefs

In 1975, the year of self-government in the Solomon Islands, but still three years prior to independence, the primary body of local government was the district council. In the case of Santa Isabel, the district was co-extensive with the island; and the district council was made up of fourteen elected members, each chosen from a designated sub-district. Many of the members were young men who had been to secondary school and had some knowledge of English. Others were known as successful entrepreneurs with experience in organizing economic projects.

The council meeting was convened by the clerk who had greeted me at Buala wharf. He sat at a table in front with the council president, facing the members seated on benches. The discussion that followed covered a range of matters both routine and not-so-routine. In addition to reviewing the council budget and capital improvement projects (such as surveying for a Maringe road or building school classrooms), the council also took up questions related to its own legitimacy. Specifically, the members discussed the council's relation to two other loci of sociopolitical activity: the church and local chiefs. Here again, three of the sectors of Isabel society diagrammed by Bishop Tuti at the Jejevo meeting surfaced once more as objects of discussion, addressing another facet of the multifaceted concept of *kastom* and its significance within contemporary society.

Santa Isabel is perhaps unique in Melanesia as an island its size with nearly the entire population belonging to a single church (the Church of Melanesia).[3] With church and state on Santa Isabel co-extensive in scope and structure (both organized into subdistricts with representatives responsible to island-wide leadership), the need for coordination is a frequent topic of conversation. In the council meeting members discussed the possibility of inviting church leaders (such as Bishop Tuti) to council meetings. After reminding the members that church representatives could attend, but only as observers without a decision-making role, the clerk said he would in the future send invitations to Tuti and selected church leaders.

The issue of *kastom* was raised in a debate about the role of chiefs, particularly that of "paramount chief," in local government. I had already encountered this topic in Honiara, when one of Isabel's two representatives in the national government council, Willie Betu, showed me a plan he had drawn up to install chiefs from each major clan and region in a proposed system modeled on the structure of the district council. But this was my first indication that the issue of chiefs, and of a paramount chief, were being actively debated. As will become obvious in later chapters, these concerns were not limited to council members, but were widely recognized in Santa Isabel, and had been for decades. The council deliberations on this occasion marked a moment in a long and ongoing process of transformation – a process that continually finds chiefs at center stage, as both agents of change and mediators of conjoined structures.

The dilemma faced by council members and, indeed, by Isabel people generally can be summed up as how best to construct the status of chiefs within the context of modern (colonial) institutions connected to a complex and changing world political economy. It is widely recognized on Santa Isabel that chiefs continue to have sociopolitical significance based on their roles as lineage leaders and community representatives and on their close identification with *kastom* and all that that entails. The council's approach to the issue of chiefs at this time involved a proposal to establish a "committee of chiefs" whose members would attend council meetings and advise about the effects of council actions on *kastom*. While there was agreement about the merit of the general idea, there was disagreement about how to institute it. How many chiefs would attend meetings? How would they be selected? Would a paramount chief be selected? If so, how?

After some debate about the appropriateness of electing chiefs – wouldn't the most populous villages get their way? – the members decided that each village could elect a chief, and that the chiefs would decide among themselves who would attend meetings. One of the members suggested that the chiefs could also select a paramount chief from among their number, but others argued that people from other areas would not recognize him as such. So, according to my notes, the idea of a paramount chief was rejected as inappropriate and possibly causing undue conflict. When, six months later, virtually the whole island mobilized to install Bishop Dudley Tuti as paramount chief, I would look back at this meeting and wonder about the variability and fluidity of local political discourse.

In connection with their ruminations about the problem of chiefs, several members spoke to the need to teach young people about *kastom* so that they would learn the stories of their ancestors, "our stories," not just the stories of "whitemen." There was general consensus on this point, but also agreement that this was the province of chiefs, not council members.

Even though I had not yet settled down in the village setting which I envisioned as the proper place for the work of ethnography, my first few days on Santa Isabel provided a condensed view of themes and complexities that continue to engage people in managing their lives. My own movements back and forth, from Buala to Vavarenitu and back to Buala, were symptomatic of people's involvement with institutions beyond the village. Each occasion (the Jejevo business meeting, the land inquiry and the council meeting) was a reminder that the cultural world does not end at the peripheries of the island's geographic terrain. Each event, quite different in purpose, occasioned a discourse of self-understanding in which assumptions about identity, community and history were recreated and transformed in speeches, debates and decisions dealing with the problems of the day – problems that arise in large measure at the junctures of local communities and larger, encapsulating forces of institutional power.

The apparent irony in this sort of reflexive discourse is that it originates in colonial institutions of church and state (business, court, council), but concerns itself overtly with the promotion of indigenous culture or *kastom* (cf., Keesing 1989). But for many Isabel people who talk about their society in overtly adaptive and syncretic terms, there is little sense of contradiction. Rather than read this difference as a lack of insight on the part of "natives," I take it as an opportunity to problematize terms such as culture, tradition and history that are often taken for granted as the bedrock for comparative analysis (Jolly 1990; Toren 1989). The extent to which modern discourses of *kastom* are regarded as contradictory stems in part from our (Western?) inclinations to dichotomize "tradition" and "modernization" – with the former connoting structure and fixity, and the latter implying process and change. Rather than approach the problems of sociocultural change in terms of the grating of whole systems or institutions upon one another (a process too easily mapped in terms of reified oppositions such as indigenous/Western, traditional/modern or local/national) this volume examines some of the ways that processes of culture contact and change are taken up by local actors as issues of voiced concern. Each of the meetings I sat in on during my first week in Santa Isabel generated talk about society, about *kastom* and forces of change – talk that, by its very nature, historicizes identity by situating self and community in relation to a shared past and a desired future. By noting that local traditions and social change are focal topics of conversation in meetings and other contexts, we may begin to ask how culture and history are constituted in subjectivity and social process.

3

Portraits of the past

We are what we remember: the actions we lived through or should have lived out and which we have chosen to remember.

Albert Wendt (1987: 79)

This chapter continues the narrative of arrival already begun, and in the process broaches other narratives – stories that Isabel people tell about their own past. It is more than coincidental or fortuitous that such stories mediated my first encounters with Maringe villagers. I suspect that in most rural Solomon Islands communities the arrival of visitors, particularly Westerners unfamiliar with local ways, evokes a discourse of self-represen-tation in which distinctive local customs are explicated and contrasted with the ways of an imagined West. Since much that is now regarded as notable or remarkable in local culture is associated with abandoned practices of the pre-Christian past, such reflexive accounts often focus upon "old" ways and the historical events that have changed them. In my case, these explications were particularly appropriate, since I identified myself as someone who had come to study local culture. It seemed straightforward, then, when my hosts arranged an excursion to see certain sacred places associated with pre-Christian life. While not apparent to me at the time, that tour and the running exegesis accompanying it afforded an oppor-tunity for enacting understandings of self, community and history that would emerge repeatedly during the months to come.

When I first visited the village of Vavarenitu where I took up residence, Eric Ehamana informed me that he had discussed my arrival with local leaders and that they had already decided that Vavarenitu would be the appropriate place for me to reside. It was, he explained, a central location from where I could easily walk to several nearby villages. (It no doubt seemed only natural to add an anthropologist's house to the nucleus of modern institutions already there: school, clinic and tradestore.) During the time it would take to build a house in Vavarenitu, I could live in an unused building next to the clinic – a neglected structure of concrete floor, iron roof and dilapidated thatched walls. However, before any of that got underway, I was invited to participate in a small feast that Eric and his relatives were preparing in a nearby village named Togasalo to mark their reunion. Having spent my first night in Vavarenitu, I set out the next day with two companions for four days in Togasalo where preparations were underway. The track to that village follows a river through a narrow valley before ascending steeply to the top of a ridge two miles inland where the settlement perches at an elevation of about 1,000 feet. This is a walk which local people, often carrying heavy loads, do in less than an hour. It took me more than two hours, with help.

Groping up the slippery trail, I wondered why people continue to reside in the interior when they can choose to live closer to the coast, as most do these days. Once we reached the ridgetop where Togasalo is located, the appeal became somewhat more understandable. Emerging from the forest onto the village clearing, we were met with a cooling breeze and a panoramic view of the valley and ocean below. Aside from these aesthetic attractions, however, there are other reasons people make their homes in the uplands away from the coast, as will be discussed below.

Togasalo showed few of the signs of development evident in Vavarenitu and Hofi below where the clinic, school and tradestore are visible manifestations of modernization. (One reason for this is that Togasalo is one of eight satellite villages that utilize and support those facilities.) In its size, arrangement, and physical appearance, Togasalo was then, and is now, typical of Isabel villages since conversion to Christianity: clusters of thatched dwellings and cookhouses dispersed around a well-manicured plaza with a larger church building visible at one end. By my count, Togasalo at that time consisted of ninety-two people living in some sixteen households.[1] There was considerable variety in the composition of these households, but the modal type consisted of husband, wife and children, with elderly parents and occasionally a sibling of the husband or wife added in. In some cases a married child and his or her spouse continue to reside with the parents until they have children and establish their own household. It is common for men to live in their wife's village, but this uxorilocal "rule" is frequently reversed by influential men who desire to remain in their village of origin with their sisters and sisters' husbands assisting with family and clan activities.

Even as we arrived in Togasalo the manner and rhythm of village life began to make itself apparent. As we headed for the resthouse, women could be seen returning from their gardens – walking with huge net-bags filled with taro or sweet potato hung over their backs. Others were off to the stream or viaduct used for bathing (one for women, one for men), getting ready for the evening prayer service. The sound of slit-gong drumming calling people to church marks the beginning and end of the cycle of daily work.

We had arrived on a Wednesday and many people were preparing for Eric's feast on Saturday. My hosts lost no time in educating me in matters of tradition. In fact, the next day, just five days after stepping ashore at Buala, I had my first and perhaps most intensive lesson in cultural history. First introductions are frequently the richest in information and insight, but they come at a time when one is least prepared to understand them. The day after my arrival in Togasalo, I was given a walking tour of the past – a brief survey of some of the sacred sites of the pre-Christian world.

My hosts suggested that I go along with a group of men going out to find two of the family pigs (allowed to forage in the forest) needed for the upcoming feast so that I could view some of their *kastom* places identified with the ancestral past. Two of the senior village men, Josepa Lokutadi and Forest Voko, led the way so that they could explain the significance of the places we visited. A younger Togasalo man, Hudson Lagusu, recently ordained as an Anglican priest, accompanied us and acted as translator.

The Knabu: ancestors and identities

I had almost no conception where our small expedition was heading, except that we were going to places of special importance. We set off along one of the paths leading out of the village, first down from the ridgetop, then across a stream and up and around the side of another ridge. The going was slow and before long I lost any sense of direction. Later, looking at a map, I would see that we actually traveled little more than a mile from Togasalo in straight-line distance, but probably three or four times that distance in the circuitous, up-and-down route we followed.

After we had been walking for some time, our guides indicated that we had arrived at one of our destinations. I could detect little that distinguished this place from the surrounding forest, but my companions began clearing away the thick underbrush as Josepa and Forest talked more concertedly. Fr. Hudson translated. The first piece of information I jotted down in my notebook was the placename: Sithalehe. Indeed, what seemed to me like continuous undifferentiated forest was for my hosts an elaborate patch-work of significant named places, each harboring its stories of persons, events and spirits associated with that place. In later walks along bush trails, I would listen as companions kept up a stream of narrative about places and features of the natural landscape that figure in stories about historical and mythic events.

Sithalehe, my guides informed me, is a place where sacrifices had once been offered to the spirits of deceased ancestors. The offerings included taro and other garden crops, pigs and, on occasion, humans. Most importantly, it was *their* ancestors, a people known as the Knabu, who performed these rites. The Knabu, they said, had migrated to this region from a nearby area named Korogha. The people of two intermarrying clans, Posamogo and Thauvia, were said to have moved into the area together and built shrines such as Sithalehe for making sacrifices. With this brief explanation, the two elder Togasalo men had, within minutes of arriving at Sithalehe, narrated a condensed account of traditional life around the key features of locale, descent, intermarrying clans and propitiatory rites. As we talked further at that site, and later went on to view others, they expanded and elaborated their narration in a variety of ways. Before continuing with their reminiscences, however, a brief digression will help to clarify the nature of these anchor points of collective identity in the "life before."

Prior to the creation of large Christian villages during the era of conversion (to be taken up in subsequent chapters), geographic regions with names such as "Knabu" that refer both to place and people were significant loci of sociopolitical activity. Usually no more than a few square miles in size, each region was ideally inhabited by people of two exogamous and intermarrying clans, such as Posamogo and Thauvia for the Knabu.[2] In societies as yet unaffected by the advent of church and government, ties of kinship, formed particularly by descent from matrilineal ancestors and attachments to ancestral lands, constituted basic parameters of social life. Lineages of people who could trace descent from a common ancestress composed the primary landholding groups, as they do today. Then as now, each lineage was associated with one of two or three exogamous clans (*kokholo*, literally "type" or "kind," connoting common origins or substance) found throughout the Maringe area. These relations of codescent and clan membership could then be extended outward through intermarriage and identifications with prominent chiefs acting as leaders of clan and regional affairs.[3]

The matrilineal idiom of descent among Cheke Holo speakers is clear and unambiguous. For example, descent groups are typically referred to as *thi'a* (literally, "belly"), signifying their uterine origins, whereas genealogical segments descended from male relatives are sometimes termed *grege lehe* ("dead branches") – branches that are customarily pruned from oral and written genealogies. And, as is often the case in kinship terminologies associated with matrilineal descent, the sociological importance of the relationship between mother's brother and sister's son is marked with a distinctive, reciprocal term, *nebu* (see White et al. 1988: 270–1).[4]

Beyond these linguistic reflections of unilineality, what are the contexts and activities in which shared descent takes on social reality for Cheke Holo speakers? Here the significance of land looms large. It is obvious that in a subsistence economy where people cultivate most of their own food, and where most efforts at economic development require a land base, land will be a highly valued resource. However, to understand the cultural significance of land in Santa Isabel, it is necessary to consider the range of social practices within which land obtains utility and meaning. The most consistent way in which land figures in daily life is through the constant round of gardening that keeps most family cook houses well stocked with a supply of root crops (sweet potato, yams, taro). In the usual gardening cycle, men clear a garden plot of trees and overgrowth, and women perform the work of planting, weeding, harvesting and, ultimately, cooking its produce. This process allows nearly everyone on the island to maintain a regular diet of these staple foods. Beyond these consumption practices, garden produce enters into a variety of exchange activities that are constitutive of social relations. These exchanges, ranging from informal sharing among kin to elaborate feast distributions, create and maintain relations among those involved. As much as anything, it is the cooperative activities of producing, exchanging and consuming the fruits of the land that constitute shared identity among lineage mates and other kin.

In symbolic concordance with these practices, notions of shared descent and collective attachments to land connote fertility and nurturance. Some of these connotations were articulated for me by a man named John Gebe – a man from the Gao area recognized for his knowledge of local culture. Prompted by narrower questions from me about kinship matters, Gebe began talking in more metaphorical terms about relations between matrilineal kinship and the productive capacities of both land and women.

In our custom, it is the women who came first. This is still true. In the stories in the Bible, it is always the men who stand for the family and clan. In our custom, it is the women who are like that. Land is like a mother. It is the earth which feeds you, gives you drink, clothes you and puts you to sleep. In your life and your ways, the land is your mother. When you go searching for something to put in your basket, it is from the land that you will eat, from the land that you will drink. Trees are cut from the land in order to build canoes. These are the thoughts behind our custom that the woman comes first in our clans and families. It is true enough that the man puts the seed in the woman in order to make a person. But in matters of land, it is the woman's name which is the highest, not that of men. Men are for leading, for speaking, and for working – these kinds of things. Women's names are on the land and on the families.

Even though most people would not intellectualize about the rationale for matrilineal descent in this way, Gebe is here articulating quite general understandings about the nature of person and gender salient in people's thinking about land, kinship and *kastom*.[5] When people talk about indigenous ways, it is the ability to produce, share and exchange food that emerges again and again as a prime signifier of local identity and traditional values. It is here, in the social and political organization of these productive activities, that ideas about kinship and descent have retained their greatest resilience in the face of dramatic sociopolitical change since the time the Knabu made sacrifices at Sithalehe over one hundred years ago.

While the ideology of matrilineal descent remains unambiguous, the range of contexts in which lineage and clan membership *matter* are greatly diminished. The cultural and political significance of descent-based activities have been transformed by processes of Christianization and colonization, as will be seen in subsequent chapters. While descent and region continue to be highly significant in many contexts, these constructs are often submerged in other agendas, and are no longer the overarching terms of reference they once were. Group activities such as defense, raiding, propitiation and large-scale feasting that once activated descent relations have either declined or been appropriated by other institutions. These shifts are evident in the relative lack of interest in matters of ancestry and clan history today. For the average person, genealogical memory for the names of ancestors extends no further back than grandparents; and even the names of paternal grandparents are frequently forgotten. One old man of recognized knowledge and authority could elaborate from memory genealogical information extending back four ascending generations. Not surprisingly, totemic food tabus (*dangna*) and mythic stories about clan origins have also been largely forgotten.[6]

The context where genealogical knowledge is most concertedly displayed today is in disputes over land. It is quite common for senior lineage men to possess written lists of serially linked names documenting matrilineal ancestry, sometimes stretching back ten or more generations. But this type of information usually cannot be recalled from memory, and seems to have little relevance for other dimensions of social life. For example, the most valuable commodity for most people's participation in the cash economy is coconut trees (used to produce copra), and these are frequently passed from father to son in ritualized exchanges that transmit property other than land across lines of matrilineal descent. And, since Santa Isabel is still relatively sparsely populated and garden land is plentiful in many areas, the question of land ownership often does not arise in the context of subsistence needs (although this is changing as the phenomenal population growth of recent decades begins to produce overcrowding). And these changes are exacerbated by contemporary plans for the commercial development of land in the form of plantations, forestry and mining, making land an increasingly politicized subject of dispute and controversy.

For the most part, it is land located along the narrow strip of level, commercially valuable coastal regions that is the object of contention in contemporary disputes. To some extent, these disputes replicate well-established patterns in which power is constituted in rights to speak about plots of land and determine their use. The problem of sorting out issues of land ownership that now plagues Santa Isabel is associated with more general political processes and with the status of "traditional chiefs" in particular. For it is chiefs as lineage leaders who represent ancestral heritage and land. But the current value of land is increasingly defined in commercial terms often disconnected from the sorts of cooperative productive activities that valorize understandings of common descent and place. In contemporary debates about land ownership and use, old shrines and other relics in the forest associated with early ancestors and chiefs are regarded more as boundary markers, as evidence to be used in support of land claims, than as symbols of shared place and history. Places such as Sithalehe iconically recall a nostalgic past made up of social meanings and spiritual powers that have been overtaken by sociopolitical transformations, just as a thick layer of forest now overgrows them. But this is jumping too far ahead of the narrative where this digression began.

Shrines and scenarios

The Togasalo men hacked away at the underbrush to clear vines and dense growth, gradually exposing two stone structures – a pyramidal (once rectangular?) shrine and a low bed of flat stones. When finished, they had exposed a sacrificial altar said to have been used to make offerings to the spirits of powerful ancestors. About ten feet long, five feet wide and two feet high, the structure was constructed with wide, flat stones forming straight sides and a level upper surface.

With the shrine as a visual reminder of the past, Forest and Josepa launched into a story about the site's most dramatic purpose: human sacrifice. Adding immediacy to the account, Fr. Hudson assumed the posture of a sacrificial victim to demonstrate the procedure for ritual decapitation (up to a point).[7] He sat down with his back against one end of the shrine, leaned his head back, and stared upward with neck exposed. He and the others then described the scenario for human sacrifice, carried out to enhance the strength of Knabu warriors. About forty men would assemble in a line extending away from the altar. Once the victim was decapitated, the severed head would be handed down the line "like a coconut" so that the warriors could drink its blood.

In its stark simplicity, this scenario is typical of the overdrawn images of violence often heard as characterizations of pre-Christian life. As my guides continued to talk, they elaborated their description. They noted that after the beheading the headless body might, by reflex, run a short distance before collapsing. The warriors, they said, would laugh at this, even putting an axe in the grip of the macabre figure as it ran along. To this the translator added his own footnote: "What a cruel people they were."

Continuing with the story of human sacrifice, the narrators noted that the procedure also included the consumption of human flesh. Presided over by a ritual specialist or priest, the body was cut up and the flesh cooked in an oven near the altar. Portions were then allotted according to status considerations. Skulls of human victims were kept around the altar and in a nearby ceremonial house, visible testimony to the strength of the Knabu people.

Josepa and Forest pointed out that a renowned chief was buried at this place, his bones encased in the shrine or *phadagi* – a block-shaped or pyramidal structure just four or five feet high constructed out of large stones piled one on top of another (see Riesenfeld 1950). *Phadagi*, which still dot the Maringe landscape (even though overgrown by bush), were once the centers of ritual activity that tied together land, chiefs and kin groups in a single potent symbol. Since each shrine was named according to its locale, a shrine name was both an index of ancestral lands and an emblem of descent group identity. As noted earlier, shrine names continue to be used in the context of land disputes as a shorthand for claims to ancestry and connections with place.

The altar we uncovered was but one piece of a shrine area used for rites of propitiation. For these rites, descendants of the ancestor(s) enshrined there would gather to offer sacrifices of garden produce, pig meat or human flesh under the direction of a priest (*mae fafara*, "sacrifice man"). The Knabu men explained the purpose of these offerings as an attempt to enlist the aid

Plate 2 Fr. Hudson Lagusu demonstrates use of sacrificial altar

of ancestor spirits (*na'itu*) in gardening, hunting and other risky activities.[8]
Beyond the narrow functionality of bountiful gardens and the like,
maintaining a ritual dialogue with ancestral spirits was the primary means
of acquiring spiritual power (*nolaghi*, mana) – the ultimate source of
personal strength, well-being and success in worldly affairs. Speakers of
Cheke Holo refer to spiritual potency as *nolaghi*, and readily equate the
term with the word *mana* used by their Bughotu neighbors. The activities
described by Josepa and Forest resemble the general pattern of traditional
religious practice described widely in eastern Oceanic societies where rites
of propitiation at shrine sites are the centerpiece of ritual activities aimed at
achieving specific worldly ends as well as more diffuse personal and
collective powers (Codrington 1891: 128–44; Hocart 1922; Keesing 1982;
Scheffler 1965: 244).

The two elders noted that it was strictly tabu (*blahi*) for women to enter
the altar area, with the exception of the wife of a chief. Since both ancestors
and ghosts of sacrificial victims were active in the vicinity of shrine areas,
these places were regarded as highly dangerous, especially for children and
women. Encountering a sudden proliferation of snakes is thought to be a
sign that a tabu area has been violated. Furthermore, any such trespass
would be likely to result in sickness or even death. At this point my notes are
ambiguous. At first one of the guides said that these ghosts are still active,
that strange noises and other signs of ghostly presence continue. Then
someone else indicated that signs of resident spirits diminished with the
advent of Christianity. In fact, they said, Christian priests had come to
kneel and pray at this shrine to dissipate its threatening power – using the
power (mana) of Christianity to neutralize its threatening forces (see
chapter 6). Since that time, they noted, the area has been safe, even for
women and children.

The ambiguity on this point reflects deep ambivalences and variation in
local beliefs about the persistence of the indigenous spirit world in the
Christian present.[9] In this instance, my presence and that of a young,
educated priest certainly affected the manner in which the sacred sites were
represented in our conversation. Upon returning to Togasalo, I heard other
views about the continuing danger and potency of traditional shrine sites.
The next day a woman commented to me that she and other women had not
seen the places Josepa and Forest showed me because they are afraid of the
consequences. Some believe that violating the boundaries of a shrine area
will cause thunder and lightning. As someone told me, the reason this did
not happen in our case was that we were accompanied by the two elders.[10]
It is also possible that the Christian priest went with us to add a further
element of spiritual "insurance."

We moved on from the Sithalehe shrine to the second site on our itinerary: the grave of an important Knabu chief named Patrick Maneaja. At this location my guides pointed out a feature of the landscape that distinguished it from the surrounding forest: cordyline plants (*nahogle*). (In addition to marking the boundaries of shrine sites and other sacred areas, cordyline plants are used in religious and healing practices of all sorts, as they are in many parts of the Pacific.) Maneaja had converted to Christianity and was living in a newly formed Christian village, Salanisi, when he decided to return and live in this area just prior to his death. He had wished to be nearer his ancestral lands, to be buried in the sacred burial ground where the bones of other Knabu chiefs lie. His grave, now marked in the contemporary fashion with a flat cement tombstone, was the only one visible. But, my informants assured me, were I to dig at this site, I would find lots of bones because it was once a burial ground (*thututamnu*) for Knabu chiefs.

The story of Patrick Maneaja's return led to another narrative: that of the conversion of the Knabu to Christianity. The three guides jointly reconstructed the story of the Knabu's first contact with Christianity and their subsequent movement toward the coast. Christianity, they said, was brought to the Knabu by Walter Gagai, one of the first Isabel catechists trained by the missionary Henry Welchman. Gagai came up to the Knabu from Bagovu, a Christian village on the coast. When he appeared, the chief (Krogamana Iho, later baptized Matasi) blew a conch shell to signal his warriors and followers to assemble. When the warriors gathered they threatened Gagai, but he was saved by the chief's wife (Mabel Ngoha) who hung a tapa cloth necklace on him, signifying that he should be spared. The tapa, given by a chief's wife, was a sign of life – sufficient to save a condemned person. This was said to be the beginning of the church among the Knabu. Later, they said, another catechist, Wilson Bana, came to stay with the Knabu. At that time there were nearly 300, all living in an area named Sosrogha. Bana, they continued, persuaded them to establish a single, large Christian village (Salanisi) nearer the coast where it would not be so difficult for the bishop to visit them. Salanisi later splintered into three villages that remain to this day, of which Togasalo is one.

An important feature of this account of Knabu conversion is its close attention to places and movements. The narrative is topographically organized such that events are mapped onto features of the landscape (see Parmentier 1987). In our short journey, a sequence of place names codified a sequence of historical events. As Renato Rosaldo (1980) discovered in listening to the Ilongot of the Philippines tell elaborately detailed stories about their movements in the forest, place names are a ready mnemonic for social history. In similar fashion, the three men I listened to traced a narrative path connecting the places of the Knabu past (the shrines and burial sites of their ancestors) with the Christian present, following their ancestors as they moved from Sosrogha to the large Christian village of Salanisi and then Togasalo.

Diklo and the feasting process

Leaving the burial ground with its boundary of cordyline plants, we moved on to another location a short distance away. The third feature of the Knabu landscape which Forest and Josepa wished to display was the site of a former ceremonial house and dance ground. Once again, the area was heavily overgrown, and it was only after hacking away the brush that a prominent stone foundation became visible. This place was named "seven fathoms" (*fitukhangafa*) after the height of the house, seven fathoms tall. My guides underscored the extraordinary size of the structure by telling of how the central houseposts had been erected by men standing on adjacent hills, pulling on ropes and signaling each other with conch shells to coordinate their work. The walls, they said, were decorated with patterns of plaited bamboo; and the posts embellished with designs woven into the rope lashings.

In listening to Forest and Josepa recall these details of the extraordinary ceremonial house – including the skulls that once lined its rafters as trophies of war – it became apparent that these memories were about more than an impressive piece of architecture; they also constituted a sense of vitality and accomplishment. *Fitukhangafa* called up recollections of an active ceremonial life centered upon large feasts and associated ritual practices. As Forest and Josepa described it, Knabu chiefs would periodically invite neighboring chiefs "from east and west" to gather with their followers for eating, oratory and ritual exchange (as well as singing and dancing). The ability of Knabu chiefs to call in prominent leaders from surrounding regions and participate in a cycle of exchange would have betokened their own power and prominence in regional politics. These largest of feasts are referred to in the Cheke Holo language as *diklo*, a word that is both noun and transitive verb. As a verb, *diklo* is an activity directed toward the guests and recipients of the feast. However, an equally important aspect was the presentation of gifts and the performance of speeches and songs directed toward the sponsor(s). *Diklo* feasts are conceptualized as reciprocal exchanges between chiefs acting as regional leaders. As such, they were a primary arena for interregional politics where reputations were made and relations formed that could have wide economic and strategic repercussions. In light of the importance of feasting as an opportunity for collective self-fashioning, consider briefly the remembered form of *diklo* feasts.

Much anthropological ink has been devoted to the analysis of feasts and ritual exchange in Melanesia, and space does not allow a detailed accounting of the material organization of these events in Santa Isabel (but see also chapter 4). However, feasting is a major form of social and ceremonial activity, and contributes importantly to the formation of identity at the broadest levels. It is clear that in nearly all parts of the Pacific feast exchanges are a primary mode of political action. Indeed, much of our understanding of the Melanesian "big-man" (stereotypic as this may be) is based on observations of competitive feasting in which aspiring leaders mobilize followers in producing, amassing and distributing food and wealth (see, e.g., Oliver 1955). Interpretations of these activities have focused mostly on their political and economic functions, with some marginal interest in the personalities of their big-man sponsors. But feasting as a process does not simply presume or affirm social relations, it also creates them. Feasting constitutes identities and relations in at least two ways: through the coordinated productive activity required to organize a large distribution of food, and through the speeches, songs and other performances that represent the meaning of the event for its participants. More appropriately thought of as an extended process (*eigano*, "make a feast") than a single occasion, organizing and preparing a feast activates social ties among the sponsors – whether a family, a lineage, a village or an entire region. Equally important is the simple fact of bringing people together in a large public gathering that then becomes a context for collectively externalizing shared interests and identities. In oral, face-to-face societies where communal consciousness is shaped through public performance, the politics of identity depends upon the ability to attract an audience and create the appropriate "stage" for dramatizing social statements.

Diklo feasts were the largest stage with the highest political stakes. The power and resources commanded by chiefs and their communities were indexed by the food and wealth that could be amassed on the occasion of a feast – an occasion that could only be enacted as part of a cycle of reciprocal exchange with other chiefs and regions. The entire *diklo* process was conducted in a reciprocal cycle such that the recipients of one exchange would, two or three years later, host a return feast of comparable size and value. The interval between *diklo* was necessary for feast organizers to have enough time to plant sufficient gardens, raise or purchase mature pigs, and conduct hunting and fishing expeditions in preparation. This pattern and many of the details of exchange resemble closely the *kelo* exchanges described by Scheffler for neighboring Choiseul (1965: 214–16).

In the prototypic form of *diklo* exchange, the sponsors distributed food to the guests who in turn presented shell valuables to the sponsoring chief. The return presentation, in which visiting chiefs presented valuables in the form of shell money and bodily decorations to the sponsor, was a focal point of the exchange. These presentations would have been accompanied by speeches and/or songs commemorating the meaning of the event, valorizing relations among the participants, and lauding the status of the sponsor. The significance of *diklo* as exchanges between chiefs was underscored by the fact that most of the wealth exchanged was in the form of personal adornments worn by chiefs. In precontact times, chiefly status was indexed by decorative regalia such as shell armlets, clamshell pendants, and porpoise teeth bracelets, necklaces and belts. And it was these items, in addition to strings of shell money (*vilihei*), that circulated among chiefs participating in cycles of reciprocal *diklo* exchange.[11]

Before leaving the site of the "seven-fathom" house, Josepa and Forest asked me to take their picture standing in front of the stone edifice which had been the front of the building. I had been taking pictures of each object cleared from the bush by our party, but this was the one that the two older men specifically requested. Their request underscored what was already obvious: that the old Knabu sites, and the ceremonial house in particular, were places of considerable sentimental attachment.

The fourth and final stop on our *kastom* tour was, appropriately, the last shrine where sacrificial rites were practiced and where some of the last major Knabu chiefs are buried. This place, Kokhoilapa, was a more recent shrine than the one we had seen earlier at Sithalehe. Fr. Hudson observed wryly: "The pride of the Knabu invades the present."

The central object of interest here was the shrine where the skull and bones of a renowned Knabu chief named Osei are entombed. As the three worked to hack away the underbrush, they described the traditional mortuary procedure whereby the body was bound in a sheath (*saosago*) and placed in a tree to decompose. Sago leaves were, they said, spread underneath so that the sound of the decomposing flesh dripping onto the leaves signaled the state of the body. When the dripping sound ceased, descendants knew it was time to remove the skull and collect the bones for placement in the shrine.

When the three had finished clearing the shrine, they summoned me closer for the tour's climax: viewing the bones encased within. Josepa had carefully dislodged one of the large, flat stones near the top of the structure so that it was possible to peer inside. Sure enough, as I climbed into position to look inside, there in the exposed cavity was a yellowing skull, presumably that of Osei, with a few other bones also visible. I took a couple of pictures and gingerly stepped down from the side of the structure. Osei's shrine was never used for human sacrifice. Only pigs and garden crops are said to have been offered there. Another Knabu chief, Paul Riju, who had been baptized, is also buried at this site and his cement gravestone lies just adjacent to the stone shrine. My guides also noted that a second man is buried alongside the shrine as well, but they did not know his name.

Josepa called attention to a weathered conch shell perched on top of the shrine. With a hole bored into the side, conch shells were an effective means of trumpeting a signal through the valley. In particular, that conch was said to have been used by chiefs to signal that something important had occurred, calling others to gather at the chief's compound. Implicit in this scenario is the significance of chiefs for the social life of a region. The conch-blowing scene symbolizes the chief's role as one who initiated and focused collective action on a regional scale, particularly in response to events that might impinge upon the area from "outside," such as approaching raiders.

In this instance, the conch on Osei's tomb turned out to be an animated sign. It was said to have changed position from time to time without any person having visited the shrine. The implication is that the roving conch is a sign of spirit activity. Small anecdotes such as this are the stuff that animate the Maringe world with spirit presences – presences that proliferate beyond the bounds of the village where signs of spirit activity (*khofuboboi*, spirit "sign" or appearance) are frequently noted. In addition to the shrines, particular locations in the forest are associated with specific, named spirits (*na'itu kahra*, "live spirits"), often identified with individual or clan "owners" who may have the *kastom* knowledge and power to treat illness caused by them. Although spirit abodes, like shrine sites, are normally avoided, people do report personal encounters with spirits, sometimes close to or even in their villages. Numerous people I talked with reported catching glimpses of spirits at night, appearing as a faint glow, or as a cluster of fireflies. Encounters with forest spirits (*na'itu mata*) are almost always frightening and can have serious effects such as illness or craziness. One such example of this is given in the next chapter. Among the milder effects reported from encounters with malevolent spirits is the experience of disorientation, of becoming lost in otherwise familiar areas.

As the last Knabu shrine, Osei's *phadagi* evoked another narrative of transformation: this one about the era of increased raiding and headhunt-ing that ultimately forced the Knabu to migrate out of this area and take temporary refuge at the southern end of the island near Bughotu. Forest and Josepa here summarized the well-known story of this epoch in the Maringe past: marauding headhunters emanating from the western Solo-mons and Kia at the western end of Santa Isabel made raids along the Isabel coast, forcing less well-armed people to take refuge in hilltop forts or flee southeast (returning to their homelands only after pacification, see White 1979). In the case of the Knabu, they abandoned their lands and shrines and sought protection through alliance with the renowned Bughotu chief, Bera, said to have had a considerable military force (see chapter 5). But once the headhunting threat died down, the Knabu returned to their home region and, unlike others who had been converted while in the Bughotu area, the Knabu remained in a resolutely heathen state.[12] It was not until the legendary visit of Walter Gagai that they turned toward Christianity.

Having replaced the stones in Osei's shrine, and finished with the narrative and photographic record of our visit, we headed back to Togasalo. Before long we ran into the others we had started out with, now carrying two pigs trussed up and tied to poles.

The Knabu epic retold

Walking through the forest offered an opportunity for listening to the Togasalo men talk about aspects of their past that they regard as significant and also of interest to an outsider. I thought at first that these musings might have been more for my benefit than an expression of living concerns. But I was later persuaded otherwise as some of the same stories surfaced in other contexts for other audiences. Missionary encounters, such as the story of Walter Gagai meeting Matasi Iho and the subsequent conversion to Christianity, are regularly memorialized on various ceremonial occasions. Only a couple of months after I had heard the story of Knabu conversion told (in Pidgin translation) walking through the forest, I had the opportunity to record a somewhat longer version narrated in Cheke Holo.

Acts of reciting history are recognized as a special type of speech activity. Termed *susurei*, historical recitation is usually performed in the context of feasts and ceremonies. To *susurei*, whether in song or oratory, is to reconstruct historic events so as to communicate their collective significance. The narratives frequently focus on important persons, especially ancestors, enumerating places they lived in, locations of shrines, migrations, marriages and notable accomplishments of chiefs (which in the past would have included their successes in raiding or peacemaking). A skillful orator can weave together an account of key events interconnecting families, clans and regions in a shared history of mutual involvement.

One of the most evocative forms of historical narrative is a type of sung lament termed *thautaru* (verb form: *tautaru*). *Thautaru* are composed for particular ceremonial events, usually performed at moments of presentation to a feast sponsor or recipient. A *thautaru* is typically sung by a chorus of persons representing one "side" of the two groups involved in the exchange. These songs are sung in a subdued, lyrical style with the tone of a lament, expressing sorrow for deceased ancestors and nostalgic attachment for places of past residence.

The most frequent occasion in which I have heard *thautaru* performed is in a type of exchange in which a young man makes a ritual presentation of substantial amounts of food, trade goods and money to his father. Termed *faghamu thaego* (literally, "feeding the caretaker or guardian"), these exchanges are enacted with the expectation that the son acquires rights to certain of the father's possessions, primarily coconut and betel nut trees. These presentations are usually accompanied by a tearful *thautaru* that reviews the father's devotion to his children, interpreted as an expression of the child's gratitude and warm feelings toward his father. Although avowedly about personal and familial attachments, these *thautaru* usually bracket their message with allusions to places and events that represent shared history and collective identity for wider groups of people participating in the exchange. The opening lines of a *thautaru* performed at one such exchange in Togasalo illustrate this type of lyrical history:

Come listen	*Ke fanohmo mei ghu*
May you, father	*Iagho ia ba mama*
Children sing (*taru*) forth	*Ke sua taru ari ghu*
We (all of us) kindred	*Ghetilo tabusigna*
When living on	*Aui me au*
Salanisi ridge	*Ghukhui Salanisi*
There they lie (in death)	*Me thuru ari nodi*
Our grandfathers, grandmothers	*Ku'eda kaveda ra*
Our mothers, our fathers	*Idoda kmada ra*
The Salanisi church	*Khilo'au Salanisi*
Because of that	*Naugna teuana sini*
Grandfather in his thought	*Ku'e nogna gaoghatho na*
Decided that	*Me ghatho au ni nga*
They should come together	*Me salo mei di nga*
Grandfathers, grandmothers did	*Ku'e kave ra neku*
There at Sosrogha	*Ka photukui Sosrogha*
And then arriving at	*Meke tapla mei nga*
Togasalo ridge	*Ghukhui Togasalo*
Clearing gardens	*Me tobi ni thobi na*
Building houses	*Me banai suga na*
Was how it went . . .	*Ame ghu ari neku*

Notice the extent to which this song reflects the stories told by Forest and Josepa walking through the nearby forest. Like their story, the song refers to the movements of the Knabu as they converted to Christianity and first established a large Christian village on a neighboring ridgetop. Simply singing the name of that village, Salinisi, evokes a larger narrative about events of considerable significance for most people of Togasalo and their relations.

During the months following my first climb to Togasalo, I returned periodically to fill in various sorts of background information about the place, and on occasion for ritual events of importance to the community. One such occasion was a feast sponsored by several of the prominent

Togasalo families to mark the arrival of Christianity among their ancestors. About four months after my initial visit I once again ascended at the invitation of others, only this time for a special church service and feast. The event, I was told, is observed annually on the day of Pentecost – said to be the day on which the first Christian catechist, Walter Gagai, ventured into the area and made contact with the Knabu chief Matasi Iho. On the Sunday I visited, this occasion was combined with a wedding service. Villagers today commonly combine occasions for feasting in this way. By defining multiple purposes for a feast the sponsors may expand its size and importance by augmenting the number of people contributing to the preparations, and attracting a larger number of prominent guests. Like most of the Christian occasions for community feasting, the Pentecost remembrance is an annual event marked by some form of celebration each year by Togasalo people. On this occasion, three priests and one anthropologist were among the featured guests who spoke during the festivities along with the sponsors. For this feast, the sponsoring families contributed several baskets of garden crops, two pigs and fish, augmented by rice and other store-bought foods. The featured guests went away with packets of cooked pork, fish and taro pudding.

In anticipation of this event, I hiked up to Togasalo on a Saturday, the day before the Communion service and feast. It became customary during my visits to the village to spend the evenings in the large house of Forest Voko and his wife Selina (where my wife and I slept) with an assemblage of villagers gathered to tell stories and discuss matters of culture or language, often punctuated by starting and stopping the tape-recorder. The next evening, in between Josepa's account of one of the notorious "live spirits" known to have inhabited the region, and the telling of a well-known folktale by one of his cousins, Forest interjected that he wished to tell the story of the events memorialized earlier that day – the story of the arrival of Christianity and its acceptance by his ancestor, Matasi Iho (paragraph structure is mine):

Alright, there were six chiefs in this region. But there was one man who was the leader, the one whom we remembered earlier today [Matasi Iho]. The other five men were followers of his. They were all here and made feasts, *diklo* and dances . . . They still followed the old ways of killing. They would build ancestral shrines with stones. When this was done, they stood up to make feasts, to make feasts for one another and exchange baskets of food. This is what they were doing when Christianity arrived.

The Christian men who reached this area said: "We are afraid of the Knabu because they still kill, butcher and eat people." The news that had gone out about Sosrogha scared those who had come with the church. Walter [Gagai] arrived in Baghovu to begin teaching and heard: "The Knabu are like this." Father Walter Gagai thought: "Mmm, those are my fathers, those are my mothers in the Knabu region. It's up to me to go up there." So Walter Gagai went up. It was on this day now that he went up. Father Walter went up on the day of Pentecost. He said: "I want you [pl.] who are Christian [to come up] because the Knabu are still heathen." But, [they said] "Mm! We are afraid of that, we don't want to go in there." So Walter said: "Then just I will go in there to all my fathers and my mothers" and went up on this day of Pentecost. Just about this time he went up.

Walter Gagai went to Iho, Matasi Iho. "I want you [pl.] to come inside Christianity, father," he said. So he [Iho] said: "Alright, I will call my brothers, my warriors, my men," and he called them. But then, because of their heathen ways, they arrived and wanted to kill Walter. So Matasi Iho said: "No!, leave him alone, don't attack." But they were clamoring to attack, so my grandmother [Iho's wife] jumped up and hung a tapa cloth necklace on him so that Walter lived when he came up to open up that place Sosrogha. Because of this, Christianity began to reach them [the Knabu].

The big man whom we remembered today [Matasi Iho] was a good man. He did not have any [bad] ways. He did not engage in any fighting or recalcitrance. He never talked back. He was a good man and a good chief. The big man whom we remembered earlier today was sympathetic, sympathetic with people, sympathetic with children. He died on the day of Pentecost . . . This man was the leading chief here. This big man was the chief of this area, Matasi Iho. Because of this, Christianity reached the Knabu and the teaching reached the Knabu. The teacher who came to teach the Knabu was Wilson Bana who said "I will do it" because all the other teachers and leaders were afraid. After Walter came and opened up the area, saying "I'll go to them," Wilson Bana came to teach the Knabu.

Forest's account focuses particularly on the person of his maternal grandfather, Matasi Iho. The legend is, among other things, a mythic charter for the chiefly prominence of Iho, his descendants, and chosen successors. In this respect, it is a narrative of continuity, publicly restating the historical antecedents of regional identity and power which are as important as they are tenuous in local arenas engulfed by contemporary institutions of church and state. The legend is also a narrative of transformation that uses images of person, action and identity to create a story of personal and social renewal. These cross-currents of continuity and transformation make the conversion genre an effective vehicle for formulating self-understanding in communities contending with problems of fragmentation inherent in the colonial experience. Chapters 6 and 7 explore some of the means by which conversion narratives such as the Knabu epic work to recreate desired social realities, conceptualized in the prototypic identities of "Christians" and "chiefs."

A recurrent motif in these depictions is the image of "opening" in which previously "closed" communities are "opened" from outside (but with the collaboration of central ancestor figures). The "opening" motif makes use of metaphors of enclosure to conceptualize the moment of missionary contact as a kind of turning point in "opening" access to the wider (colonial) world. The traditional Knabu world is depicted as a bounded world which, like a dwelling, may be entered and exited. Walter Gagai does not simply visit the Knabu, he goes "inside."[13] He then in turn invites the Knabu to "come inside" Christianity. But to do so they must "come out" of their old ways. The enclosure metaphor is also the basis for the vernacular term for Christianity: *Khilo'au*, literally "call outside." The parallel oppositions of LIGHT/DARK and OPEN/CLOSED converge to produce the implication that the mission called heathens "out" of their world of "darkness" into another world of "light" and understanding.[14]

The metaphor of containment is also commonly used to conceptualize the role of the chief as the guardian of community boundaries. The chief, like Iho, mediates relations between "inside" and "outside," protecting his followers by figuratively standing at the boundaries and variously "shutting" (*fotho*) or "blocking" (*nagra*) access (see next chapter). The first steps toward conversion are represented in the Knabu epic through the actions of important persons – primarily chiefs and catechists or priests – who exemplify key identities, relations and modes of action. By focusing on Iho, the narrative sustains the importance of an ancestor and chief who personifies a distinctive regional identity. The story begins with reference to Iho's position as the most prominent among six regional chiefs. It is Iho whom Gagai first encounters on his quest to convert the Knabu; and it is Iho who calls together his followers and warriors in response. And Iho's role as the "leading chief" (*mae funei ulu*) responsible for the Knabu acceptance of Christianity is reiterated again at the story's conclusion.

Forest elaborates the moral significance of his story with remarks about Iho as a person, characterizing him in terms of personal qualities. He is said to have avoided "fighting" (*mamagra*) or "recalcitrance" (*huhughu*) and, more positively, to have been "sympathetic" (*kokhoni*) with "people" and "children." Chiefs and other big-men attract more of this sort of talk about personal dispositions and character than is usual for others in Maringe society. In the following chapter I speculate about why this may be so, inquiring into local concepts of person and the contexts in which they are articulated.

The characterization of Iho as a "good" chief – one who was both "sympathetic" and "peaceful" – is consistent with another component of his identity: that of the "Christian person." Even before conversion, Iho is said to have manifested ideals of sympathy and peacefulness central to Christian ideology. He is cast as a man of peace who listens to the missionary and attempts to protect him from his own warriors. In this respect, the portrait of Iho resonates with that of the catechist Gagai who, as the harbinger of the "new way" of Christianity, more directly personifies the Christian person. Like Iho's sympathy, Gagai expresses concern for the Knabu in the idiom of kinship as his "fathers" and "mothers."[15]

Iho's demeanor contrasts most sharply with the Knabu warriors who represent the stereotypic violence associated with heathen ways. The description of the Knabu at the opening of the story as people who were feared because they "still kill, butcher and eat people" is the background against which the persons of Gagai, Iho and Iho's wife are drawn. The interrelation of Christian and heathen is established at the moment of first encounter when the warriors seek to kill Gagai "because of their heathen ways." As a catechist who presumably partakes in Christian spiritual power or "mana," Gagai is not deterred by the fact that others were "afraid" to approach the Knabu with their reputation for violence. But the story implies that not even their chief, Iho, would have been able to restrain those who were "clamoring to attack" (*heta ghedi mala a'aknu*) had it not been for the intervention of Iho's wife. The scenario which sees the humble Christian missionary threatened by violence-prone warriors is perhaps the central image in memories of first Christian encounters, with each of the protagonists typifying contrastive categories of person.

Lest it appear that all this attention to a single text gives undue significance to a single person's view of history (and a version volunteered for anthropological recording at that) I now turn briefly to the ceremonial events staged by the community in its annual remembrance of Iho and the coming of Christianity. Whatever the actual timing of historical events, it was said that Iho died on the same day (years later) that Gagai first made contact with the Knabu, the day of Pentecost. As a result, the memorial feast held to "remember" (*gatho fapulo*) Iho is simultaneously a celebration of Pentecost and the arrival of Christianity.

As in *diklo* feasts, the importance of any large-scale feast is indicated by the status of its guests. These days this is measured in part by the number of priests who attend. On this occasion, three were present: one retired (himself a Knabu descendant) and two active. The day began with a Sunday morning Communion service which included the marriage ceremony and a sermon from the retired priest alluding to the first arrival of Christianity. Following the service, everyone filed out of the church and began making preparations for the feast. Within a short time the food was distributed on mats in the village plaza and a table and chairs set up under an impromptu shelter for the priests, chiefs and anthropologist.

Once the distribution was complete and people had gathered, the familiar sequence of prayer, eating and speech-making began. One of the priests and two village chiefs rose in turn to give speeches about the significance of the occasion. The priest who spoke said that the "real meaning" of the day was to "remember" the ancestor who first accepted Christianity among the Knabu. But, being from a neighboring area, he confused the name of the ancestor in question. Rather than Matasi Iho, he named Iho's son, James

Rage, as the person responsible for the historic act. He went on to link the marriage ceremony performed earlier in the morning to the conversion theme. Referring to the married couple, he said "joining the two together" was part of the "Christian life" (*nakahra Khilo'au*) which had begun with the legendary first encounter. Marriage would "make them good" and "make them grow."

Perhaps feeling the need to correct the mistake that most of the Togasalo people would have noticed, one of the younger village chiefs, who is also one of Rage's sons (and Iho's grandsons), stood up and spoke as follows:

Alright, on this day we are doing something to remember Matasi Iho. Because he was a man who was a leader in time of peace. Before that, a man named Osei stood as chief. And he was a bad chief who killed people, whose ways involved killing [for ritual sacrifice] . . . Then [he was] replaced by Matasi Iho, a chief of peace. And then Matasi Iho stood and it was as if to the west, to the east, and in the highlands, the way of fighting and killing was finished. And thus it has gone until we reach this present time of peace. Because of this, of what this man did, Maringe is alive, because of our ancestor [big-man], we remember him today. Every year when this day comes when he died, on the day of Pentecost, we remember him. It was on the day of Pentecost that they [Walter Gagai] came with the opening of Christianity. And it was on the day of Pentecost that he [Iho] died. Because he forbade axes and shields, we are alive. We will always remember this "big man" because we were born from him.

In restating the rationale for the feast, the speaker draws upon metaphors of "birth" and "life" to connect the concept of descent with a broader image of life seen as following from pacification and Christianity. By saying that Iho gave life by "forbidding axes and shields (warfare)" the speaker states that others, in addition to those descended from him, are figuratively "born from him." In this manner the idiom of descent is expanded through the metaphor of conversion to include others in the community who would but for that not be connected through common descent.

In this excerpt, as in the longer narrative cited earlier, Iho is recalled by his descendants as a person who embodied some of the core traits of Christian identity even prior to the advent of Christianity. In contrast to the "bad chief" who preceded him, Iho was a "chief of peace." The speechgiver characterizes pacification as an act of chiefly power: "Because he forbade axes and shields, we are alive." On another occasion, I would hear this same theme echoed in the speech of a much older and respected big-man speaking to a different audience assembled for a feast in his coastal village. That man (related through marriage to Iho's descendants) painted a similar picture of Iho by contrasting his ways with those of other chiefs during the conversion era. In that speech, Iho and another chief, Gano, were said to be "together" (*fofodu*), whereas other, "bad" chiefs were "still killing and eating people."

For the small community of Togasalo, and especially the descendants of Iho and Rage who make up a significant part of that community, the Pentecost ceremony with its church service, feast and speeches externalizes and reproduces certain key social understandings. The discourse of "remembering" (*gatho fapulo*) brings several identities into play, appealing variously to the descendants of heroic actors in the conversion drama, to the Togasalo community generally (heirs to the Knabu story), and, finally, to the sense of Christian personhood valued throughout the island. The beauty of the conversion story is that it represents the drama of Christian transformation in idioms of ancestry and history, thus simultaneously localizing Christianity while revitalizing elements of kinship and place that remain anchor points of everyday experience.

As seen in a variety of contexts in this chapter, understandings about shared ancestry, place and history are the symbolic "raw materials" from which a sense of mutual interest and community may be built in certain circumstances. In each context – a walk through the forest, a nighttime storytelling session, and a memorial feast – the activity of reciting history (*susurei*) works to create images of collective identity. But these images are neither ready-made nor self-propagating and must be continually reconstituted in the talk and activity of those who share them. Principal agents in these processes of cultural reproduction are the local leaders, especially chiefs, who in life speak of history and who in death are spoken by it, memorialized in ceremonies such as the Togasalo celebration of Pentecost and Matasi Iho. One of the lessons of my first tour of the Knabu past was that the names of ancestral chiefs are inscribed in the land in places such as Sithalehe where shrines are iconic reminders of a past where person, place and power coalesced more tightly than they do today. A closer consideration of local understandings of "traditional chiefs" will provide a frame of reference for interpreting shifts in power and meaning that have left Sithalehe overgrown with forest, and that have given rise to new symbols of identity in the conjunction of local and (post) colonial institutions.

4

Chiefs, persons and power

Readers familiar with the anthropology of Melanesia will realize that talk of "chiefs" is anything but straightforward. Not only do most societies in the region lack formalized titles of chiefly status, but further ambiguities in the power and legitimacy of local leaders have been created by the colonial experience. The encounter with the West has produced new discourses of tradition that have made chiefs a focal point for ideological innovation. As will be seen in later chapters, local chiefs are being created and recreated in the context of modern bureaucratized forms of governance. One way of interpreting these changes is to see them as the gradual replacement of one form of polity (indigenous, personal, particularistic) with another (Western, rational, universalistic). However, I argue that such an approach presumes a unidirectional evolutionary process that misses the multiplicity of practices that contend in the contemporary political arena. It is as important to note that Western political forms are assimilated within indigenous frameworks of meaning as it is to attend to the "impacts" of colonial forces.

In this chapter I suggest that present-day chiefs are a focus for ideas about persons, power and political institutions – a site where indigenous and Western practices mutually shape one another. Rather than see chiefs as a shrinking remnant of precontact reality, or as an invention of colonial society, I ask what the contemporary significances of "traditional chiefs" are. As glimpsed in the previous chapter, chiefly ancestors symbolize a range of meanings and values associated with localized, descent-based identities. Why focus upon these meanings if the former status of the "chief" as dominant political and religious leader is largely a thing of the past, an object of nostalgic recollection? This chapter suggests that ideologies of chiefly leadership continue to provide potent models that shape social experience and that have contributed to periodic movements to create new sociopolitical institutions capable of reconciling tensions between ideology and practice.

By beginning with one person's account of an encounter with a spirit-snake, I underscore the fact that the Cheke Holo universe remains an enchanted one, animated with powerful unseen forces that affect people's daily lives. Although the event described is extraordinary, it points to understandings about human agency and well-being that have been at the center of the Christian transformation and remain a major source of sociopolitical legitimacy (see chapter 6). The story serves to introduce a discussion of the former significance of chiefs as spiritual intermediaries. I then go on to elaborate other facets of chiefs as an exemplar of forms of identity and action associated with a past way of life. The chapter concludes by briefly examining two key contexts of practical action – settling disputes and making feasts – in which chiefly reputations are constructed today. By considering ordinary talk about tradition and chiefs it is possible to discern the often ambiguous and contested nature of understandings that might otherwise appear abstract and uniform. It is when models of chiefs are externalized in conversation or ceremony (usually with moral effect) that they may be subject to challenge, negotiation and revision.

A spirit encounter

One day as I was recording information about magical practices used to "sweet talk" giant prawns out of their holes in the sand at low tide, the speaker recalled an incident in which he had experienced a frightening encounter with a spirit (*na'itu*) snake several years ago. This person, whom I will call Thomas Mereseni, is known for his expert knowledge of magic used in fishing and healing. Experiences such as that which he describes below have enhanced his reputation in this area. I give only the beginning of his account (in translation), which went on at some length about the subsequent effects of this encounter on his mental and physical state.

One day I was thinking that I should go to do some garden clearing, and Samu and Robeti were supposed to go up and do their own clearing as well. They were going up to do their own clearing, and I was going up with my two dogs also. So we went up and reached a place that was sacred (*blahi*, tabu). Beginning long ago, the old men wouldn't do any clearing or anything at that place because that was a very sacred burial area of theirs. If anyone went and cleared there he would get sick, or die, or get injured. They had left their *kastom* at that place that was really very powerful (*nolaghi*, mana), but I mistakenly thought that since the church was already strong (*hneta*) that those *kastom* things would be "covered over by" Christianity. That's what I was thinking as I went to clear that area.

So Neni and Lithu are clearing the forest over in one direction, and I'm clearing another garden. As I clear and cut, working up the side of the hill, I look and see a large stone. "This looks like a large stone in front here," I think as I keep cutting on up. And there is grass growing up around the edge of this rock so in order to get rid of it I start cutting the grass, cutting around the edge of the rock when "kle!" the knife suddenly strikes something and this big snake stands up; the stone had become a snake, that big stone had! At that I was shocked and we [the snake and I] began struggling. I fought hard but the snake was strong, too, hitting me, biting me. I was flailing about with my knife but couldn't do anything until the head of the snake banged me and I fell over, rolling down onto the flats where I stood up again. I stood up and saw the snake looking at me from up there. At that I was furious and yelled for my two dogs.

As the story continued, Thomas told of a ferocious fight in which his two dogs finally killed the snake, and the two men working within shouting distance came over to see. When Thomas returned the next day to bury the snake, he found that it had turned back into a rock (a process termed *jukhu*). At that point he tells of experiencing a kind of disorienting possession, and racing helter-skelter downhill through the forest with the two dogs following, making such a commotion that others in the area thought they must have been hunting pig (known to create a great uproar in the forest). It was only when he finally reached the sea and plunged into the water that he regained enough of his senses to find his way home and lie down.

But home was no sanctuary. He then sensed that the snake was getting on his leg and his body. It was only by clutching his decorated walking stick, blessed by a powerful local Christian priest, that he was able to ward off the snake spirit. Whenever he held the walking stick the snake would move away, but whenever he released it he sensed the snake coming to his body again. So his family urgently summoned a traditional healer from a neighboring village and the healer was successful in ridding Thomas of the spirit. Although he recovered without ill effects, both of his dogs died, which he interpreted as a sign that the spirit had lodged in them when driven from Thomas' body by the healer (*fafigri*, literally, "made to turn back"). Thomas speculated: "Maybe if the dogs hadn't died, *I* would have or something... Because of that I survived. It was a hard thing, really difficult. These *kastom* things like burial areas and sacred grounds are very powerful (*nolaghi*, 'mana-ful')."

Thomas' story is an extraordinary one, no less for Cheke Holo speakers than for others such as myself unused to vivid accounts of personal encounters with spirit beings. It is, after all, an account of a life-and-death struggle. But for Thomas and other Santa Isabel people, the story, remarkable as it is, expresses cultural understandings about the everpresent reality of spirit forces, and the constant potential for their intrusion into everyday events. Western readers might well conclude that Thomas experienced a psychotic break with vivid and disturbing hallucinations of the sort reported by schizophrenics. But Thomas is not schizophrenic. He is a family man and respected village leader. He does evince a greater-than-average interest in and knowledge of the spirit world, and is regarded as one of the most effective traditional healers, but there are numerous others who share similar reputations. For most Isabel people, the palpable presence of spirit forces on the margins of everyday life is manifest in sudden deaths attributed to sorcery, in odd noises and appearances in the forest interpreted as signs of "forest spirits," and in geographic formations regarded as the iconic traces of mythological events. Much of Christian belief and ritual has taken over the role of indigenous practices aimed at maintaining a mantel of spiritual protection against just the sort of spirit attack experienced by Thomas. Whether individual healers or the priests who enacted rites of propitiation at ancestral shrines, those who possessed the appropriate spiritual knowledge and the artifacts required to communicate with spirit beings were the persons attributed with formidable personal power or mana (*nolaghi*).

As much as any single factor, it was the ability of a person to engage in ritual transactions with the spirit world that marked the chief as a person of extraordinary power. Traditional knowledge in the form of magical formulae used for healing and all sorts of practical purposes was (and is) widely distributed among men and women who inherit or purchase it, usually within families and lines of descent. However, the most potent, visible, and collectively significant forms of religious knowledge and power in the past were those associated with ancestral shrines such as Sithalehe, and the chiefs and priests who made ritual offerings there. The role of the chief as a proprietor of one or more ancestral shrines symbolized his status as clan head, manager of lineage lands and inheritor of the sacred relics required to communicate with ancestor spirits. It was at the shrines that chiefs and/or ritual specialist priests would communicate with spirits to help ensure collective well-being or cope with moments of crisis. In addition to propitiation offerings, acts of divination were an integral aspect of communicating with ancestors. Using any of several types of divination device, priests could "awaken" ancestor spirits to diagnose the source of present misfortune or to foresee future threats to the community. The actions of a traditional priest using a divination device to communicate with spirits constitute a central image in popular conceptions of *kastom* and ancestral religious practice (see Naramana 1987: 53; Vilasa 1986).

Access to potent spirits reinforced the power of chiefs to speak for and regulate the use of lineage lands and properties. Lineage leaders controlled the use of land, reef waters and nut-bearing trees (almond, betel nut or coconut) by issuing chiefly edicts. By announcing that certain property was tabu (*soka*: "restrict by applying a tabu") and marking it with a visible token, a chief could declare that property off-limits. Such a proclamation would be sanctioned with the threat of spiritual retribution since transgressions were thought to invoke the wrath of the chief's ancestors (whose names probably would have been invoked in the *soka* or tabu).

The ambiguity in contemporary beliefs about the continuing power and danger of abandoned shrines alluded to in the previous chapter surfaces in Thomas' story when he refers to his "mistaken" assumption that the dangers of the burial ground would have been "covered over" by Christianity. The same uncertainties voiced by Thomas are widely shared by others in Santa Isabel who speculate that shrine sites and burial areas continue to be protected by *kastom* magic, and that trespassing, however accidental, may result in illness or injury wrought by vengeful spirits. Snakes, particularly the sudden appearance of a multitude of snakes, are a culturally recognized sign of such violation. I have heard numerous people tell stories of their own experiences or those of their neighbors who have had unexpected encounters with scores of snakes that suddenly appeared out of nowhere while gardening or walking in the forest. All such stories are taken as evidence of spirit manifestations, of the work of *kastom*.

The visitor to contemporary Isabel communities who attends primarily to public ritual life might be excused for making the same assumption reported by Thomas that supernatural forces associated with *kastom* have been pushed to the margins or "covered over" by Christianity. Of course, being "covered over" or hidden does not imply that such forces are no longer effective or powerful. To the contrary, it is only the countervailing power of Christian practice that establishes the protective cover. The cultural significance of many Christian practices, such as the priestly blessing that bestowed protective powers upon Thomas' walking stick, stems from the role of Christian ritual in mediating *kastom* and Christian realms of experience. Later chapters (particularly chapter 6) take up the Christian practices that have been brought to bear on the long-standing dangers of the Isabel spirit world.

Chiefs

The English word "chief" appears less frequently in contemporary writings about Melanesia than the more favored "big-man."[1] But despite its ouster by the tides of anthropological fashion, the term has a long history in the region and may be heard throughout the Solomons archipelago today (see, e.g., Alasia 1989). Indeed, talk of chiefs (or, in Pidgin, *sif*) has become a central part of political discourse in the postcolonial Solomon Islands. This chapter poses the questions: "What is this talk of chiefs all about?" and "How do present conceptions of past leadership shape present realities?"

As might be expected from any term that has been so extensively topicalized and valorized in local discourse, images of chiefly leadership are many-faceted and many-voiced. This multivocality reflects the fact that the term is constantly susceptible to rewriting within local contexts of historical transformation. However, despite this thicket of variability, the primary meanings of chiefship lie within a field of understanding that has to do with land, ancestors, power and local communities caught up in a world political and economic system dominated by others.

One of the difficulties in exploring this conceptual terrain is that it is mapped by three languages in regular use: Cheke Holo (*funei*), Solomons Pidgin (*sif* or *chif*), and, in some quarters, English (*chief*). The complications, however, also provide clues to contrasts and shifts in meaning that bear on this discussion. Consistent with European notions of leadership as political office, the English/Pidgin usage (*chif*) is often used to refer to chiefs as a finite set of recognized leaders despite the fact that the people of most communities would not all agree on which individuals are chiefs and which are not. The objectification of chiefly status is further marked by the use of the English term, "chief," as a form of address. Thus, for example, it is recent practice for letters of invitation and correspondence that emanate from local government offices to use the address form "Chief —," on the envelope. Similarly, those who chair large political meetings may now be heard to recognize speakers as "Chief —," even when everyone present speaks Cheke Holo. I take these multiple usages and the intrusion of English terminology as reflections of a long history of cultural accommodation.

The term "chief" and its Pidgin counterpart, *sif*, entered readily into political parlance in Santa Isabel in the late nineteenth century when Europeans, some with Polynesian experience, sought out leaders they referred to as "chiefs" to further their own dealings in trade or evangelism. In Santa Isabel, where distinct traditions of political leadership exist in each of the major language groups, prominent individuals are referenced repeatedly in the accounts of early explorers, traders and missionaries (see, e.g., Amherst and Thomson 1901; Coote 1883: 140–51; Penny 1888; Shineberg 1971; Wawn 1893: 219; Welchman 1889–1908; Melanesian Mission 1895–1946). The relations which developed between chiefs and outsiders were at first beneficial to both sides – a process examined in chapter 5. Local leaders parlayed entrepreneurial advantage into expanded regional influence, and Westerners gained either trade goods or converts, according to their objectives. The irony, however, is that the initially expansive contacts with outsiders ultimately narrowed the role of chiefs and diminished their power.

Parallel to the ironic story of the constriction of chiefly power is another irony: even as their power diminished, chiefs became a prominent topic in the increasingly self-conscious and bureaucratized discourse of *kastom*. Isabel people have for at least a century (and probably longer) engaged in overt discussions about the status of chiefs, seeking ways of bolstering their visibility in the local arena. Because the cultural category of the "chief" is emblematic of locally defined polities, it focuses efforts to propagate community-based definitions of power. Epitomized in periodic movements to revive the paramount chieftainship (chapter 10), these efforts externalize current understandings about relations between local communities and the wider political economy.

As discovered in my first walk through the Knabu forest, past chiefs, or at least the ones that obtained some notoriety, tend to personify collective identities. Whether the lingering presence of an abandoned shrine or an annual memorial feast celebrating ancestral heroics, tokens of chiefly status signify genealogically and geographically salient constructs. Given my own voiced interest in local culture, with its connotations of the "way before," I found that much of the information offered to me had to do with chiefs. In the following I consider how models of traditional leadership relate to broader concepts of person and interpersonal relations, beginning with some of the more prominent cultural signs that mark chiefly status.

Funei: marking chiefly identity

The Cheke Holo term *funei* ("chief," "leader" or "important person") has a range of meanings, varying from a form of polite address to the acknowledged head of a descent group or region with responsibilities and powers over land and people. Usually assumed to be male, the term is often redundantly combined with "man" (*mae*) to form the phrase *mae funei*, also read simply as "chief." The implied "woman leader" (*ga'ase funei*) is also used, but more often as a term of respect rather than as a designation of leadership status.[2]

When people talk about chiefs they often imply that the chief is somehow different from most people. In contrast with ordinary "persons" (*naikno*) or "common men" (*mae khomabro*), the prototypic chief is thought of as bigger than life, as a man who is strong, powerful and who makes things happen. Indeed, the metaphor of bigness is often used. Chiefs are "big men" (*mae bi'o*) as opposed to "small men" (*mae sitei*, also "boys") who lack their stature and accomplishments. References to chiefs and their "people" presume an opposition between the categories "chief" (*funei*) and "person" (*naikno*) as distinct kinds of social agent. This contrast effectively narrows the sense of *naikno* to that of "ordinary person" or "follower" – a connotation that was apparently picked up by the first Spanish explorers who in 1568 recorded the term *nakloni* (a cognate of *naikno*) and translated it as "vassal," noting that it was used to refer to a chief's followers (Amherst and Thomson 1901: 126). Subsequent generations of explorers made equally stark interpretations of chiefly authority, sometimes modeling their accounts on European notions of kingship (e.g., Fleurieu 1791: 140).

The nature of chiefship as a distinctive and more powerful sort of agency is related explicitly to the chief's mediating role in regulating relations between persons and spirits (see White 1985a: 340). As the one who inherited ancestral knowledge, status and sacred relics, the chief mediated transactions with spirits, and so participated to some degree in their aura of spiritual power and danger. And, like those ancestor spirits, chiefs were often regarded ambivalently as both protective and severely punishing. Just how these multivalent perceptions are organized in Cheke Holo interpersonal relations is taken up below.

When people talked to me about chiefs, they would sometimes make distinctions among types of chiefs differing in degrees of power and influence (or "bigness"). Those who achieve recognition throughout an entire region or descent group are sometimes referred to as "renowned chiefs" (*funei nafnakno*) or, in the vocabulary fashionable today, "paramount chief." At this level, there tends to be greater agreement about who are (or were) chiefs. The image of larger chiefs located above or somehow encompassing their communities is expressed in modifiers such as "covering" (*fruni*, also *kmui*) that connote the shielding or protecting function of chiefs. Similar imagery is found in other parts of Melanesia, such as on neighboring Choiseul where people say that a leader "covered his people like an umbrella" (Scheffler 1965: 189). Metaphors of "covering," "sheltering," or "blocking" express the significance of the chief as one positioned at the boundaries of his community, facing outward to meet and deflect challenges from outside. Here again the markedness of the chief as a mediator, in this instance mediating the opposition of "inside" and "outside," is fundamental to the meaning of indigenous leadership.

With the advent of an array of new types of big-men such as Christian priests, government headmen, members of the provincial assembly and business entrepreneurs, the *prototypic* chief is conceptualized through contrasts with modern leaders – the exemplar of tradition or *kastom* expressed in images of a past way of life. Even though local leaders today are likely to build their reputations in conjunction with any number of new styles, talk of "chiefs" typically refers to leaders whose power is based in microtraditions of land, descent and village. Furthermore, retrospective views of chiefly activity frequently focus on those roles connected with warfare and sacrificial rites that have disappeared with pacification and Christianization. The images of chiefly leadership most commonly articulated in stories or depicted in dramatic enactments draw upon scenarios of a chief blowing a conch shell to gather his warriors or directing sacrificial rites at ancestral shrines.

As if to highlight further the larger-than-life status of the chief, people in their discussions with me would often mention the visible wealth controlled by traditional leaders, symbolic of their extraordinary power. Regional chiefs lived in larger houses, married more wives and controlled more shell valuables than others; they were "chiefs of wealth," *funei thogha*. In my records, the greatest number of wives attributed to a single chief was seven (not all concurrently). Having more wives would have implied greater productive capacity, with wives, children and other relatives working in the chief's gardens to produce surplus food for feeding pigs and exchanging at feasts. A chief's house was said to be two or three times larger than others and marked with distinctive decorative designs of various types. Traditional valuables made of shell and porpoise teeth were the quintessential sign of chiefly status. These valuables were not merely possessions; they adorned the person of the chief on ceremonial occasions and were primary items of exchange between chiefs, as in the *diklo* feasts described in the previous chapter. Types of chiefly adornment included shell armlets (worn on the upper arm ten or twenty at a time by those of high status), bracelets, circular shell breast ornaments, and belts and headbands made from porpoise teeth (see White et al. 1988: 254–5).[3]

Memories of chiefs seem to amplify their extraordinary status, positioned apart from the usual routines of daily life. Their distinctiveness is said to have been marked by etiquette as well as the visible accoutrements of wealth and adornment. As commonly remembered, approaching a powerful chief required attention to certain tabus or restrictions. For example, only euphemistic terms for eating, defecating and urinating were to be used in the presence of a chief. Mention of his name was strictly proscribed; and stepping on his shadow was regarded as a serious offense. As people today look back, the power of chiefs to punish offenders of the moral order is sometimes stated in absolute terms. Richard Naramana's statement (1987: 45) reflects the tone of this retrospective absolutism: "The chief or the elder of the tribe was always regarded as infallible. His orders were never opposed and everyone had to obey them." Chiefs are said to have wielded the sanction of death for a range of transgressions, including personal insults, endogamous marriage and sorcery.[4]

The most distinctive signs of chiefly status – the visible tokens of wealth, multiple wives and authority to punish with death – have all passed from the modern scene. Traditional valuables have mostly been traded or given away; Christianity imposes the rule of monogamy; and the government has usurped the right to impose coercive sanctions. Despite the decline in these material conditions of power, strong images of indigenous leadership past and present remain.

"Strong men" and violent history
Impressions of past chiefly power and strength are constituted in stories about an earlier time plagued by persistent violence – particularly the upsurge of raiding and headhunting in the mid-nineteenth century. Retro-

spective accounts portray a pattern of allegiances and alliances centered upon chiefs who could command a coterie of armed men if necessary. The warrior or "strong man" (*mae hneta*) featured in narratives such as the Knabu epic epitomizes the past ethos of violence. Behind narratives of conversion lie other stories about the exploits of warriors and raiding parties – stories that dramatize and reproduce a past characterized by pervasive fear and vigilance.

One such story is recounted in the next chapter, excerpted from the recollections of an old man who was himself kidnapped as an infant, given up to marauding raiders by his besieged community. Another example is given below in which invading raiders from the western Solomons get the best of a group of Maringe men, as they often did, leaving several dead and one taken captive. The storyteller, James Nidi of Maglau, is here talking about his ancestors, including his grandfather, Breara (who was taken captive), and his grandfather's father, Kidia (who was killed). The latter, Kidi'a, however, is depicted as a "strong man" who did not retreat from the fight, and was only killed because the raiders had a rifle:

On this occasion raiders came up the coast and took my grandfather. At that time these men [my grandfather's group] were living at Khasakho'u. They all came down to the shore because there was a big low tide and they could look for fish and shellfish in the ocean. But at that time men from the west were raiding here in Maringe.

My father's father was Breara. He was following after his father, Kidia, and his father's brother, Fihu. While they were fishing there, the attackers came and killed many of them. So the others took off for Juakhau (a small offshore lagoon island). Others went and jumped into the river. Then the men from the west went around Juakhau and searched inside the mangrove and killed the men hiding there, killed the men who had run away to that island.

There was another man who was with Kidia and Breara who was washing his clothes in the middle of the river and making noise. Because of that one of the men from the west who was downriver heard him washing clothes on a large stone and looked up the river and saw him. So the man from the west came up and killed the man washing clothes there. Then the man from the west realized, "these men might be hiding right here in this river." So he began probing with his axe handle and went until he jabbed Kidia. Then the big man Kidia came out ready to fight the man from the west. When the man from the west saw what a strong man Kidia was he jumped down, went back down river and called out to his friends. "Bring the gun, you all, this man is really strong." At that point, Breara's father tried climbing a banyan tree ... Breara listened for his father but when he heard "Pho!" from the place where the men from the west shot, he knew "Oh, father must be dead."

Breara's older brother was Fole and the two of them had both been with their father. After Kidia died, the men from the west took Breara, took him captive and headed back offshore when they found Fihu. Fihu and Vihi's father were both still out on the island of Juakhau. So the attackers chased them and Fihu went and jumped up in a tree and lay down on the back of a wide branch. Vihi's father then put on shell armlets and a breast ornament just like Fihu had on. When the men from the west saw him they chased him and killed him. But Fihu was still lying there on the back of that big branch. When they were finished and had gone off in their canoes, he went back up by himself to Kasakho'u. Later, after the church arrived, my father went and brought Breara back from where he had been kidnapped to Bilua.

The occasional retelling of small stories such as this is the stuff of which images of the past are reproduced from one generation to another. The stories are notable for the appearance of named ancestors opposing faceless raiders. Interestingly, I heard no stories in which the narrator attributed actions of grotesque violence to his or her own named ancestors. Where such actions are discussed – as in the case of the Knabu warriors mocking a headless corpse, or the sacrifice of an infant crushed underneath the central housepost for a new ceremonial house – they tend to be generic, not linked to one's own ancestors.

The physical strength and ferocity attributed to warriors are manifest in the stereotypic postures of the armed "strong man" poised for attack. An old man of Gnulahaghe village named Barnabas Sati told me that as a boy he had been trained in spear throwing and in using a shield for dodging, although the Christian peace arrived before he gained actual experience in warfare. Having said this, Sati proudly got out his wicker shield and steel axe and demonstrated the techniques he had never put into practice. In crouched position with shield held in front and axe poised behind, he peered out first on one side and then the other and swayed rhythmically as if dodging blows. Even though Barnabas Sati and others of his generation have now died, the posture of the warrior, with shield and axe held in outstretched arms, is commonly displayed in dancing and ceremonial activities.

Weapons – axe, shield, spear and rifles – are a frequent metonym for the violence of the past. They readily call up scenarios of attack and violent death, as well as the fretful vigilance maintained under conditions of constant raiding. Remembrances of the past, as in the schoolchildren's essays mentioned in chapter 1, frequently make reference to weapons and the necessity of carrying them in the pre-Christian era. At the same time, however, one may also detect traces of ambivalent respect for the warrior's impulsive strength and bravado. This was brought home to me by the comments of one old man who noted with some pride that really strong warriors would notch the wooden handles on their shields as a kind of kill count.

The ideal image of a warrior is a person who was "strong" (*hneta*), "aggressive" (*faheaheta*) and "brave" (*frane*). But the warrior's ferocity had to be cultivated. On the one hand, certain individuals performed the work of "professional killers" (*khana*) who could be contracted for their services in carrying out vengeance killings or assassinations. But for the ordinary warrior, aggressivity and ferocity had to be ritually heightened on the occasion of a raid. Prior to a raid, priests were said to call upon ancestor spirits to impart greater strength and fighting ability to the warriors. With the aid of ancestral spirits, the warrior could, it is said, become nearly

Plate 3 Barnabas Sati shows off his early training with shield and axe

invincible, drawing upon spirits to confuse, blind or sap the strength of his adversaries. Spirits could help one run, paddle a canoe, jump or fight with extraordinary strength. There were also magical formulae for increasing strength and reducing vulnerability, including potions that were ingested or administered into the blood upon setting off on a raid.

Ethnopsychology of the chief

Reminiscences like Forest's and Josepa's description of Knabu rituals of sacrifice show a distinct fascination with the violence associated with earlier times. It seems obvious that images of violence maximize contrasts between past and present; but they also express a certain nostalgia for a projected way of life in which the identity and vitality of local communities were personified by powerful chiefs and their "strong men."

In the course of listening to stories about raids or about warfare in general, I occasionally heard references to a well-known chief named Rekegau, notorious for his exploits as a warrior. One person described him as the "strong man" for Matasi Iho (implying a separation between the warrior and the "good chief"). Indeed, Rekegau is mentioned in missionary diaries as one of the intransigent leaders who led his followers away from the Bughotu area and back to Maringe to avoid contact with the mission (Welchman 1889–1908). I was quite eager to hear more about such a prominent "strong man," so I sought out Rekegau's descendants in a neighboring village for more information.

As it turned out, an old man, Timothy, who had been a regular informant on matters of *kastom* and genealogy, was Rekegau's sister's daughter's son (a direct uterine descendant). On one of my visits to his house I asked Timothy if he would tell me about his ancestor. I posed my request by asking him to talk about Rekegau in an open-ended way, simply to "narrate" (*toutonu*) rather than answer specific questions, thinking he might describe a specific raid, or perhaps recite parts of his life history. Instead, he offered a kind of verbal portrait of Rekegau as a person:

When Rekegau was growing up and could understand things, his father decided to teach him how to fight. But he was certainly not taught to kill indiscriminately. Rekegau didn't think: "I can simply attack and kill people." His kinsmen, offspring and sisters were all his friends. Rekegau didn't kill anyone without a purpose. He didn't look for compensation payments or attack unprovoked anyone who passed in front of him. If he was eating and someone went to defecate, he wouldn't get angry and strike the person. He was restrained with all his friends. Even though someone would defecate, or urinate, or speak harshly and swear, he would not get angry with them. Rekegau was like that. He didn't kill or harm others needlessly. He was sympathetic with people and with his fellow clan members. It was Rekegau's way to take care of people. He was a strong man and he did kill. But other chiefs would summon him before he would do any killing. He wouldn't simply say: "I am going along [on a raid] in order to kill." Before he would go out on raids, chiefs from other places would say: "Come along on a raid against this village, friend. You accompany us and we'll all go to attack these people." It was not the way of Rekegau simply to say: "I am going to attack the people of that place." But in standing as a heathen, Rekegau was one man in this area who was strong in times past.

As I listened to this account, I was surprised and a little disappointed. It was not what I had expected. Timothy had described his ancestor as a "sympathetic" person of balanced temperament. Where was the Rekegau whom others had referred to as the epitome of the fierce and even ruthless warrior? One possibility is that the portrayal was tailored for the occasion: tape-recorded remarks elicited by an anthropologist. But there is more to it than this. On closer inspection, the narrative does portray Rekegau the "strong man." In fact, it presumes those qualities and, for that very reason, focuses on other facets of Rekegau as a person in the context of his relations with "friends" and "kin" – one of whom is the narrator.

It is significant that Timothy talks in person-centered terms, describing Rekegau's personal dispositions and relations with others. He gives a generalized portrait of his ancestor, just as Forest Voko did in his recollections of his mother's father, Matasi Iho. In both cases, the distinctive qualities of chiefs emerge in the course of reminiscence. Timothy begins his account with a statement that Rekegau learned how to fight and kill, reminding us of his reputation as a "strong man." But the focus quickly shifts to his "restraint" in everyday life, especially in interactions with friends and kin. Rekegau is described as "sympathetic with people" (*kokhoni di naikno*), as someone who "took care of others." Much of the narrative is concerned with qualifying Rekegau's reputation as a "strong man," with mitigating his remembered potential for harming others, except in specific contexts.

The language and phrasing of the narrative reinforce the characterization of Rekegau as "sympathetic" – an attribute usually applied to powerful persons (and, nowadays, to God) to indicate that their relations with less powerful others are, ideally, tempered by compassion. The implication is either that the powerful person will "take care of others" or, at least, that he will not indiscriminately harm them. Along these lines, much of Timothy's portrait is cast in terms of what Rekegau was *not*: he did not get angry, even at violations of etiquette which might be expected to produce anger, and he did not "kill or harm others needlessly." These attributions temper the inference that a "strong man" such as Rekegau would be volatile or destructive in his daily encounters with others.

At first glance it seems dissonant that Rekegau is both a killer and "restrained." However, these characterizations are indicative of the highly contextual, relational nature of local person concepts (cf. Read 1955). Rekegau's aggressive actions ("killing") are conceded, but placed in the context of legitimate leadership activities – in this case, cooperating with other chiefs who requested his assistance in attacking mutual enemies. In this way, his qualities as a fierce killer are directed outside the boundaries of kin and community. Even though a person, especially a chief, may be characterized with global descriptors such as "strong" or "sympathetic," these attributes pertain to persons-in-relations rather than to individuals as social isolates, independent of social context. The specific problem or dilemma articulated in Timothy's description of his ancestor appears to be the moral formulation of the strong man's potential for violence – locating it in appropriate contexts (vis-à-vis enemies) and excluding it from others (in kin relations).

Timothy has, in the above passage, articulated a major theme in the anthropological literature on Melanesian big-men. Since big-men are said to achieve their influence more through personal qualities than inherited or ascribed rights, considerable attention has been paid to the "personality traits" of traditional Melanesian leaders. The anthropological discourse has concerned itself with both cultural *beliefs* about personality as well as the actual personality types of leaders (frequently assuming a convergence between the two). Numerous writers, commenting on the ideal traits of big-men, have pointed to the salience of strength and aggressiveness as characteristics of successful big-men (see, e.g., Oliver 1955; Sahlins 1963; Valentine 1963; among many others). At the same time, many have noted the problematic nature of aggression for big-men who risk alienating their followers if they are too demanding or intimidating (what Sahlins [1963: 293] referred to as the "Melanesian contradiction"). The dilemma was succinctly stated by Watson (1967: 103) for a highland New Guinea society: "The political ideal rather calls for the leadership of men of strength but, when they arise, the Tairora often experience with them the moral conflict expressed in characterizing them as 'bad.'"

Many ethnographers have sought a conceptual resolution of the dilemma of dominance in the personalities of successful big-men. The model of traditional leadership posed by Read (1959) for the Gahuku Gama has been widely cited as a prototype. In its simplest form, Read proposed that Gahuku Gama understandings about personality are organized in terms of two basic dimensions or orientations: "equivalence" and "strength." The difficulty is that these two dimensions may be regarded as "antithetical" (1959: 427) since "equivalence" represents notions of fairness and compromise which may be overridden by unrestrained "strength" or "bigness." Traits of "strength" are regarded with wariness and hence pose a problem for aspiring big-men who, ideally, exhibit both types of qualities (1959: 434–5):

As a rule the ideal masculine type is found toward the extreme of "strongness" and "bigness." Yet it is not the men who most closely approximate the stereotype of the "strong" man – not the truly "big" – who tend to be the most successful leaders. Indeed, extremes of "strength" and "bigness" are probably incompatible with the role of leader ... the truly "big" – if we accept the descriptions given by informants – are characteristically aggressive, somewhat compulsive and overbearing. These may be valuable assets in warfare and raiding ... But the precipitate, compulsive individual may be a constant source of irritation or disruption in his own group, where the use of force or the threat of force is proscribed under the ideal of group consensus.

Read's formulation focuses upon the person of the big-man, but does so without an explicit account of Gahuku Gama concepts of person, of how they are applied to big-men, or how they may or may not map onto our own assumptions about "personality." In another article (1955), Read raises more fundamental questions about the Gahuku Gama concept of person, noting its highly contextual character (see also Leenhardt 1979). In that work, he lays the groundwork for a somewhat different resolution of the moral dilemma of big-men. There he finds the resolution more in the social organization of the person than in the personal organization of society. Only by examining local ethnopsychological formulations more directly, particularly in regard to big-men, is it possible to determine the extent to which dominance constitutes a moral dilemma and is in fact variably evaluated across a variety of contexts.

Analysis of Cheke Holo concepts shows that, at a general level, linguistic descriptions of persons tend to cluster together into two distinct dimensions which I have interpreted broadly as "solidarity" and "dominance" (White 1978, 1980a).[5] Keeping in mind that there is nothing sacred about these particular English labels (i.e., that they are an approximation of themes suggested by semantic similarities among Cheke Holo words), they bear an uncanny resemblance to Read's (1959) dimensions of "equivalence" and "strength."

One possible explanation for the parallel between the Cheke Holo data and Kenneth Read's model is the universality of meaning in interpersonal language at this level of generality (White 1980a). However, the structure of Cheke Holo person concepts also speaks to the moral dilemma noted by Read (1959) when he characterized the principles of "strength" and "equivalence" as "antithetical." The dimensional model of the Cheke Holo lexicon shows dominance to be *morally ambiguous*. If we take the opposition of "solidarity" and "conflict" to express the most evaluatively loaded dimension of meaning (anchored in the contrast of words like "kind" and "sympathetic" versus "greedy" and "recalcitrant"), then the moral significance of traits of dominance ("strong," "commanding") or submission ("fearful," "obedient") is less predictable. Without a specific context to fix their moral implications, words such as "strong" and "commanding" are as likely to connote conflict ("recalcitrant," "greedy") as they are harmony or solidarity ("sympathetic," "kind").

In practice, however, talk about persons and social action is never neutral. It is always evaluative, implying that actions or events are either desirable or undesirable from the speaker's perspective. And, upon closer scrutiny, the apparent ambiguity of Cheke Holo terms for personal "strength" disappears once they are contextualized. When people explain the meanings of descriptive terms in their own words, they inevitably situate terms within a field of action and identity. For example, in asking people to explain the meanings of words such as *faheaheta* ("aggressive"), I found that traits of dominance are inextricably bound up with the social contexts of chiefship. Talk of dominance (at least among men) usually evokes reference to the roles and activities of leadership: speaking at meetings or feasts, directing and organizing work activities, engaging in transactions with spirits, and, in the past, raiding and fighting. Each context establishes a framework that fixes (or at least narrows) an action's moral and emotional meaning. One older man with particular insight into his own language reflected upon the alternative moral possibilities for the term *faheaheta* ("aggressive"). When I asked him to explicate the word, he traced its ranges of evaluative meanings by shifting its context, linking it first to the activities of "making feasts" or "talking about plans for working," and then to prototypic expressions of conflict ("fighting or stealing"):

A man can be *faheaheta* in talking, in working or in the bad ways of fighting. Chiefs can be *faheaheta* in making feasts, or in talking about plans for working or leading people. Another meaning is the way of fighting or stealing. A person may be *faheaheta* not because he is really bold, but because he is fearful or angry.

In this example, the speaker focuses on the alternately positive and negative meanings of aggressive behavior (*faheaheta*). In doing so, he invokes the status of the chief as a frame that legitimates assertive action, giving them positive significance.

Very similar reasoning is evident in another person's explication of the term "quarrelsome" (*mamagra*, from *magra*, "fight"). In this instance, the direction of reasoning is turned around. Rather than beginning with an attribution of dominance and working toward more evaluatively loaded terms, the speaker begins with one of the most negative terms in the language (*mamagra*, "quarrelsome") and works toward concepts of "strength":

A man who is *mamagra* can fight about land, about food, about almond trees, breadfruit or anything. He thinks that he is high, above others; that he is boss; a haughty (*fahaehaghe*) and aggressive (*faheaheta*) man. In the past he might be the one to give orders to go and raid people somewhere. A man who is strong (*hneta*) can do anything because he is strong, that's how he can fight (*magra*). He isn't sympathetic, he's a fighter.

The chain of association here reveals just the sort of moral ambivalence noted widely in perceptions of Melanesian big-men. Highly negative attributes such as "quarrelsome," "haughty" and "aggressive" all bundle together in images of leadership. Notably, however, the one who "is boss" or who would "give orders" is associated with the past, as one who would likely "go and raid people," who would be a "fighter." The moral quandary arises from the fact that such a person "can do anything because he is strong." Effective action and personal "strength" are seen as desirable and important elements of the image of the traditional chief. And yet, such a person is said not to be "sympathetic," as Rekegau was said to be by his descendant Timothy.

The contrast between this generalized, faceless portrait, and that constructed by Timothy for his ancestor Rekegau, is sharply drawn. Rekegau was both "fighter" and "sympathetic." The implication of the above passage is that one excludes the other. The difficulty for the aspiring leader, then, is to demonstrate "strength" and the "ability to do anything" without being cast as "haughty" – a problem which is not only Melanesian (see, e.g., Kirkpatrick 1981).

Metaphorical language used to characterize chiefs also reflects ambivalent emotions surrounding chiefs and dominance. A recognized traditional leader is one who is said to be the "first man" or the "man in front" (*mae ulu*). A powerful *funei* is not only "big" (*bi'o*), he is figuratively "above" (*au fakligna*) or "high" (*au fahaghe*). Accordingly, followers of such a person show respect by "looking up" (*filo fahaghe*), as in the English idiom. However where a person is not regarded as a *funei* representing the interests of others (which itself is likely to be a variable judgment) those very same metaphors may easily express negative valuations. Without legitimation dominance may connote self-aggrandizing actions that run counter to the goals and interests of others. The potential for ambivalence here reflects a sociology in which leadership status is often ambiguous and contested, extending across multiple and overlapping collectivities. Consider the language of illegitimacy. One who is seen to assume leadership status inappropriately (as in attempting to direct a work task, without actually doing any work), may be said to "make himself big" (*fabibi'o*), "put himself above" (*fakliakligna*) or "make himself chief" (*fafuefunei*). As if to counter the problem of self-aggrandizement symbolically, Cheke Holo speakers reverse the metaphors of prominence to say that an ideal leader "puts himself behind" (*au faleghu*) his followers.

These concepts of relative status or importance are expressed in locative metaphors (above/below, in front/behind) that conceptualize social relations in terms of spatial positioning. A person described as "making himself high" (*fahaehaghe*) is, by implication, "making others low" (*fapaipari*). The relational structure of these images reflects local assumptions about the fundamental interdependence of persons in society. Construing a person as "putting himself high" is a commonly voiced verbal weapon turned upon those whose actions are regarded as individualizing or self-centered.

As moral claims are advanced in contexts of ordinary talk and interaction, concepts of person and chiefship are more readily externalized and debated. Consider briefly one example in which understandings about chiefs were invoked to argue about how a particular incident of village conflict should have been handled by the parties concerned. The interlocutors in this exchange, two cousins named Kesa and Bilo (pseudonyms), are arguing about whether or not the police should have been contacted when Kesa's son was beaten up by a gang of boys led by Bilo's son. Bilo, whose son was ultimately taken to the local court and fined in this affair, suggests that village chiefs would have been a better means of handling the conflict. In raising this possibility, Bilo touches upon the more basic conceptual opposition between chiefs and modern leaders, and, more broadly, between tradition and modernity.

The discussion between Kesa and Bilo took place in a village meeting called for the purpose of airing bad feelings associated with past conflicts (see White 1990). Kesa's claim that the incident would have been better handled outside of court produced some illuminating dialogue about the significance of "chiefs" in contemporary life. The two men disagree about the role of the police, the court and chiefs in this particular incident, but share certain assumptions about typical modes of chiefly conduct. In particular, their comments reflect a view of the chief as a symbol of tradition and community-based practices, in contrast with the institutions of modern government such as police and courts. The following exchange is excerpted from a longer sequence in which both men recalled the details of this incident and their responses to it.

KESA Suppose you, older brother Bilo, or John Maghati [the catechist in Bilo's village] had gotten up and just come straight to me and said: "These boys have done this [beaten up Kesa's son]. What are we [all of us] going to do about it, man?" Then maybe that would have been the end of what the three boys started, of the news about the fight. If it had been up to us [inclusive] maybe that would have been the end of it, in the way of togetherness (*fofodu*), of discussing (*roghei*) things. But with the police in it, our [inclusive] part was finished. But this is what I thought afterward when it was too late.

BILO . . . In my opinion, when these things happen we should first work them out among ourselves. We handle it ourselves before concluding: "This business is bad, it's suitable for that place [the district court]." That could have happened with this business. That's what should have been done first, rather than hurriedly by-passing it. Chiefs are supposed to do this, are supposed to decide about these things with us [inclusive] . . .

I said: "Alright, it's that way. The way of that place [the district court] is on the rise; this way of paying fines is on the rise . . . This is what is happening at the present. Modern ways are alive now. The way previously would have been to be sympathetic (*kokhoni*) with a person before going that way [to court] . . . That still seems the best way – the way my two eyes didn't see, although they were open; my ears didn't hear, although I was listening . . . We could have taught them, but it seems too late for that. We have gone by that. We have gone straight into the live fire . . ."

KESA At the present time, this is what things are like. The police look for whatever we people do or say. Even if the village chief doesn't know about something, it gets outside. And the police will take a man to court. These days the police don't ask or anything. They just come to collect a man, whoever he may be, and take him to jail. They don't ask the chief or any man in the village. It's just they themselves who hear the path of talk and follow it to the people, to a village where they ask questions because of whoever started the talk. It's at court where people go and say: "We did this and we did that." That's all the police are doing. This life today is no longer up to the village chiefs. It was during the time when police hadn't come that village chiefs would straighten out affairs before sending them to court. Now they just come and simply take [someone] according to talk.

Kesa and Bilo disagree about how the council constable, the police, and the court came to be involved in this affair. But they both presuppose understandings of chiefly behavior that contrast with "modern ways" of police or government. At the heart of this contrast is the culturally constituted theme of solidarity discussed above. In this case, the chiefly posture of being "sympathetic" and first talking things through stands in opposition to the actions of police who ". . . don't ask or anything. They just come to collect a man, whoever he may be, and take him to jail." Kesa's statement about the "way of togetherness, of discussing things" is echoed by Bilo who talks in the past tense about the customary way of being "sympathetic with a person" before seeking legal redress. Both of them regard the chief as personifying traditional means of resolving disputes through talk, although they differ about the extent to which chiefs have been marginalized in contemporary society. Their statements recall images of the "good chief" that temper chiefly potentials for unrestrained "strength" or dominance. The concerns with dominance are here transferred to government agents (police) characterized as acting without regard for prior social relations or any kind of shared history of mutual involvement.

The exchange between Kesa and Bilo reflects conventional knowledge about the progressive narrowing of the power of local chiefs as government institutions encroach upon their spheres of activity and legitimacy. But this is a longer story of historical accommodation to be taken up in subsequent chapters. The argument I have been making here is that these ongoing processes of historical transformation are constituted in and through cultural understandings about persons and chiefs. The chief is a prominent topic of conversation and interest because he mediates the (shifting) boundaries of community that constitute the collective "we," differentiating "inside" and "outside."

By noting various points of disjunction between ideal models of chiefs and contemporary realities, it is possible to look at social process in terms of the diverse meanings and ideals that vie for legitimation, with some emerging as authoritative and others remaining submerged, such as the village chiefs ignored in Kesa's court case or the "tabu place" stumbled across by Thomas Mereseni. But these apparent oppositions – between chiefs and courts or *kastom* and Christianity – are by no means separate or disconnected. To the contrary, they are mutually constitutive, such that each defines the other as they are invoked in contexts of practical action, whether in encounters with dangerous spirits, in village disputes or, as already seen in the previous chapter, in feasting.

Feasting and the practice of chiefship

Among the recurrent contexts for chiefly action are the many feasts large and small that punctuate village life. For reasons discussed earlier, the former *diklo* feasts organized as exchanges between chiefs were probably the single most important arena for constructing and validating regional leadership status. While the reciprocal cycle of feasting has been altered by Christianization (see chapter 6), the feasting process – planning, organizing, and exchanging accumulations of food and gifts – continues to be politically salient. As noted earlier, the productive activities required to sponsor feasts underlie the multifunctional roles of local leaders as lineage heads, managers of land and gardens and village spokesmen. Even as the occasions for large feasts have been appropriated by the institutions of church and government, feasts continue to valorize constructs of place and descent that are central to images of traditional leadership. As chiefly roles in warfare and ancestor propitiation have been stripped away or transformed by the tides of change, the practice of feasting remains a primary activity for constituting power and identity in the local realities of ancestry and land.

Sponsoring feasts requires resources. The larger the feast, the more extensive and diverse the resources required. At a minimum, feasting necessitates the accumulation and distribution of food – food to be consumed at the time of the gathering and to be taken away by the guests in the form of cooked pork, fish, turtle and pudding, as well as baskets of uncooked food. To say that one went away from a feast hungry is to say that the hosts failed to meet normal expectations for such an event. Garden produce provides the staple foods for these purposes, supplemented by meat, fish, nuts and other delicacies, as well as store-bought foods such as rice and corned beef. Even though money (which has itself become an exchange item) is now used to purchase many of the most prestigious items distributed at feasttime (such as bags of rice or cases of canned meat), the bulk of foods eaten and distributed at feasts continues to depend upon the productive capacity of the hosts and their network of contributors. At the core of such networks are overlapping relations of kinship, marriage and coresidence that become the paths for coordinating the work of cultivating gardens, tending pigs and going out on hunting and fishing expeditions. It is practices such as these that give substance to the roles of local chiefs as matriline heads and village spokesmen.

Large feasts like the *diklo* exchanges of old are a kind of processual litmus test – sampling, prodding and momentarily validating social realities that emerge in the activities of production, exchange and ritual performance. The more ambitious the feast, the wider and more diverse the network of people who must be drawn into it as sponsors and recipients. Most of the smaller feasts sponsored by one family or localized descent group tend to be associated with life-stage transitions, such as birth, marriage, honoring the father, or death. Although the scale of these varies depending upon the abilities and ambitions of the sponsors, these events typically draw upon well-established social relations and expectations for their enactment. Larger events on the scale of *diklo* would require (and hence demonstrate) a more extraordinary level of political power. Today, as before, the prominence of a chief depends upon the degree to which he can extend his influence in demonstrable ways beyond localized groupings of kith and kin.

One of the largest feasts put on in Maringe during my first period of fieldwork was a Christmas feast sponsored by a local leader named Charles Bice Thegna. In many ways, Charles fits the image of a modern Melanesian entrepreneur. He is the son of the former district headman, Frederick Pado, who was the most prominent political figure in the region during the postwar period (very aged at the time of the feast, he died a couple of years later). Although not the oldest son, Charles is regarded by many as the successor to his father's position of influence in the region. He is knowledgeable about matters of land, ancestry and *kastom*, and also active in the spheres of government and development, having been elected to the local council (now provincial parliament) and organized a commercial agricultural project. At the same time, he is one of the most visible feastgivers in the region. From the time I first heard of this feast, it was clear that it was "Charlie's" initiative. And yet it was defined as an occasion with several purposes. In addition to celebrating Christmas (which would not in itself evoke an extraordinary effort such as this), the feast was planned to mark the establishment of a new inland village on ancestral lands by some of Charlie's relatives and associates, as well as to give testimony to his status as a chief. Additionally, a priest (the newly ordained Fr. Lagusu who translated on the Knabu tour) would be married in the church service planned for the occasion (Lagusu is also Charlie's lineage mate and cousin (MMMZDDS)).

As the sponsor of this event, Charlie relied upon a core of people associated with him through descent, marriage and village residence, most of whom were also cooperating with him in the new agricultural project. There was here a mutuality of purpose. Those involved with him through these various connections could themselves identify with the Christian event as a celebration of their collective resources and accomplishments in other spheres. At the same time, to the degree that they acted upon this, their expectations would be validated in the scale of the distribution. As Charlie and some of his closer relatives talked about the rationale for the event, they referred to the need to remind themselves and others living along the coast that their ancestors once lived on lands in the area of the new village of Kolokofa. For example, in one village meeting three weeks before the feast, Charlie's sister prodded some of her neighbors about their slack attitude toward preparing for the event by reminding them that their ancestral lands are in the Kolokofa region, and that one day the coastal landowners (where their present village is located) might remind them of that fact. By alluding to ancestors and land, the feast sponsors invoked potent symbols very much like those that emerged in the reminiscences of Forest and Josepa about the Knabu past.

The larger and more ambitious a feast, the more likely that the meanings and motivations for collective participation will be challenged and negotiated in the organizational process. And this was indeed a large feast, on the order of the *diklo* feasts referred to by the early missionary Henry Welchman as "great feasts." The Christmas feast was about three years in the making, and attended by an estimated 500 people drawn mainly from six villages. The logistics of feeding and housing this many people required lengthy planning which had begun from the time Kolokofa was first settled. Preparations for the feast included the construction of five large thatched shelters in Kolokofa as temporary housing for the guests. In addition, the village church was extended in size, nearly doubling its capacity so that the planned Communion service and wedding could be accommodated. Construction of four of the shelters was done by men from two nearby villages and the fifth by men from Charlie's and one neighboring village. Charlie paid for this work by "chartering" the construction of each shelter at ten dollars each (equivalent to twenty US dollars at that time) – money available to Charlie because of his commercial activities. After the feast, Charlie made a gift of the materials used in building the shelters to the Kolokofa people for their contributions to the feast.

One way of measuring the size and importance of a feast is the number of pigs that are butchered for the occasion. In this instance, about thirty-three domestic pigs and forty-two wild pigs were cooked. I was told that nearly forty domestic pigs had been raised for the feast, but since they were not penned, several could not be located. Charlie, together with his wife and several close relatives (especially a half brother (MS), a cousin (MZS) and his wife's father – all in his lineage), had been acquiring pigs regularly during the three years and sending them to Kolokofa where residents of the new village looked after them. Hunting and fishing expeditions mounted intensively during the month preceding the feast produced the forty-two wild pigs and hundreds of parcels of cooked fish (one person estimated that 1,000 were distributed). Two or three men from each of five villages did much of the pig hunting in a less populated region of the island where wild pigs are more plentiful; while the fishing was done primarily by men from two of these villages along the coast. In addition to the gardening, hunting, fishing and construction work, money also had to be raised to purchase rice, navy biscuits, canned meat, tea, sugar and other store-bought items now expected on such occasions. Some of this was contributed by Charlie himself, and the women of Kolokofa raised $100 by working for four days on a nearby church-run agricultural project. Other contributions were raised from relatives of Charlie and the Kolokofa people working for wages off the island.

Although timed to fit the annual celebration of Christmas, and further rationalized as a commemoration of the new village, the social meanings that emerged in the feast process centered to a large degree upon the person and career of its sponsor. At one point this was made explicit in plans to "ordain" (*taofi*) Charlie as a (the?) leading chief in the area. Some of his supporters conceived of this as a kind of rite of succession – a ceremonial enactment of Pado's wish that his son continue his generalized leadership role in Maringe (in fact, since Pado's death, Charlie has adopted his father's name and is now known as Charlie Pado). But, in the end, no such ordination was attempted. One person explained to me that Charlie's sister had ridiculed the idea of "ordaining" a chief, saying that this was reserved for priests, not chiefs. There was also some concern that such a public display might attract sorcery attacks. As will be seen in later chapters, however, the notion of using Christian ritual to sanctify the power and status of a traditional chief was not without precedent (most recently in the ceremony to "anoint" a new paramount chief held just five months earlier). The very fact that the feast was considered as an occasion for enacting an "ordination" is testimony to the continuing force of the *diklo* model in which sponsors were the recipients of ritualized acts of recognition. The imagined ordination sought to reinject chiefly practice with an element of spiritual authority – an authority long since appropriated by the church. Like any concept that ventures a novel recombination of cultural elements, the ordination idea risked resistance. Even though it was ultimately rejected, similar models of chiefly practice had emerged previously in Isabel history (see chapter 9) and would again in years following 1975.

Even though the Kolokofa feast did not explicitly "ordain" Charlie, it did link him with the institutions of spiritual (Christian) power by engaging the bishop and priests as honored recipients of gifts and speeches. Although no longer defined overtly as transactions between chiefs engaged in cycles of reciprocal exchange, feasts are still conceived largely in terms of the leaders who initiate them and the prestigious guests who attend them. Only now the invited guests come largely from the institutions of church and state (bishop, priests, members of parliament, etc.); and they generally do not present the sponsor(s) with gifts or shell valuables. On the contrary, it is the *guests* who are the primary recipients of ritual presentations, effectively reversing the *diklo* pattern. In this feast, the guest of honor was the Bishop of Santa Isabel (and recently installed paramount chief), Dudley Tuti. A focal point of the event was the presentation of a series of gifts (net bags, mats, shell armlets) to him. Other prominent invitees included four Anglican priests and the head of the government council (who did not appear).

Just as the ritual presentation of gifts enacted a linkage of *kastom* and Christianity, speeches and songs performed for the occasion also wove together images of indigenous and Christian identity, much as Forest and his relatives did in their celebration of Pentecost. This melding of images was accomplished in somewhat different ways in a *thautaru* sung by the Togasalo people to Charlie, and in Charlie's welcoming speech to the bishop. The welcoming speech, which was read by someone other than Charlie himself, consisted primarily of a succinct narrative history of events preceding the establishment of the village of Kolokofa. The speech, quoted in part below, opens with a brief description of precontact life and Christianization that resembles the portrait of Knabu life painted by Forest and Josepa in the preceding chapter. Indeed, Charlie's speech intersects directly with the earlier narrative at one point when he refers to the Knabu chiefs who first accepted Christianity and called others, including those living in the Kolokofa area, to assemble in the new Christian villages closer to the coast. But Charlie extends the narrative further, bringing it up to the present to recount his efforts in re-establishing Kolokofa after it had been previously dissolved as part of an earlier wave of church-sponsored and government-sponsored movement of villages to coastal areas.

Alright, this place, Kolokofa, that we are in the middle of now had its beginnings during a heathen generation. These two clans [attending the feast] were both here, along the valley, along the river, along the mountain, with their shrines for making sacrifices, their burial grounds, their forts for escaping to – chiefs, warriors and noble women of this place, Kolokofa.

Then for some came the way of destroying each other [warfare]. Some ran away to where there was peace. Others ran to where there were strong men in order to live in safety – to Hograno, to Bughotu, to Gao, to Kia, and scattered all around Maringe. Others went so far away that we don't know where they went. Others who stayed scattered completely, dispersed all over. And so they remained until the news of the church arrived. With the church came the way of peace inside it; togetherness and kindness, same father and mother – all brothers not fighting each other.

Then the Knabu chiefs said: "You all go down to this church," and they gathered together and established the church with the Knabu. That's where they were when their chiefs and church teachers said to move to the coast to be near the bishop and priests. With that the church split a second time and this church at Kolokofa was established. The people had already been here for many years, months and days when the word of the church and the government reached them saying: "You all move down; you all gather together." That's what happened with all of us when this was just torn down [moved]. Some of the old women cried, some of the chiefs were sad hearted, and the children were confused as they just spread around to the west, to the east, inland and to the coast in those bygone years. Because of that I started to listen and think; "Hey, this is really confusing, making decisions like the ways of the whitemen." And I went and fought with some of my friends in the council to move it [the village] back. With the help of you, father bishop, talking about this place, the church was again established here at Kolokofa. And because of that we are all gathering together one day here at Kolokofa – children and people of Kolokofa – in order to be together with our bishop, our priests, other chiefs and teachers, children and respected women . . .

In stating the meaning of the Kolokofa feast for those attending, Charlie (or his spokesman) articulates a rationale for his leadership on the basis of shared descent, land and history. This is accomplished in large measure through allusions to the common historical experience of conversion to Christianity. As in the case of the Knabu legends, an epic story of warfare, dispersal and decline, followed by conversion and revitalization, constitutes a kind of myth of common origins (or at least a common past) that may be used in a variety of ways to construct shared identities that are at once highly general ("Christian persons") and yet anchored in the specific places and persons of a particular locale. The next chapter turns to the epoch of crisis that emerges repeatedly in Isabel recollections as a precursor to the momentous events of conversion and the origins of Christian identity.

II   *Transforming*

5

Crisis and Christianity

Life was not easy in Santa Isabel during the years preceding the turn of the century. It may not have been as bad as the darkness and death depicted in mission journals of the day, but there is abundant evidence that Isabel society was indeed a society in jeopardy, suffering widespread dislocation and serious population decline at the hands of raiders armed with newly acquired weaponry. Stories such as that told by James Nidi in the preceding chapter remind present generations of the once-upon-a-time vulnerability of their ancestors.[1] Other accounts are even more immediate, told, until recently, in the first person. Christian Odi, an old man of Koviloko village now deceased, tells of his experience as a child being kidnapped by raiders:

At first we were located at Kolokofa. Then when the raiders started coming, we all fled to Kubolota where there were many others in our Thauvia clan. But Nagu and Jra'i, two chiefs of the Nakmerufunei clan, thought that we were becoming too numerous. So they sent a pouch-payment to Goregita for him to come and wipe out our Thauvia line . . . When the payment reached Tuarughu in Hograno, Goregita said to his followers: "Nagu and Jra'i have sent us a pouch-payment, so we are going to raid Kubolota." At that time some Kia men came up to pay Goregita a visit. There were eight of them who came to Tuarughu . . . and Goregita said: "Tomorrow we are going to Kubolota in order to raid them. You eight men follow us in order to camp at Kubolota." The eight Kia men who had come up said "okay."

So they came to Kubolota where there was a very steep fort. The fort had a rope ladder like the ones on ships, only made out of lawyer cane, which could be lowered and raised. When it was evening, the people would pull the ladder up on top. Then in the morning they would lower it down so people could go and look for food . . . The raiders and the followers of Goregita came up even though it was difficult. They began to wait until those of us in the fort would get hungry and come down. But there was a lot of food in the fort at Kubolota. The men down below waited a long time and when they ran out of food they went to the gardens to get more. They waited, they ate and they built thatched shelters for themselves. No people went down until finally four women from the clan of the two chiefs Nagu and Jra'i climbed down . . . But before they climbed down they put on shell armlets and porpoise teeth necklaces (indicating high status). When they were not killed, we thought it would be safe for another four of us to go down . . . Myself, my mother, Taki and Kinahe were the four people who climbed down . . .

By then news had reached the men of Baghovu, Fitupogu, Kmaga, Klolo, Boromani and others to the west that "the enemy is attacking our fellow kin and our children." The many chiefs said: "Let's go attack and save our children, our sisters, our nephews." . . . But when they reached Kubolota, all of Goregita's men had left . . . We had already gone down to the base of Kubonitu. The women and I were gone.

The women took turns carrying me on their backs, even though I was already growing up and had begun to talk. When we reached the shore the Kia men boarded a canoe with the rest of us following them. No one was left with Goregita. The men from Kia bypassed him with the eight people and went out to sea to the island of Nanuhana. There we slept. At nightfall the women looked back at Kubonitu and began to sing and cry. [One of the Kia men] said: "Hey, I feel sorry for them. They're crying. Why not take them back and put them down on shore?" But other men stood up and said: "You're just like a woman, man. If they're supposed to die, they'll die. If they're supposed to live, they'll live. What's the use of putting them down on shore?"

Odi, obviously, survived his harrowing childhood experience. As the story continued, the party traveled on to Kia where Odi, his mother and two other women remained under the protection of the leader Rona. The other four captives were sold to men from New Georgia for guns, axes and shields. Those four were but a few of the scores of Isabel people who were taken as captives to the Roviana area. Some captives met an ignominious fate in the sacrificial rites of their captors. However, many were simply incorporated into New Georgia society, where large numbers of their descendants may be found today. Odi, like Nidi's grandfather Breara, remained in Kia. This proved to be fortunate for him when in 1911 several visiting Maringe men recognized him as "one of us" and took him back to Maringe.

Odi's narrative has poignant salience – for him, his community and their collective past. The story was offered without solicitation the first time I visited Odi in his home. It is a story, no doubt revised and refined during periodic retellings, that succinctly depicts several aspects of Isabel society and history discussed in previous chapters. Prefatory to the kidnapping episode, the story outlines the relations of rivalry and alliance between regions, clans and chiefs that structure and motivate intergroup hostilities. (The Thauvia clan was "becoming too numerous.") Plans for the treacherous raid follow the script-like scenario of "sending a pouch-payment" to enlist the support of another chief and his warriors. The past practice of raiding, like the major *diklo* feasts, both expressed and constituted ties between chiefs, engaging them in reciprocal exchange and alliance-building. If a chief wanted to organize a raid he is said to have sent gift-payments to the chief(s) whose support he wished to enlist. Termed "sending a pouch-payment" (*fatali gnhaka*), these payments were made in the form of a pouch or netbag filled with shell valuables. By accepting the payment the recipient chief signaled his willingness to cooperate. In this way, the process of organizing and carrying out raids externalized and reconstituted the current state of interregional relations. In this instance, the alliances extended outside Maringe to bring in raiders from Kia. The planning of the raid, the siege of the fort, and the eventual seizing of captives jointly compose a portrait of a treacherous past in which communities were vulnerable to attack without mercy ("If they're supposed to die, they'll die").

Like many who narrate the past, such as Forest and Josepa talking about the Knabu or Charlie's speech at the Kolokofa feast, Odi concluded his story by referring to the coming of peace and the arrival of the church. Even if he had not stated it, the link to the Christian present is implicit in the fact that stories of raiding and warfare prefigure accounts of conversion and peace. How are we to understand the significance of these narratives that, even though cast in a variety of forms and contexts, all recreate mythic histories of transformation that are as much about the present as about the past? Rather than answer this question by separating past historical events from present cultural meanings, the approach taken here is to examine social history and cultural narrative in dialectic relation. I presume that the significance of past events for the people of Santa Isabel can hardly be understood without reference to their own interpretive frames, and that the stories themselves obtain meaning and value in the context of social and political processes of long duration. It is with this in mind that this chapter begins an account of Christianization and colonization in Santa Isabel drawn from documentary sources and local recollections. This sketch of social history is the necessary prelude for a closer examination of the local histories that reconstruct these events taken up in chapters 7 and 8.

Mae vaka: "ship men"

When Alvaro de Mendana sailed from Peru in 1567 with two ships in the hope of discovering the fabled gold-rich lands of King Solomon, the first high island he sighted, eighty days after setting sail, was given the name Santa Ysabel, after the patroness of Mendana's voyage.[2] The record that Mendana and his navigator, Quiro, have left us of their experiences in Santa Isabel suggests that some of the patterns of power and meaning embodied in chiefly leadership today were also evident then. While we cannot hope to ascertain the thoughts and perceptions of those who greeted Mendana in the sixteenth century, and while the Spaniards' diaries say as much about themselves as about those they describe, the initial encounter and the interactions that ensued distinctly reflect various aspects of local models of the chief, particularly as these pertain to dealings with powerful outsiders.

The Spanish ships made landfall at a bay they named Estrella Bay – a region probably inhabited by speakers of a Cheke Holo dialect. As the ships approached the Isabel coastline, "there came out many small canoes with Indians all equipped for war, with bows and arrows and lances of palm wood" (Amherst and Thomson 1901: 108). Signs of peace were exchanged and small colored hats thrown to the islanders, a number of whom quickly overcame their timidity and climbed on board ship where they ate, mimicked the Spanish language and received small presents. This was the first encounter between Isabel people and that class of white-skinned person who, in subsequent centuries of contact, came to be known as "ship men," *mae vaka* (see Bennett 1987 for a comprehensive history of Western involvement in the Solomons). The local attitude toward the newcomers was a bold one. Mendana commented that several men remained on board to urge him to "choose the port in his district" (Amherst and Thomson 1901: 109).

The Spaniards were not only initially welcomed, they were briefly incorporated into existing networks of chiefly alliance and rivalry. A chief who resided inland from Estrella Bay was among the first to visit the ships. He exchanged names with Mendana and later sought his assistance in raiding a nearby enemy. Mendana cooperated in this alliance, sending off thirty of his soldiers with four local men in the ship's boat. They returned with a "chief's son" and four captives to be used as "interpreters" (*ibid.*: 21–2). Mendana and his crew of about 150 anchored their ships in Estrella Bay and began building a sailing vessel with which they could explore the extent of their discovery without endangering their only means of return to Peru. They reported encountering large populations in the western region of Santa Isabel which is now only sparsely inhabited. Before they left the Solomons, they repeatedly engaged island warriors in armed conflict.

After Mendana's departure Santa Isabel was, incredibly, not visited again by Europeans for 200 years (Jack-Hinton 1969). The next contact was with a French expedition that anchored in Kia and remained seven days (Fleurieu 1791). By the mid-nineteenth century, European whaling and trading ships visited the Solomons archipelago with increasing frequency in search of turtle shell and bêches-de-mer. Then, in the 1860s, labor recruiters began seeking islanders for labor on plantations in Queensland and Fiji. Most of the exchange was carried out with local leaders who gained reputations as entrepreneurs controlling resources desired by the Europeans.

The traders concentrated their efforts in areas with good anchorages. The New Georgia group, with its vast lagoons, many reefs and islets, became an active center of trade. On Santa Isabel, the primary trade locations recorded in European journals are Kia, or Port Praslin as it was often

Plate 4 Early sketch of Bughotu people and canoe

called, at the northwestern end of the island and the Bughotu area to the southeast (Fiji Agent of General Immigration). Kia, like the New Georgia area, boasts many reefs and small islands surrounding a sheltered inlet. At the opposite southeastern end of Santa Isabel, the name of the harbor off the Bughotu coast, Thousand Ships Bay, speaks for its value as an anchorage.

Chiefs who controlled trade and labor recruiting in their regions seem to have become adept at dealing with Europeans and profited considerably from the exchange. The most significant technological innovations introduced in this trade were improved weapons, primarily steel axes and guns. These quickly captured the imagination of local leaders whose tastes for the new weaponry developed rapidly. As early as 1844, the people of Simbo and New Georgia refused to exchange turtle shell for anything except steel axes (Shineberg 1971: 311, cited in McKinnon 1975: 294). By 1889, New Georgians would bargain only for breech-loading rifles and ammunition (Captain Hand of the HMS *Royalist* to Rear-Admiral Lord Charles Scott, WPHC 268/1889, in McKinnon 1975: 303).

Trade for improved weaponry created a self-propagating cycle in which a few dominant leaders gained unprecedented ascendancy in the western Solomons (see Jackson 1975). Increased military power was used to expand control over reef-waters harboring turtle and bêches-de-mer. In this way a group actively trading for weapons could gain access to even more resources to be used for obtaining more weapons. As a chief's reputation for military prowess increased, he would have been better able to create alliances and garner support for more distant raids. With resources (and victims) in the western Solomons becoming more scarce, raiding parties began to range further afield toward Choiseul, Santa Isabel and even Guadalcanal (Chapman and Pirie 1974: 16).

The spiral of trading and raiding was associated with the spread of headhunting and the ritual practices associated with it. In New Georgia and surrounding regions raiding expeditions acquired captives who, in some cases, were the source of human heads placed as offerings or tokens of mana and accomplishment at shrines and ceremonial sites. Occasions such as the death of an important leader or the consecration of a new canoe or canoe house required that humans be offered in propitiation. As noted earlier, an unknown number of Isabel captives met their fate in the context of such sacrificial occasions. In a passage quoted by Bennett (1987: 67), a Canadian trader named John Macdonald reported witnessing the ritual killing of a boy captured from Santa Isabel as part of the launching of a new war canoe at Nono in New Georgia. After the boy had been exhausted by repeated dunkings in the sea, the chief took up a 12-inch trade knife and with a gash across the child's throat and then a chop the head was off and the blood streaming from the neck. The man still carrying the child on his back then ran round and round the [canoe] house as before scattering the blood on the house and the ground until the body ceased to bleed. It was then thrown down in front of the house . . . [It was] afterwards eaten with the other bodies and the child's head was stuck up in the clubhouse.

Although stark and disturbing, the trader's account, however accurate, resembles much of the imagery of pre-Christian savagery that circulates among Santa Isabel people today. However they, or we, choose to interpret them, such acts of ritual violence must have occurred with some regularity in the rather exceptional circumstances of the nineteenth-century western Solomons. The victims' skulls that adorned shrines and canoe houses were visible testimony to the power obtained through raiding and ritual practice. Captives such as Christian Odi or Nidi's grandfather also had economic value. They could either be adopted into the community or traded to allies for weapons and other goods.

In this complex of trading, raiding and ritualizing, the canoe was a highly strategic device that also acquired considerable symbolic significance. Canoes allowed the most intrepid raiders to travel across long distances, and so move anonymously to seek wealth outside the encumbrances of local networks of obligation or intrigue.[3] The large war canoes were both a means to wealth and a symbol of power, particularly spiritual power that could be evoked and enhanced through ritual propitiation such as that described above. In several instances, headhunter chiefs photographed by European photographers pose alongside their canoes or canoe houses (see, e.g., Woodford 1890).

On Santa Isabel the pattern of trade allowed the more seagoing peoples of Kia and Bughotu to dominate Cheke Holo speakers in the central regions who participated very little in European trade and labor recruiting. Steel axes were commonplace in the Maringe hills by the late nineteenth century, but guns were much less available. In the nineteenth century only a handful of traders attempted to base themselves on Santa Isabel (and these all in the Bughotu area), and none seem to have established enduring stations as in the western Solomons (Bennett 1987: 382). Most of the Isabel trading was carried out with visiting ships. Records show only a small amount of recruiting along the central coasts of Isabel, although evidence for the early period is sketchy. Saua Bay, an unprotected anchorage in the Gao area is the only site often mentioned in the journals of British agents from Fiji on board recruiting vessels after 1876 until the end of recruiting in 1914 (Fiji Agent of General Immigration).

The Kia people at the northwestern end of Santa Isabel participated in exchange networks that included Choiseul and New Georgia, especially Roviana. Links between Kia people and their neighbors to the west were utilized in the expanding cycle of trading and raiding, contributing to the increasing range and scale of raids such as those described by Nidi and Odi, and noted by numerous European observers. In 1880, a trader gave the (no doubt exaggerated) report that he had sighted 1,000 to 1,500 canoes "leaving New Georgia for their annual turtle and headhunting raid on Santa Isabel" (McKinnon 1975: 303). Even allowing for exaggeration, there is substantial evidence of the extraordinary raiding expeditions being mounted out of the western Solomons at that time. There is no shortage of accounts such as Woodford's observation on his first visit to New Georgia in 1886 that ". . . no less than forty heads, besides slaves were brought back from Ysabel in the course of my stay of two weeks" (Woodford 1909: 510). The brunt of the raids were aimed at the central part of the island, but extended ultimately into the Bughotu region. The extent to which Isabel people were captured and brought to the west may be measured by the sizeable population of descendants of Isabel captives now residing in the Roviana area of New Georgia.

In Bughotu, a leader named Bera expanded his reputation by trading for weapons and by mounting raids into other parts of Isabel and nearby islands. Because traders and recruiters repeatedly tended to contact leaders known to them, their reports probably give a distorted picture of the power and authority of those individuals. Nonetheless, it was precisely such repeated contacts, combined with European expectations that chiefly "kings" constituted individualized centers of authority, that would have focused and enhanced their influence in the conjunctive world of trading and raiding (cf. Douglas 1982). Bera is the most frequently mentioned contact for labor recruiters in the Thousand Ships Bay area. His success in obtaining weapons through these dealings is indicated in one transaction in which he "sold" the infertile and deserted island of San Jorge (believed to be the home of ghosts) for 70 dozen axes, 44 dozen knives and 136 muskets (Jackson 1975: 69). Through exchanges such as this Bera and his followers built up a considerable arsenal. The first resident missionary, Alfred Penny, described Bera's personal armory: ". . . besides the numberless trade guns and old rifles he has got two splendid breech loading rifles of some foreign make and a regulation Schneider – added to which one of the best revolvers I have ever seen. All in excellent order" (Penny, Diary: September 26, 1879). This collection must have done much for Bera's reputation throughout Bughotu and southern Isabel. He is known to have organized raids and headhunting expeditions along the entire Isabel coast, as well as southward as far as the islands of Nggela and Savo.

Grikha glehe: "flight from death"

Raiding and headhunting forays from 1860 to the end of the century put enormous pressure on the Cheke Holo population. The heightened level of violence originating outside the region also intensified fighting within. Headhunting expeditions exploited regional rivalries to recruit allies familiar with local terrain. Headhunters traveling by canoe from more distant places are said to have enlisted local men along the coast to guide them to settlements in the interior. People in the "bush" responded with counter raids against coastal groups, or those suspected of collaboration, contributing to the depopulation of coastal regions.

At the peak of the headhunting era, over one-half of the island between Kia and the Maringe Lagoon was almost completely deserted. Charles Woodford, before he became Resident Commissioner of the British Solomon Islands Protectorate in 1896, anchored in the Maringe Lagoon and reported clearings and gardens visible on the mountain slopes which convinced him "that there is a considerable number of natives living in the bush" (Woodford, Diary: November 7, 1888).[4] He saw forty or fifty people who came down from the hills and hesitantly approached his ship in canoes. They were armed with axes, shields and spears, but no guns. Of the remainder of the island to the west of Maringe, Woodford wrote: "I found no natives that were living to the westward of the Maringe Lagoon, but the deserted sites of some villages and plantations which had been devastated a year or two previous were pointed out to me" (Woodford to High Commissioner, August 27, 1898: WPHC 295/98).

The killing and kidnapping resulted in widespread dislocation and heavy attrition among Cheke Holo people. In some cases raids were not aimed simply at taking a few captives, they wiped out whole communities. One Maringe man remembered his parents telling him about a raid that killed so many people, and left so few survivors that they could not observe the proper burial practices for everyone. Instead, bodies were simply heaped up under the shade of a mango tree. Those who remained began their migration to other regions. The widespread flight from raiding and massacre is remembered as the *grikha glehe* ("flight from death").

For people in the Maringe area there were two responses to the intensified killing. Some sought refuge in inaccessible, fortified locations at high elevations in the interior, such as the fort where Odi's group took refuge. Others fled to the extreme southeastern end of the island, as in the case of the Knabu ancestors of Forest and Josepa. These migrations involved movement away from ancestral lands and the sacred sites of burial and worship. Chiefs who led their followers into the Bughotu area had to establish alliances with Bera or his successor, Soga, the dominant chiefs in that region. The migration toward Bughotu further enhanced the power of Bera and Soga among segments of the island population not previously within their sphere of influence.

Those who remained in the high mountainous areas formed alliances among themselves and consolidated their settlements around ridge-top forts (*thoa*). Tree houses (*thori*) built during earlier times were useless against rifle-toting enemies (Brenchley 1873: 292; Coote 1883: 140). These defensive alliances and nucleated settlement patterns must have also affected the political ecology of the region in so far as they expanded the scale of chiefly polities, giving greater prominence to those few leaders who attempted to bind together formerly dispersed peoples. One of the largest fort-settlements in the central mountains was named Khakatio, constructed near the peak of Kubonitu mountain (Mt. Marescot), on a plateau sloping off sharply on three sides. The name of the location was taken from the term for "lime gourd" (*khati*) because it, like a lime gourd, was something to be shared by people regardless of common ancestry. The fort was built when Rogna, one of the major chiefs in the area, had a vision in which his ancestor spirits revealed to him that the answer to the headhunting threat lay in the unification of dispersed people around a single fortified settlement (Naramana 1987: 43). At least four major chiefs and their followers clustered together at Khakatio, making it a bastion of defense throughout the headhunting period. In 1890, the first European missionary to trek into the Kubonitu area, Dr. Henry Welchman, described the Khakatio fort as follows:

The fence is set at an angle of forty-five degrees, and cross posts, set along, serve as standing places for the defenders in case of attack. Plenty of large stones lay all along inside. There are three gateways, which are nightly secured by logs. Outside, the ground has been cleared all round, and the sides of the hill have been all dug away so as to make a nearly perpendicular wall beneath the fence. The houses were well built and large, some thirty-six in number. The chief's is the largest of all in the centre of the castle. It is about sixty feet by thirty feet . . .

In the village are about forty fighting men, but within call are another 150 scattered about among villages and hills.   *(Diary: July 30, 1890)*

Although Khakatio was apparently never attacked, others were subject to siege, as testified to by Christian Odi. The Khakatio fort and its complement of armed warriors may have constituted a deterrent to raiding in the area. Working in the western Solomons where most of the raids originated, Hocart (1931: 304) recorded an account of a raid by men from Simbo against a Maringe settlement in which the Simbo party laid siege to a fort, but were driven off by a large force of about 200 warriors from Khakatio. Note that Hocart's figure of 200 agrees closely with Welchman's estimate of the size of the fighting force available at Khakatio and its environs (190).

If societal disruption was great among those forced to aggregate around fortified locations at high elevations, the dislocation was even greater among those who fled into the Bughotu area. Migrations are recalled as events initiated and led by chiefs who managed the resettlement and represented their followers in establishing relations in a new region. In some

Plate 5 Isabel tree house

cases, shrines were dismantled and the skulls, bones, and even some stones were taken to construct new shrines. But confidence must have been shaken in the ancestors, priests and chiefs to whom people looked for protection. Even the chiefs who expanded their influence through defensive coalitions were frequently attacked.

The Maringe exodus which left much of the population dispersed and unimposing, is now reconstructed as an epoch of violence, fear and vulnerability; but the period is also remembered as a time that held the seeds of its own transformation. Enacting a salvation drama which they "co-authored" with the Isabel people, Christian missionaries working on the island throughout the headhunting period supplied the ingredients for cultural reformulation, and these were variously taken up, put to use and transformed in the conversion process. Pacification was largely propagated by influential chiefs who seized upon Christian dogma to organize further defensive coalitions and suppress local raiding (White 1979). This process was rationalized and fostered by the mission ideology of peace that dictated the elimination of raiding and killing as accepted practice. One of the ironies in this is that newly converted warrior chiefs played a role in imposing the new peace, but acceptance of the new moral order led to the demise of the "strong man" ethic and its contexts for building chiefly power. Furthermore, the "new way" was much more than simply a release from the cycle of raiding; it was also regarded as a path to greater knowledge and power that could renew the envelope of protection once provided by ancestor spirits, priests and chiefs.

Soga: Christian chief
The work of the Melanesian Mission in converting the people of Santa Isabel to Christianity was one of its most publicized successes – a success chronicled at length in mission publications such as the journal *Southern Cross Log* and other books (e.g., Armstrong 1900; Wilson 1935). On this island, the mission strategy of converting people through their "chiefs" worked out better than in many Melanesian isles. Missionaries there rightly perceived that the disruption created by raiding and the concentration of power in the hands of a few renowned chiefs created fertile conditions for rapid socioreligious change. The conversion of a chief necessarily entailed conversion of his relations and followers. And, because a number of chiefs used their influence to propagate peace and Christianity under their aegis, Christianization followed even more rapidly. The most notable of these was Soga who converted with seventy of his followers in 1889. The phenomenon of "mass conversion" has been noted in other island communities where conversion to Christianity was produced (and probably experienced) as a collective rite of passage (Monberg 1962).

A unique aspect of the Christianization of Santa Isabel is that it was accomplished by a single church, the Anglican Melanesian Mission.[5] This feat followed from the sociocultural consequences of headhunting as well as the sphere-of-influence policy established by Resident Commissioner Woodford to restrict competition between missions (Laracy 1976: 39; Hilliard 1978: 134). The first attempt at missionization on Santa Isabel misfired when the Marist Catholic Bishop Epalle was killed the first time he set foot in Bughotu in 1845. Following this setback, the Catholics did not return to the island. The next attempt was by Bishop Patteson of the Melanesian Mission who visited Bughotu in 1861. Most of the early evangelization was carried out through the mission ship *Southern Cross* which visited the area repeatedly during the next decade, engaging in trading but making little headway with Christianization. But the seeds for later progress were sown as young men were taken away to mission schools for training as missionaries. These efforts produced a cadre of catechists (also called teachers) who played a major role in the conversion drama, as already glimpsed in the story of Walter Gagai's ascent to the Knabu.

Most of the evangelical work on Santa Isabel was done by Melanesian catechists trained in Mission schools. In 1874 a catechist from the Loyalty Islands named Wadrokal succeeded in establishing a church school at Nuro in Bughotu. The school was later moved close to Bera's village. But it was not long before Wadrokal and Bera came into conflict, resulting in the shooting deaths of two of Bera's men (Armstrong 1900: 187). It was obvious that Bera was not to be the key to Christianization in Bughotu.

After Bera's death the mission finally began to make some headway. The key to progress was Bera's successor, Soga. The context for this progress was forty years of escalating headhunting raids. The reality of violence and the promise of peace during this period constituted a unique historical moment in which a new sort of chief emerged – one who had established his reputation partly through military strength, but who now actively espoused the Christian peace. The everpresent threat from raiders who might descend at any moment provided added incentive for those who came to hear about the new message of peace.

Alfred Penny, the first European missionary to take up residence in Bughotu, observed in 1883 that "a very considerable influx of Bush men [speakers of Cheke Holo] had come in since I was here last year" (Diary: June 4). As this was chronicled in mission history: "A horde of bush people in terror of headhunters had come . . . to place themselves under the protection of Samson Ino, the fearless chief, and this would, it was hoped, lead to a general Christianization . . ." (Armstrong 1900: 233). Although Samson Ino was not to be the one, the mission hope that a "fearless chief" would produce "a general Christianization" was soon to be fulfilled, almost as if a script was already there, waiting for the right actor to galvanize a collective response.

Not all refugee colonies of "bush people" in Bughotu immediately embraced Christianity. Some groups, such as the Knabu, eventually returned to the Maringe area after headhunting raids waned at the turn of the century. But the climate of killing and fear must have disposed chiefs and their followers to new solutions or formulae for protection and prosperity. (This, it should be noted, is not an explanation posed by local histories which focus rather upon the power of missionaries and miraculous events, without directly raising the issue of disillusionment with indigenous institutions.)

For the missionaries, the first step in converting a community was obtaining the permission of a chief to allow a teacher to move into his area, set up a "school," and begin instructing interested people in Christian belief and ritual. What, then, attracted local chiefs to mission teaching? On the one hand, teaching offered a new source of knowledge, especially sacred knowledge, and all that that implies. Yet, the "new way" exacted a heavy price with unforeseeable consequences: the new knowledge emanated from, and was regulated by, outsiders. Conversion might augment the community's knowledge pool, but it might also undercut the status of local chiefs and priests as proprietors of the spiritual domain, and guardians of people and land.

The "solution" was for the chief himself to become a primary channel for the infusion of the new ideas and practices. By taking on Christian identity, and gaining access to the social and spiritual world of the mission, chiefs such as Soga could tap into an important new source of mana and, in doing so, become agents of new and possibly powerful forms of ritual practice. And, as has been noted in many accounts of conversion in the Pacific, Isabel people were also motivated by the hope of gaining access to the practical and material benefits associated with Western ways and technology. In Bughotu, where the mission first began its work on Santa Isabel, one of the practical benefits came in the form of assistance with defense. The missionaries helped bolster defenses at a time when raids from the western Solomons were increasingly troublesome, made ever more destructive by the introduction of breech-loading rifles (some supplied by European traders stationed in New Georgia (Bennett 1987: 61)). Although it was mission policy not to supply weapons, resident missionaries sanctioned their use and worked to organize more effective defenses. Alfred Penny described their efforts:

The natives keep watch when they hear tiding of the enemy, but after a desultory fashion: there is no organization or unity about their efforts. The Mission Stations at Ysabel now have men told off for this duty. Weapons and ammunition have been purchased by them from the traders, or contributed by returned laborers. The night divided into watches, and the watch is mustered and changed by ringing the school bell. The result has so far been satisfactory.   *(Penny 1888: 218)*

Welchman, who resided in Bughotu off and on between 1890 and 1908, and ultimately oversaw wholesale conversion, also encouraged an organized defense. At one point he proposed to Charles Woodford that he take two Bughotu leaders on board the mission ship *Southern Cross* to visit New Georgia in order to take a peace offering to Ingava, a notorious Roviana headhunter (Woodford to High Commissioner, August 27, 1898: WPHC 295/1898).

The mission contributed more than just improved defenses. It also introduced ideological and ritual practices that functioned in much the same way that ancestor propitiation did, only without the links to warfare or killing. The mission claimed to offer a new source of power and, to the extent that its enclave was prosperous and protected, gave some evidence of its effectiveness. Some chiefs, pressured by continuing raids, made the pragmatic decision to let a new kind of ritual specialist in their midst, Christian catechists. The attitude of Goregita, the chief who sponsored the raiders who captured Christian Odi, reveals some of the assumptions that lay behind acceptance of Christianity. Welchman visited Goregita at his fort and asked him about sending a catechist to teach him and his people the "new way":

Goregita told me, in answer to my question, that he was anxious to have a teacher to live with him. I asked him why, and he said he had been much troubled by the enemy, who harried him continually, and, within a month, they had forced him to give them two of his people as captives: he had noticed that where there was a teacher, the people lived in peace, and they were seldom or never disturbed by raids. So he thought if I would send him a teacher, he also would be left alone. "Then you don't want your people to be taught?" I asked. "No, I only want one of your teachers to come and live here."   *(Melanesian Mission 1899: 8)*

Soga was the most prominent of the chiefs who first saw the potential benefits of Christianity – a prominence magnified in both written and oral histories of the conversion period. With his village Sepi centrally located on the Bughotu coast where the mission first established itself, he was well positioned to observe and inquire into the work of the missionaries. It was not long after the death of his predecessor, Bera, that Soga approached the resident missionary, Alfred Penny, about inviting a teacher to live in his village. Penny noted this event in his diary as follows: "Soga and Voo came to see me. They are very amenable to have a teacher, we have arranged for Devi to go there and begin a school" (Penny, Diary: May 22, 1884). Five years later, in 1889, Soga was baptized along with his wife and seventy followers (Armstrong 1900: 273). He took his Christian name, Monilaws, from the middle name of the resident missionary during that period, R.M. Turnbull.

From that time until his death nine years later, Soga used the mission's ideology of peace to rationalize and form alliances extending into every corner of Santa Isabel. His exploits are portrayed extensively in the mission journal *Southern Cross Log* as one of the dramatic examples of Christian transformation. Despite the inevitable enhancement of Soga's heroic image

Plate 6 Monilaws Soga and Anika, his wife

in mission writing, it is clear that he was an exceptionally talented individual who probably saw the mission as a source of knowledge, prestige and power for himself and his community. Under the tutelage of Dr. Welchman, he learned to read the mission *lingua franca*, Mota, and eagerly sought out available texts. In his diary, Welchman describes regular conversations in which Soga questioned him closely on religious and historical points raised in his readings. The two of them – English missionary and Bughotu chief – formed a symbiotic relationship in which each contributed to the legitimacy of the other. Welchman provided advice and mission backing for Soga's activities as peacemaker; and Soga lent chiefly power and influence to Welchman's attempt to spread Christianity. Through the agency of Soga and other converted leaders, the suppression of local raiding and the evangelization of Santa Isabel proceeded hand in hand. By the turn of the century, the entire Bughotu population was baptized and nearly every part of the island had been contacted by mission representatives.

In the early stages of mission work the strength of regional chiefs was more important for defense than the organizational efforts of the mission. Like Bera before him, Soga had already established a kind of political hegemony in the Bughotu region through his dominance in the cycle of trading and raiding. Soga expanded his influence by forming alliances widely throughout Isabel, Nggela and Savo. These pacts, together with the suppression of local raiding, strengthened his ability to withstand head-hunting attacks from the western Solomons. But there were setbacks, even after he converted to Christianity. In 1891 about 150 New Georgians forced him and his followers into their ridgetop fort where they were helpless to prevent the plundering of their village and gardens below. Ultimately, someone from their ranks had to be offered in ransom, much as Odi described in his account of the Maringe siege (Armstrong 1900: 292). Following this raid, however, Soga repelled major headhunting forays on at least two occasions. The following year he successfully turned back an attempt by a group of thirty headhunters to purchase a victim from his group. And in 1897 eight canoes of New Georgians were surrounded by Soga with a large force and sent away in defeat, apparently without loss of life (Melanesian Mission 1898: 1–3, 7–8).

Those within the mission orbit on Santa Isabel regarded the missionaries and colonial officers as allies against the headhunting threat. In this attitude the Isabel Christians differed markedly from some in other parts of the Solomons, such as New Georgia or Malaita, where colonial officers were seen as threats to the power of local leaders (Keesing and Corris 1980; Zelenietz 1979). As far as Bughotu and Maringe people were concerned, the British ships and patrols provided a welcome antidote to the troublesome raiders from the west. By mounting a few punitive expeditions, such as that by the naval vessel HMS *Royalist* in 1891 against headhunting villages in New Georgia (Somerville 1897), the British demonstrated their military superiority just as they were establishing a colonial regime.

The British declared a protectorate over the south and central Solomons in 1893, while Santa Isabel and Choiseul remained under Germany until 1899 (Morrell 1960: 343). German sovereignty was little felt on Isabel where Anglican missionaries were the only sustained European presence on the island. In 1896 the British Protectorate took on greater reality with the appointment of a Resident Commissioner, Charles Woodford, who gave much of his attention to the suppression of headhunting. In a series of punitive forays with a small corps of police, Woodford attempted to discourage further raids by headhunters. On Santa Isabel, Soga began reporting headhunting raids to Woodford (Woodford to High Commissioner, August 27, 1898: WPHC 295/98), even though it was not until 1899 that Santa Isabel, Choiseul and the Shortland Islands were transferred formally to the British Protectorate (Morrell 1960: 347).

In that same year, 1899, the last fatal headhunting raid was made against Bughotu. It drew a quick response from Woodford. A single Roviana headhunting canoe with some Kia men on board claimed six lives, including a catechist. Woodford led a reprisal against the offending Roviana settlement and succeeded in killing one of the raiders and scattering the remainder. A canoe said to have been one used in the raid was discovered and destroyed (Woodford to High Commissioner, January 14, 1900: WPHC 56/1900). On another occasion, Woodford recruited Soga's successor and twenty followers to attack a fleet of forty war canoes reported in northern Isabel. The Bughotu men boarded the government vessel and were issued rifles and drilled in their use for the fight. The headhunting canoes, however, were never encountered and the contingent returned home empty-handed. It seems likely, however, that experiences such as this would have impressed the Isabel people with the ability of their new allies to mount a show of force. In any case, it was not long before headhunting raids waned as a result of both government punitive sanctions and changing economic circumstances (Zelenietz 1979).

The mission's ideology of peace was by no means entirely unfamiliar to local orators used to invoking their own images of solidarity and reconciliation in regional alliance building. But the new message did offer a new twist on the old rhetoric of peacemaking: it called for a cessation of *all* raiding and killing, rather than an alliance between particular groups (possibly for the purpose of raiding third parties). The avowed goal of evangelization was to reach all people on the island, regardless of traditional divisions and antagonisms. In carrying the peace message forward, the new Christian chiefs had the opportunity to expand their influence more widely than ever. Soga was the most successful (and best documented) of the peacemakers. It is largely for this reason that he is today recalled by many as Santa Isabel's first "paramount chief" – a fact indicated by the appropriation of his name, Soga, as a title for the paramount chief.

The degree to which Soga's remembered influence extended into Maringe is reflected in a story about a plot put forward by several Maringe chiefs to deceive and wipe out a rival group in a "final killing." But the story tells of how the plotters abandoned their plan out of fear of retribution from Soga for violating the new peace. The plot called for inviting the intended victims to a large feast so they could be attacked when they were unarmed and unsuspecting. However, one of the important chiefs invited to participate in the attack is said to have refused, exclaiming, "What! The church has already come to Sepi [Soga's village] and is established at Lagheba [colony of Maringe refugees], isn't it? We're ashamed [at the suggestion of killing]. Soga has said: 'Don't kill!' His word has already come and that makes it impossible." Whatever the accuracy of this account, it shows the extent of Soga's prominence in local recollections. As a Christian peacemaker, his influence is thought to have stretched across the island and across language boundaries. As an indication of this, the Cheke Holo chief Figrima of Khakatio sought to establish an alliance with Soga by inviting him to a large *diklo*-type feast in 1895 and presenting him with pigs and shell valuables.

Soga's most remarkable accomplishment as a peacemaker was his alliance with the Kia leader, Rona. A meeting with Rona and other men at Kia produced an agreement to cease headhunting raids against Bughotu (Melanesian Mission 1896: 1). A few years later, Soga acted as middleman in attempting to establish peace between Rona and his enemies in western Santa Isabel. Accompanied by two hundred men and a fleet of canoes, Soga traveled to Korighole in the northwestern part of the island and convened a meeting of leaders who settled upon a truce. As part of the agreement, one of the Kia groups sent a boy for mission schooling (Melanesian Mission 1900: 91–3).

Ironically, the rapid Christianization of Santa Isabel, which sought to extinguish the violence associated with "strong men," depended upon the ability of Soga, Figrima and other Christian chiefs to bring coercive force to bear on reluctant communities. Even before Soga was baptized, it was noted that he "had enforced discipline on a disorderly tribe near Vulavu, making them build a (mission) school-house, where service was held every Sunday by one or other of the teachers" (Armstrong 1900: 273). The use of punitive measures by local mission leaders eventually became a matter of concern to colonial administrators. Prior to becoming Resident Commissioner, Woodford wrote that catechists and deacons on neighboring Nggela were assuming undue coercive powers. In 1888 he commented on the "high-handed" actions of catechists there who burned a village that refused to accept a resident teacher (Woodford Papers, No. 29, Diary: September 24, 1888). On at least one occasion, a similar incident took place on Santa Isabel when one of the mission's deacons called for the destruction of a pagan settlement.

Soga's reputation, backed up by a corps of warriors, allowed him to issue and enforce a prohibition against raiding in the region. Beginning immediately after his conversion in 1889, he made armed expeditions to various parts of Isabel and to the islands of Nggela and Savo in order to urge the cessation of raiding and the acceptance of mission teaching. In 1890 he led a large party of armed men in war canoes to the neighboring Gao area. Upon seeing them, most of the residents were said to flee into the hills. Despite that, Soga landed and held a parley with some of the Gao chiefs, even presenting them with a shell-valuable as a gift (Armstrong 1900: 282). Following his Gao visit, Soga went with Henry Welchman on board the mission ship *Southern Cross* to visit nearby Savo and Nggela (Welchman, Diary: September 9, 1890). At Savo, he is said to have "warned the chief there that if he began a fight he would have to reckon with the whole of the people of Bugotu and Florida (Nggela) who could be called together to punish him" (Wilson 1935: 17).

Although Soga was the most prominent, he was by no means the only chief to capitalize on the new ideology of peace. The Khakatio chief Figrima had decided to enter the Christian fold after a visit from Welchman in 1890 (see chapter 7). Like Soga, he also used the mission rhetoric to consolidate regional alliances. Having first organized a feast signifying his alliance with Soga in 1895, five years later Figrima sponsored another major feast to mark the onset of peace in the region. On this occasion he is said to have issued an edict against raiding just as Soga had. When a rival group violated this proclamation by carrying out a raid against a distant people, killing several and taking others captive, Figrima called for a counter raid to chastise the offending group by destroying their houses and gardens. When this measure apparently failed to humble the offenders sufficiently, Figrima organized a more deadly raid by sending a pouch-payment to neighboring allies not yet converted, and so not constrained by Christian strictures against killing. The resulting raid ended with the killing of several of the targeted group and dispersal of the rest (Melanesian Mission 1903: 93–4). The leader of the raid apparently felt that he had fulfilled the wishes of the resident missionary and sent word to Figrima that he had successfully "carried out the orders of the Dokita (Dr. Welchman)." This incident was a mild embarrassment to the mission, but not so much that it was not publicized in the mission journal *Southern Cross Log*.

Both chiefs and catechists became arbiters of the new syncretic morality. Acts of judging infractions publicly asserted the ascendancy of the "new way," demonstrating the ongoing shift in the sources of power and legitimacy toward the institutions of the mission, centered upon the emerging relations between chiefs, missionaries and catechists. In one example of Soga's role as arbiter of the "new way," he is described in mission history as punishing another chief for an assault characteristic of "the old traditions":

> ... at Pirihadi a man complained of a serious assault made upon him by the chief of his village. Dr. Welchman advised him to report the matter to Soga which he did, and the day was fixed for inquiry. The great chief arrived with his court "in five decorated canoes, manned by about thirty men paddling together in perfect time, a pretty sight to see as they came in." A clean mat was spread on the beach for Soga; his bodyguard stuck their axes, on which they hung their spears and their shields, into the sand, then disposed themselves comfortably around. The court was opened and the two men called up. It was a simple case, and there was nothing aggravated in the assault. The assailant had, in a passion, struck the other with a paddle; he was now very sorry for it, and Soga let him off with a public rebuke, reminding him of his position which should have restrained him from conduct befitting the old traditions, but not fining him as he was penitent. *(Armstrong 1900: 270)*

This passage, based on Welchman's description of the events, reveals the manner in which the presence of the mission shifted existing political practices, recentering them in new forms of conjunctive power emerging between missionary and chief. On the one hand, Welchman's role in the case is clear. It is he who advises the complainant to seek redress through Soga. His directions and his support of Soga illustrate the manner in which Welchman's actions shaped the emerging notion of a "paramount chief" – one to whom grievances could be channeled within the new moral order. On the other hand, the presence of armed men who hang their shields on axes planted in the sand indicates the continuing reality of the "old."

These new experiments in combining missionary and indigenous practices must have been fraught with ambiguities, since any given instance of conflict could be interpreted and acted upon in relation to multiple frames of reference contending for legitimacy. One of the core ambiguities during the period of conversion was the value placed on violence and chiefly dominance in the "new" moral order. More than any single element of social life, the peace and the suppression of aggression came to represent the Christian transformation. This theme is inscribed in narratives of conversion that feature early Christian chiefs such as Matasi Iho of the Knabu disavowing the ways of "killing, kidnapping, and eating people." Less well remembered in local histories are the activities of the powerful Christian chiefs such as Soga and Figrima who used their influence garnered from killing, raiding and control over powerful spirits to bring about an enforced adherence to the ethic of peace.

In light of the avowed ideals of peace and nonviolence, the maintenance of social order in new Christian communities was problematic. Henry Welchman, who was himself continually involved in adjudicating the new moral order, recognized this as a dilemma for Christian chiefs and sought to bolster their influence publicly. On one occasion he counseled Soga:

> ... it would never do for the people to think that now he was a Christian and would not murder them that they could behave as they liked toward him with impunity ... when he summoned them to trial, he was to accept no excuses and punish them severely if they did not appear. That Christianity did not take away his power but rather established it in righteousness.   *(Welchman, Diary: August 23, 1892)*

Welchman's ruminations on this occasion were by way of justifying his advice to Soga to go ahead with a raid against an accused thief who had not responded to Soga's summoning. Soga's men summarily raided the offender's compound, burned his house, destroyed his gardens and brought him back for judgment and fining.

Periodic displays of force, although inconsistent with the ideal of nonviolence, were essential to the maintenance of Soga's political power which had proved a great asset to missionization. In 1898, Soga traveled with a retinue of twenty-two large canoes and about 400 men to a village on Nggela in order to exact payment for violation of a tabu he had placed on some coconut trees there (Woodford to High Commissioner, May 15, 1898: WPHC 204/1898). He not only collected payment from four men who had broken the tabu, but his followers went on a rampage destroying several houses, two canoes, coconut trees, and other property, apparently leaving the residents in a state of fear and intimidation.

Despite the displays of force by Welchman's chief ally, Soga, missionization inevitably did erode the power of local chiefs. It could hardly have been otherwise. In hoping that Soga the chief might remain strong so as to advance and bolster the new mission society, Welchman did not recognize that the indigenous model of leadership was not so easily compartmentalized, that personal reputation, political authority and spirit power are closely integrated, each informing and validating the other.

As Christianization proceeded, it did so through transformations of social and ritual practices closely associated with chiefship. In the process much of the significance of the "chief" was appropriated by a new cadre of local leaders – the catechists and priests who directed ritual life and the formation of new settlements. The next chapter tells the story of conversion by examining the ideological and political processes that intertwined and reinforced one another in producing the remarkably rapid and comprehensive changes that are now recalled in stories about the transition to a "new life."

6

Conversion and consolidation

. . . we proceeded to a small island at no great distance, and climbed the hill to a place where there were four well-built tombs, surrounded by skulls, each with the death blow in evidence. There was a momentary hesitation, – it is not a particularly cheerful business to defile your grandfather's grave, and to burn his bones, even for a brown man, – but it was only momentary, and the stones were rolled down the hill into the sea, and the bones in them made into a heap with the skulls of the victims who had been sacrificed to the dead man and a huge bonfire lighted over them. It is only a beginning; it will be a work of time to get rid of them all for the tombs are scattered all over the mainland.

Henry Welchman *(Melanesian Mission)*, Southern Cross Log *(1908: 45–6)*

With the Tindalos [ancestor spirit, na'itu*] the power of the chiefs has greatly declined. This was inevitable: a chief was powerful because he possessed a powerful Tindalo. I do not speak of this as a benefit. Were it not that in Christian unity at least an equivalent can be found, I should consider it a loss.*

Alfred Penny, Ten Years in Melanesia *(1888: 216–17)*

Even missionaries espoused some degree of ambivalence regarding the ancestor spirits they sought to subvert. But it was just this recognition of their centrality to the pre-Christian socioreligious order that led early missionaries such as Penny and Welchman to focus evangelical attention on them, ultimately transforming spirits, *na'itu*, into "devils," *devol*. In the first passage quoted above, Henry Welchman tells of putting a number of baptism candidates at Kia village to a test in 1907 by having them destroy several of their ancestral shrines. Even though the neophytes were already attending the village church school and participating in Christian services, the ritual exorcism was necessary to confirm their commitment to the "new" forms publicly by destroying the material and symbolic centers of

the "old." The subtext of such ritual acts, however, pronounces the
continuing reality of the "old" as a complex of powers and principles that
exist in opposition with Christian forms and must be contended with
through acts of ritual expiation. Physically dismantling the shrines did not
so much destroy the powers that reside there as signify the ascendancy of
one set of institutions and practices over another. As discussed earlier,
ancestor shrines and the rites enacted there expressed and constituted
relations of power embodied by chiefs and priests acting as proprietors of
the shrines. The act of tearing down the shrine was also an act of
domination, giving performative testimony to the shift in power that was
taking place from chiefly polities to the mission institutions that had come
to encapsulate them.

For most of the Maringe population Christian conversion entailed
migration to relatively large coastal villages where catechists conducted
teaching and worship in village churches. Recall that Forest and Josepa
touched on this aspect of the conversion story when they told of the "three
hundred new Christians" who gathered together to form the new village of
Salinisi. The Christian settlements being formed at that time differed from
previous residence patterns based on close identification with lineage
estates and their chiefly representatives. In the earlier pattern, attachments
to land were established through descent and regional activities organized
by chiefs. *Diklo* feasts, propitiation rites and raids had all been occasions
for constituting social relations rooted in land, ancestors and chiefs.
Residences were dispersed and quickly changing, but land, shrines and
chiefs provided symbolic anchors. Moving away from those anchors could
only be accomplished through a realignment of definitions of community
and the ritual and narrative practices that create them. Just such a
redefinition was accomplished through conversion and the acquisition of
new histories and identities as "Christian persons."

The new villages created a social environment conducive to the rapid
spread of Christianity. At the same time, mission ideology gave meaning
and purpose to the new sociopolitical order. By altering the constellation of
beliefs and practices centered on ancestor spirits and chiefs, the wholesale
transformation attempted by the mission, at once ritualized and politicized,
was probably more easily accomplished than piecemeal change could have
been. It is these concurrent processes of pacification and conversion that are
represented in narratives of sudden, holistic change such as the Knabu epic
and others of the genre taken up in the next two chapters. As will be
discussed later, these narratives recreate mythic accounts of the origins of
Christianity in terms that are at once local and global, simultaneously
localizing the social meanings of Christianity while Christianizing local
identities. Parallel transformations are evident in the full range of ritual

practices that constitute Christianity as a social reality in Santa Isabel communities.

During the first decade of this century, pursuit of the "new way" in the Maringe area reached millennial proportions. Welchman wrote in 1903 that "one great feature of this year's work is the demand for schools in the bush, and among bush people who have come out into the open" (Melanesian Mission 1904: 37). In talking about the geographic move of "bush people" down to coastal areas where Christian villages were established, Welchman here employs the metaphor of "coming out into the open" commonly used by missionaries of the time and now reproduced in local histories of conversion. Just as the Togasalo people remember Walter Gagai as "opening" the Knabu region, so Welchman here describes the movement of inland people to Christian settlements as an outward movement that has the effect of making them visible. From the perspective of the bush communities, however, these ideological transactions were also expressed in metaphors of incorporation, of "bringing in" rather than "going outside." The attitude is expressed in the words of one local leader who was noted to have asked: "What will it cost us to buy the new teaching?" (Hilliard 1978: 170).

Even before the British flag was raised on Santa Isabel, roughly one-fourth of the people living on the island had been baptized (923, mostly in Bughotu, out of an estimated population of 4,000 for the whole island; Melanesian Mission 1901: 143). At that time there were forty-one catechists and fourteen mission schools already established on the island. Once headhunting raids dwindled at the turn of the century, the process of setting up village church schools with resident catechist-teachers accelerated rapidly. In 1903 Welchman established a mission station on the small Bughotu island of Lilihigna, renaming it Mara-na-Tabu ("Sacred People," or "All Saints"). This station became a base for Welchman's work instructing catechists and coordinating their work around the island until his death from malaria in 1908. In 1903 a school had been established in Kia at the opposite end of the island, the number of catechists had grown to fifty-seven, and Welchman could report that ". . . there is a great falling off in the number of adult baptisms in Bughotu. This is due to the fact that now all the people are Christians" (Melanesian Mission 1904: 40).

Transformations in ritual life

Conversion required a period of instruction in which neophytes acquired knowledge of the Anglican creed and ceremonial life.[1] The village church was the center of ritual activities, where twice daily services confirmed the new identity through prayer and hymn-singing. Consistent with indigenous notions of reciprocity, new converts enthusiastically gave food and money in church collections (Wilson 1935: 17) – an enthusiasm also noted in other parts of the Solomons (e.g., Hogbin 1970). The personal and collective meanings of this new ritual regime follow from the cultural understanding that power (mana), protection and prosperity may be enhanced through ritual relations with potent spirits. The church rites offered a new and potentially even more powerful way of accomplishing those ends. Not to do so, particularly when ancestral shrines had already been abandoned, would leave one vulnerable to the ravages of sorcerers or malevolent spirits such as the snake encountered by Thomas Mereseni (chapter 4). Consider, for example, the comments of a man at a village meeting who suggested that a recent death was attributable not to sorcery as had been rumored, but simply to ignoring church strictures: "The man who died at Heva didn't follow the doctrine. He didn't make offerings or stay within the church. He followed his own way so that when he went pig-hunting he died, even though some said Ko'u made sorcery against him. The church is powerful ('hot') through offerings and prayer."

To a large degree, the significance of shrines as sacred centers where priests would ritually "awaken" the spirits of powerful ancestors and call upon their assistance to divine or resolve vexing problems was transferred to village churches, the new locus of ceremonial activity and spiritual power. But the shrines retained much of their potent significance, with

Plate 7 At Dr. Welchman's school, Mara-na-Tabu

Christianization even solidifying their malign aspect. These lingering ambivalences gave particular meaning and force to Christian practices as a ritual antidote to the dangers that emanate from the traditional spirit world. To counter these threats, shrine proprietors sought symbolic solutions that variously made the "old" "new" and the "new" "old." For example, some incorporated shrine stones in the foundation of new churches, while others enacted Christian rituals to neutralize or, as some say, "baptize," the spirits lingering at old shrines (see below, p. 110).

For Santa Isabel communities, the functional relations between Christian and customary practices were not covert or left implicit. Defining and manipulating the opposition between these domains, each shaping the significance of the other, continues to be an object of discussion. For example, the analogy between sacrificial rites practiced at shrines and prayer services in village churches has not passed unnoticed. Today the commentary is being produced in the writings of a new generation of educated Cheke Holo priests who address the ambiguous and often contradictory relations between the discourses of Christianity and *kastom* (Lagusu 1986; Vilasa 1986). More ordinary, oral commentaries may also be heard. The Maringe priest who served our village of Vavarenitu gave a sermon one Sunday as part of a Communion service in which he drew an analogy between the "shrine" (*phadagi*) and the church, and between "propitiation" (*fafara*) and taking Communion: "Whatever thing you or I want, come here [the church]. Ask for it in His name . . . To get what? To get mana (*nolaghi*) and strength. This is our shrine. Jesus Christ, his body and his blood, come to help you on this morning. This is our shrine . . . It is just one name for us to receive mana." The Holy Spirit is present in the Communion service much as ancestors were present at the shrines that encased their skulls. Additionally the symbolic blood of Christ parallels the actual blood of sacrificial victims said to have been consumed in former times by chiefs and warriors.

Functional parallels between ancestor propitiation and church rites have been widely noted (e.g., Hogbin 1958: 180; Tippett 1967: 291). But here local notions of spiritual power, danger and protection expressed in ideas about mana and the ritual means of enhancing it appear to have indigenized the analogous, but more abstract ideas of European Anglicans. Indeed, the immediacy or intensity of church rites for Isabel Communicants was noted by missionaries who described the excitement with which people participated in Communion ceremonies. Welchman wrote that "it was pleasing to see how eager people were for Holy Communion . . . It was almost greedily accepted, the Communicants in many cases coming from a distance. Those who lived away in the bush stayed for days in order to make the most of the opportunity" (Melanesian Mission 1904: 37). It is still the case today that

Communion services typically draw a large attendance, with some attending from surrounding villages.

In the passage cited at the outset of this chapter, Henry Welchman stated his desire to "get rid" of the scores of shrines that dot the Isabel landscape. However, no such destruction ever took place, in large measure because the approach of indigenous catechists and priests was quite different from that of Welchman. Rather than destroy or desecrate shrines, the indigenous specialists attempted to transform them ritually with Christian practice. Acts of "blessing," "anointing" and "baptizing" were (and still are) the weapons in the spiritual arsenal of indigenous Christians. Local catechists and priests were sympathetic to the substantial continuities of the past in the present, of the old in the new. Their model of transformation was not one of rupture but of reformulation. They perhaps understood that the meaning and vitality of the "new" practices depended upon the continuing reality of the "old."

Forest, Josepa and Fr. Hudson had talked about the efforts of early Knabu Christians to do just that at the shrines we viewed. Led by a catechist, villagers were said to have organized one or more ceremonial processions to pray there. Complete with processional cross, candles and incense burner, these visitations were performed to "bless" the shrine with a ceremony that included reading from the scriptures, singing hymns and kneeling in prayer as the catechist invoked God's power to dissipate the power of the spirits residing there. The act of "blessing" is termed, literally, "making sacred or tabu" (*fablahi*, formed by prefixing the causative, *fa*, to the stative verb *blahi*, "to be tabu"). Note the inversion of meaning expressed in the act of blessing: a Christian "making tabu" is used to negate an ancestral one. The indigenous concept of *blahi* or "tabu" implies a prohibition backed up by threat of ancestral retribution. In this sense, the shrine was already a sacred or tabu place regarded as powerful, dangerous and restricted. The Christian "blessing" does not so much remake the area as sacred or tabu (as the term "making sacred" would imply) as it neutralizes the harmful ancestral powers, thus ending the restrictions associated with the threat of spirit attack against trespassers.

But, as noted before, the effect of such blessings seems not to be permanent (or perhaps not fully guaranteed). Many people continue to regard shrines as places best approached with caution, and only then by men accompanied by priests or knowledgeable elders. In other words, an element of ancestral tabu remains such that thoughtlessly violating these kinds of sites may risk spirit-induced illness or injury. Similar consequences may follow from unfortunate contacts with any of the broad range of spirits who inhabit the forest, as Thomas Mereseni's story (chapter 4) amply illustrates. In addition to ancestral shrines and innumerable forest spirits (*na'itu mata*), many areas around the island have one or more named "live spirits" (*na'itu kahra*) whose abode, noises and activities are well known to local villagers. These spirits, often associated with a particular feature of the landscape, such as a cave, hole or rock have also been the subject of ceremonial blessings enacted to dissipate their power. The priest who was most active in conducting these sorts of prayer rituals during the postwar period was Fr. Eric Gnhokro, a Maringe priest who died in 1974. An account of one of his processional expeditions will serve to illustrate the manner in which spirit presences are perceived and dealt with in these activities.

One of the men who accompanied Fr. Gnhokro in several of his ghost-busting missions recalled for me an expedition that he found particularly unnerving. On this occasion men from the neighboring island of Nggela (also an Anglican area) had heard about Fr. Gnhokro's successes is praying at spirit enclaves to "make them better" or "drive away" the dangerous spirit(s) and so sent an emissary to request his help. The speaker recalls how, once arriving in Nggela, several local men led Fr. Gnhokro and him to the spot in question:

We went in a dugout canoe until we reached a mangrove passage . . . The spot where we landed was where that spirit was, the one that they were afraid of, so they didn't go there often. If someone went there to work on their project, they would run into it, then go back to the village and get deathly sick. That's why they wanted Fr. Eric to go and pray, so we went to that place and he asked them: "Where is it?" "Underneath that mangrove tree," they said to Fr. Eric. So we all went. But those who knew about it were really afraid and wouldn't lead . . . Since they knew about the ways of that spirit thing and were afraid of it, just the two of us went in front to that place and took a look and saw a hole worn smooth (as from use). "So, this must be it." "You stand on one side of the hole, I'll stand on the other side of the hole," said the priest. There he told us what hymn to sing, and since I was always the one to lead off, I led off the hymn, with the other people singing in back. The hymn that he picked out was "The Church is Strong (*hreta*)." That's the hymn he said and I led off. When that was done he turned to his prayer book. At that point I wasn't looking at the book but just listening. Then somehow I looked down and spotted this thing that was very shiny like a coconut crab – shiny like that, but big. Then it moved forward at the mouth of the hole and startled me and I got scared as that thing started moving toward the side where my foot was, so I let out this big scream. At that the priest stopped in the middle of his prayer . . . When I shouted I also jumped and grabbed onto a hanging vine to jump up because it had come out to my foot, so I jumped up with a shout. Because I did that the thing went back into the hole and stayed until we finished the prayer. When the prayer was done, its smell came out, rotten, like the smell of something that has already rotted. That's what it smelled like. So the priest talked to us. "Now you, all of us, have smelled this rotten stench. Since we persons have smelled that thing that has rotted and died inside here, it's not alive. Otherwise that spirit that you all were afraid of might still be alive. But it has died and already stinks. This is what we are smelling. Perhaps if this man had not gotten startled, it would have gotten out. This thing might have gone out and gone off and died somewhere else. But we would not have seen its body coming out, we might only have seen the grass shaking around in the forest, like the movement of the wind. That's probably all we would have seen, we wouldn't have seen its body. We would have seen it rustling through the grass or shaking the trees. But since now we smell this rotten smell coming out, we can believe what we have seen." That's what he told us.

Having confirmed that the spirit presence had in fact "died," Fr. Gnhokro proceeded both to "baptize" and "bury" the spirit, thereby leading it through the cycle of Christian personhood. To do this, he went to a nearby graveyard and, with the others, brought back stones and coral to cover over the hole. He then conducted a brief baptism ceremony, giving the spirit the Christian name "John," and proceeded to bury (*gigilu*, specifically, "bury the dead") him by covering over the hole. Note the difference between Fr. Gnhokro's approach as an indigenous priest, and that of Fr. Welchman. Whereas the former enacts a cycle of blessing, baptism and burial, performatively reconstructing relations with the un-known presence (even giving him an identity), the latter's approach evinces detachment and lack of connectedness, regarding the spirits as an alien other, conceived as evil spirits or "devils" to be expunged from the human world.

One of the most dramatic examples of the use of Christian ritual to transform a sacred area is an expedition that went right to the heart of the traditional spirit world. In both the Cheke Holo and Bughotu regions, the island of Tuhilagi (also San Jorge Island) off the southwestern coast is believed to be the abode of ghosts of the dead (presumably those not present at shrines). In 1924 the first two Santa Isabel priests, Hugo Hebala and Ben Hageria, organized a party of catechists to trek to the island's highest point, called Tohebakala, and hold a Communion service. They arrived in the evening and held a prayer service in preparation for Communion the next morning. During the night, the party reportedly heard odd noises indicat-ing evidence of the presence of spirits. The next morning Communion services were held to make the area safe for visitors (again, to remove the tabu or restricted state of the place). But in this case also, there appears to have been no spiritual "guarantee" to the blessing, as both Hebala and Hageria led subsequent expeditions to bless Tohebakala.

Even though pacification ended the overt threats associated with raiding, unseen threats from malevolent spirits, sorcerers and hostile others contin-ued. Some say that these latter dangers even flourished after pacification. As one person put it, in the old days sorcerers known to have killed members of the community could have been killed by chiefly edict. But now modern morality and laws have eliminated this means of dealing with sorcerers. Christianity, however, offers alternatives. As in their ritual dealings with shrine sites, catechists and priests have historically taken the lead in using Christian practices to confront suspected sorcerers. In Maringe, Hugo Hebala, the first Isabel priest, is remembered as having initiated an areal campaign to confront sorcerers and eradicate their destructive powers. During the 1920s he enlisted the assistance of the catechist Walter Gagai in a prolonged "search and destroy" mission. Writing about this effort for the mission publication *Southern Cross Log*, Hebala described the process as follows:

This last year I determined hotly within myself to make a thorough search amongst all the people for every old heathen thing that still remained hidden in their hearts, to get rid of them entirely. And one man was appointed, Walter Gagai by name, to go through all the villages, seeking out every person, and questioning them. And he succeeded completely. He sought for and found some things belonging to old times that they were still keeping hidden. And they all made full confession of everything, great or small, not one thing of any kind could they keep hidden in their breasts; and all of them in every village promised earnestly to renounce entirely those bad things of olden days, and to cleave with all their might to the teaching of Jesus Christ.

(Melanesian Mission 1925: 123, cited in Hilliard 1978: 219)[2]

Some of the sorcerers so identified were then escorted to Hebala's village, Buala, where he conducted a spiritual cleansing. For each alleged sorcerer, Hebala conducted a ceremony in the Buala church in which he asked the person to renounce sorcery and give up any ancestral relics or ritual paraphernalia connected with the practice. Hebala's son Nathaniel remembers that as a boy he was awed by the pile of sorcery objects that accumulated in the Buala church from this procedure. Whether the person admitted to practicing sorcery or not, he or she was required to kiss the Bible as a sign of disavowal of any further involvement. It is generally believed that if anyone were to conceal sorcery in this situation and still kiss the Bible, he or she would suffer death within a matter of weeks as retribution from God. After Hebala, it was the priest Eric Gnhokro who, as we have seen, was most active in leading the ritual campaign against malevolent spirits and sorcerers.[3]

Most recently, an anti-sorcery revival movement led by a charismatic young priest, Fr. Ellison Vahi, emerged in the Maringe area in the mid-1980s. Until his somewhat reluctant departure when he was posted off the island by the church hierarchy, Fr. Vahi stirred renewed interest in the dangers of sorcery and the power of syncretic Christian ritual to combat it. Giving their movement the ironic appellation *meomekro*, "crazy" (anticipating the response of many in the wider society), followers of this latest manifestation of ritual enthusiasm appear motivated by the same concerns and fears that made the work of Gnhokro and Hebala so compelling for Maringe people in earlier decades. (In this case, the addition of two women attributed with divination powers when possessed by angels added a new twist to the otherwise familiar church services and ritual processions aimed at countering threats from the local spirit world.)

In addition to these more exuberant uses of Christian ritual, the mission introduced other, quieter measures of protection as well. One of the most popular are the Christian crosses worn on necklaces, much as amulets had

Plate 8 Hugo Hebala, Buala village (1906)

been previously. This type of substitution was encouraged by missionaries, such as Richard Fallowes (an English priest who worked in Isabel during the 1930s). In a letter to his sister, Fallowes asked for crosses to be mailed to him: ". . . inexpensive small crosses for wearing round the neck. Charms were very much in demand in days gone by and the people feel happier wearing the Sacred Symbol round their necks" (Letter: November 17, 1932).

Mission practices were applied to treating illness as well. Since the most powerful healing practices draw upon spirits of all types, Christians turned to prayer, hymn-singing and blessings (as well as to Western medicine) to replace or supplement traditional medicine. The new ritual specialists, catechists and priests, have from the beginning been in high demand as healers. With the movement into large mission villages the population was even more susceptible to infectious disease; and epidemics of whooping cough and influenza swept the island in 1895 and 1896. Armstrong (1900: 339) describes the ritual remedies sought for one such epidemic in Bughotu:

. . . the whooping cough continued raging, and a day was fixed for fasting and prayer, which was kept by all the Christians of Bugotu . . . at midday there was a special service for the removal of the sickness, at which a collection was made for the Mission. The churches were crowded at this service, the collection was equivalent to £10 of our money, a great sum, for Bugotu is very poor.

Prayer, hymn-singing and applying holy water blessed by priests are all used regularly today as supplements to Western and customary treatments of illness.

In addition to defending against illness, injury and death, propitiation rites and magical practices were an instrumental means of ensuring productive gardens, the material basis for community prosperity. Not surprisingly, then, Christian methods were employed for this purpose as well. The same type of processions used to exorcize spirits from shrines have also been used to bless gardens. This practice has waned in recent years, supplanted by a once-a-year church service instituted by Hugo Hebala and now regularly observed by villages all around the island. Hebala proclaimed that each year on a certain Sunday in July, people may bring token quantities of garden crops to a special Communion service where they will be blessed to help ensure continued productivity. This practice is observed regularly in the Maringe area where it is known by its Bughotu name, *thavinago*.

Missionaries such as Welchman and Fallowes, as well as indigenous catechists and priests, recognized and promoted the equivalences between traditional and Christian ritual practices. In one instance Welchman substituted Christian practice for weather magic by leading several drought-stricken Maringe villages in praying for rain (Wilson 1935: 17).

The Melanesian Mission legitimized this type of replacement by making "provision for Christian blessing of canoes, nets, houses, gardens or 'whatever was the custom of the people in their heathen state'" ("The Constitutions, Canons and Regulations of the Missionary Diocese of Melanesia 1924": 14, cited in Hilliard 1978: 197). But more often than not, Christian practices are combined with, rather than substituted for, *kastom* measures. For example, as part of the preparations for a turtle hunting expedition that I participated in (a lengthy and complex process), a *kastom* specialist with the appropriate net magic quietly uttered his spell over one of the net floats just moments before a priest led a procession to bless the nets in a more elaborate, collectively enacted ceremony.

Europeans in the Melanesian Mission understood the pragmatic significance of traditional magical procedures and saw value in replacing them with Christian practices. However, as glimpsed in their approach to ancestral shrines, European missionaries tended to see Christianization as replacement or substitution for traditional practices, whereas indigenous specialists see a confluence of models and methods. In various ways, Christian practices were themselves assimilated and transformed as they were applied to culturally constituted concerns with spirit threats and the ritual means for dealing with them. Furthermore, these syncretic practices did not emerge in a sociopolitical vacuum. Transformations in ritual life worked to express and constitute new sources of power and knowledge once centered upon the status of the chief.

Villages and churches
Whereas new ritual practices externalized Christian identity in periodic collective activities, shifts in patterns of residence and leadership created a social environment conducive to propagating and institutionalizing these activities. Mission policy aimed at concentrating dispersed peoples in a smaller number of accessible Christian settlements, thus extending the residential amalgamation which began in some areas as a response to raiding headhunters. Bishop Cecil Wilson of the Melanesian Mission described the process as follows: "In our large islands . . . there are no villages until we make them . . . the people live in hamlets . . . When we get Christians in any one spot, we gradually gather all the people together from that neighborhood so that we form a village in time. When the number is finished, and all the people have gathered together, there may be 150 of them" (Melanesian Mission 1910: 41–2, cited in Chapman and Pirie 1974: 2.31).

Nine villages were formed in the Maringe area between 1900 and 1910 (see White 1988), ranging in size from about 100 to 300 residents. During this period, most of the regional population came to reside in these new village conglomerates. Once a Christian village was established and a building constructed to serve as church and school, people residing in the environs could be attracted into the village, perhaps forming an additional hamlet (*gruru*). Through this kind of accretion, villages typically grew up as a collection of named hamlets. In this manner, the hamlets, each with one or more representative chiefs, continued elements of chiefly polities in a more muted or encapsulated form.

In the long run, maintenance of many of the Christian villages formed as amalgamations of previously dispersed peoples proved to be unworkable. Five of the nine villages formed in Maringe during the conversion period (1900–15) eventually segmented into smaller splinter villages. The most commonly mentioned reasons for these divisions are conflicts associated with sorcery and adultery. The pattern of village formation in Maringe reflects accordion-like tensions between the centrifugal forces that fragment groups along lines of descent and chiefly rivalry, and the centripetal forces of aggregation fostered simultaneously by Christianization, colonization and the economic/commercial attractions of living along the coast.

In the new settlements, as in Isabel villages today, churches have an important dual significance as symbols of identity both old and new – a kind of architectural locus of transformation. On the one hand, shifting the focus of religious practice from ancestors to the Christian God removed an important context for articulating ties of kinship and regional affiliation once expressed in rites held at ancestral shrines. On the other hand, churches continue to represent connections to localized conceptions of place and the past. This was particularly true in the first generation of churches that often incorporated stones brought from former ancestral shrines in their foundations. Although churches are named in Anglican fashion after a saint, the names of important ancestors are often found in shell-inlaid inscriptions on beams, altars and other carved objects in the church. In the case of Togasalo, where people annually commemorate Matasi Iho, his name and that of his son are inscribed on an elaborately decorated candleholder standing to one side of the altar. Similarly, the lectern of the Buala church is marked with the initials "HH" for Hugo Hebala.

The significance of churches as a new kind of ancestor memorial was succinctly stated by Timothy Lehemae, the man who talked about his ancestor Rekegau in chapter 4. As a descendant of Rekegau, Timothy had spent part of his boyhood in the village of Sugarege formed by his lineage-mate George Giladi. He recalled that Giladi exorted his followers: "Build a chapel! One big house for the Christian village and the Church I'm working in; as a memorial for Hofi and Baghovu [two villages] as a memorial for our ancestors, for Legese and Lehetilo, Rekegau and Marigi. This will be a memorial for my grandfathers and fathers . . ." An inspection of the

genealogical relations between Giladi and the ancestors he saw memorialized by the Sugarege church indicates that three of the four are uterine
ancestors: mother's mother's brother, and two brothers of his mother's
mother's mother (see figure 1). Of course, Sugarege consolidated several
lineages, and Timothy's recollection of Giladi's rationale speaks primarily
to the interests of his descent group in that village. Nonetheless, for him the
remembered significance of the Sugarege church was as a shrine and
memorial to prominent ancestors in his descent group.

Timothy went on in the same conversation to talk about his own
rationale for building the church in his village, U'uri. Even though U'uri is a
relatively small village with only about fifty residents, the church was one of
the largest on the island when it was built in 1970 – an impressive structure
made out of modern materials of cement, sheet metal and louvered

Figure 1 Ancestors named in rationale for church construction

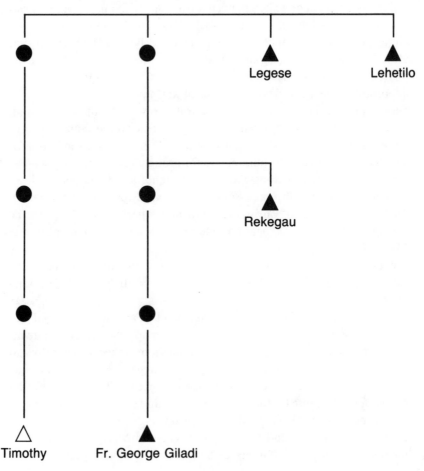

windows, with carved ebony posts and decorated beams. Timothy said that the church is a "memorial" (*thutuana*) for a number of ancestral shrines and listed the names of eight former shrines, going on to say: "These are ancestral shrines which, gathered together, make one shrine, U'uri. Those are ancestral shrines and this one shrine of Christianity is put at U'uri . . . However many shrines there were before, this is one shrine now. In order to gather together these various shrines, we call the chapel 'all holy men' [All Saints]."

Maringe churches, then, perpetuate and transform the social and iconic function of ancestral shrines. Although Christian services in village churches do not foreground genealogical connections among those who worship together, they often preserve them in more subdued forms. But these genealogical relations are often submerged in the complicated dialectic of descent-based identities and village unity. One of the important innovations of Christianity was that it introduced a single deity, God, who potentially transcended the social distinctions between particular individuals and descent groups. By invoking one spirit for the same purposes that many spirits had been called upon previously, connections between ritual practice and descent-based identities were inevitably loosened.[4]

Chiefly priests

As caretakers of the village church and proprietors of new ritual knowledge introduced by the mission, the early catechists and priests acquired many of the roles once performed by traditional priests and chiefs presiding over ancestor shrines. The rise of Christian priests and the social order of the church needs to be understood in relation to the concurrent decline of traditional priests and chiefs. With the passing of the first generation of Christian chiefs, their successors could no longer establish reputations as "strong men" and "men of mana." The cultural bases of knowledge, power and legitimacy were being redefined by the activities of missionaries and catechists as the new "men of mana." As Guiart described for Vanuatu: "Leaders now had to be experienced not in pig rearing, but in the Work of God. Teachers and deacons were, naturally enough, the new men of authority in the world of Christianity that had been accepted, with its promise of a glowing future" (1970: 135). Missionization thus seemed to dislocate the sources of personal and political power, displacing them from the traditional arenas of chiefly activity. But when indigenous catechists and priests established themselves in new Christian villages (sometimes in their own ancestral communities), they became mediators capable of accomplishing a degree of recentering.

As Maringe people today assess the ways in which their communities have changed over the years, many draw an analogy between the traditional pattern of regional chiefs and the close identification of renowned priests with localized areas or "districts." Now that the first generation of Isabel priests have passed away, there are further indications of the significance of priests as symbols of identity among their followers and descendants. A pattern is emerging whereby deceased priests are treated as renowned ancestors by honoring them with memorial feasts (*ghato fapulo*) and church services, and by naming newly built schools, clubs and stores after them.

Most of the early catechists working on Santa Isabel were trained at the Melanesian Mission's Norfolk Island school, far from the Solomons. After 1896, training was carried out at Siota on nearby Nggela. Catechists came away from mission teaching with knowledge of Anglican religious belief, and with the ability to speak and write the mission *lingua franca*, Mota. The absence of catechists from local life for extended periods of schooling allowed them a degree of detachment from ongoing rivalries and disputes. They also brought with them the mystique of foreign, Christian knowledge and power.

Just as chiefs had worked to build and maintain a following, catechists and priests such as Hebala and Giladi worked at forming and maintaining the unity of the Christian villages, often in conjunction with local chiefs. Timothy recalled from his boyhood in Sugarege that Giladi would call frequent village meetings and admonish the village residents: "You people must not go out (leave the village). Stay here from generation to generation." In order to validate the new amalgamation in Sugarege, he proclaimed that anyone who was born in the village automatically acquired rights to land in the region. The disruption and depopulation of Maringe during the previous half-century made such a proclamation feasible.

Catechists wielded potent spiritual sanctions in maintaining the new social order, and many are remembered as having been strict disciplinarians. Giladi punished minor infractions against the new moral code in Sugarege by having the offenders carry stones up from the coast for use in building the stone foundation for the new church. The most important sanction available to catechists and priests was their ability to prohibit their followers from participating in prayer or communion services for a period of time. These were weighty sanctions because they removed an individual from the protective envelope of God's power, leaving him or her vulnerable to the dangers of the natural world and to spiritual retribution. In essence, putting someone "outside" the church took away their Christian identity, placing them back "inside" the world of pagan dangers. In commenting on the powers of catechists on the neighboring island of Malaita, Hogbin (1958: 198–9) observed: "His authority to suspend members of his congregation is almost as powerful a weapon as that of the administration to pass sentences of imprisonment."

European missionaries on Santa Isabel also used these sanctions to bolster the unity of Christian villages. Richard Fallowes wrote in his diary that he had met with people in one of the coastal Maringe villages and "... discussed at length the departure of certain people, 12 in number, from Nareabu. I made the rule that anyone who left a church village to live in a village where no church existed would remain excommunicate. The people concerned agreed to return to Nareabu" (Fallowes, Diary: November 7, 1931). Mission leaders were thus able to tap deeply held beliefs in the power and immediacy of spiritual sanctions to sustain the Christian social order that emerged during the era of conversion. Nonetheless, the tension between mission ideals and the numerous opportunities for transgression and conflict is evident in the high rate at which Isabel people were placed "outside" the church as punishment by early missionaries. During 1908, one-tenth of all the converts on the island were excluded from church services for some period of time (Hilliard 1978: 174).

Whereas most of the early catechists simply struggled to make headway with the work of conversion, and many themselves fell into moral "disrepute," a small number built upon their position as moral and ritual leaders to establish a much broader base of sociopolitical power reminiscent of the earlier chiefs. Beginning with the ordination of Hugo Hebala in 1920, these more prominent catechists became the first generation of Isabel priests.

Plate 9 Mission teachers at Mara-na-Tabu (1906) (middle row, right to left: Hugo Hebala, Japhet Hamutagi; standing fifth from right: Ben Hageria)

These men inherited the mantle of spiritual authority associated with the succession of European missionaries who worked on the island beginning in the 1880s.[5] Local priests modeled their routines on that of the European priests such as Henry Welchman who would typically tour the island at least once a year to hold Communion services, counsel village catechists and minister to the sick.[6]

The recollections of a middle-aged Maringe man about the first time a bishop visited his village during his boyhood give testimony to the vivid impressions created by the visits of European priests on tour. During the course of a conversation in which I had asked the speaker to reminisce about events he remembered in his childhood, he offered the following memory:

When I was growing up a Bishop came to dedicate the church at U'uri. When they made the procession I saw his hat and his staff and I became really frightened. When he dedicated the church and we were praying, I was with some other small children. We made a hat like his out of leaves and also held a stick like him. I was acting with the other boys. But when I went outside like that, my older brother heard me and got angry. "This man is very sacred (*blahi*), not for making fun of. He is the Bishop." ... When we went down to Hofi (the landing place) for him to go, I saw the big ship and was frightened again. I thought it was a big canoe because I hadn't seen any ships before. My father said: "This one is not a canoe. It's a ship." At that time I held on to my father's hand because I was afraid of the Whiteman. I looked at his white skin; and I watched people give him food and load it into his boat. I saw that they had to make two trips. The first time they just took all the food out; after that the Bishop and his people.

In the course of this brief remembrance, the speaker three times refers to his feelings of fear upon observing this "sacred" white man and his imposing ship. And the "high" status of the visitor is symbolized by the large quantities of food and gifts that he was presented with – so much that it took two boatloads to transport all of it to the bishop's waiting ship.

The concept of "mana" or *nolaghi*, only dimly translated with English phrasings such as "personal power" or "spiritual power," represents the most potent forms of activity and efficacy – more a state of mind, person or being than a "power" or force. The attribution of mana follows from extraordinary abilities to affect the course of worldly events. As discussed previously (chapter 4), mana is associated with ritual specialists who traffic in transactions with spirits capable of effecting the most dramatic changes in people and events. Although all "Christian persons" benefit from the mana gained through the church, it is the ritual specialists, the priests and bishops, who are the source of exceptional spiritual power and authority. But even among the clergy, mana is not distributed equally. Only a small number of priests have achieved prominence as extraordinary "men of mana"; and they have done so by virtue of their abilities to perform "miraculous" feats. Those who have been active in using Christian ritual to eradicate sorcery, bless shrines and neutralize the habitats of dangerous spirits are the ones most recognized for their extraordinary powers. One such man was Hugo Hebala; another was Eric Gnhokro.

As already mentioned, Eric Gnhokro was the most active priest during his time campaigning against sorcery. In addition, he is remembered as having performed miraculous feats of all kinds. He is said to have used his powers to accomplish such things as halting the gradual encroachment of the ocean upon shore property, drawing water from the ground, redirecting the course of mountain streams, turning water into gasoline, stopping animal pests from feeding on garden crops, causing a killer shark to die and healing people for whom other treatments have failed. The mana attributed to present-day priests, more than any other single feature, differentiates them from other types of contemporary leaders (see chapter 9).

As if recognizing the multiple roles and realities represented by catechists and priests, Henry Welchman had sought to discourage their participation in large-scale *diklo* feasts or, as he termed them, "great feasts." It is perhaps ironic that it was the priests themselves (again, with chiefs) who became the sponsors for new kinds of church-sponsored "great feasts" modeled on the *diklo* pattern of reciprocal, interregional exchange.

The overt shift away from *diklo* feasts followed from the Christianization of the rationales for large-scale feasting, focusing instead on occasions of Christmas, Easter and village "church days" (*narane suga tarai*). As noted in the discussion of Charlie's Christmas feast (chapter 4), Christian feasts were often patterned on the *diklo* model but also altered it in significant ways. By locating sponsorship in church institutions and villages, and by defining their purpose in terms of annual Christian occasions, feasting is more detached from individual sponsors than the *diklo* feasts identified with the person and locale of the sponsoring chief(s) and their position in regional cycles of reciprocal exchange.

The most regular form of large-scale feasting today are the village "church days" sponsored annually by each village. Historically, the largest of these adhered to the *diklo* pattern of reciprocity, such that villages and regions often paired off, taking turns hosting one another in successive years. The practice of presenting the sponsors with gifts of shell valuables and the like also continued for a time, but has since vanished, probably as the reciprocal pattern itself has receded as feasts have come to be defined simply as occasions for village celebration to which guests are invited from the entire surrounding region.

Although the church may have altered the contexts and purposes of major feasts, feasting has remained the most fundamental mode of expressing collective identity and accomplishment. Far from having dimi-

nished, the scale of feasting even expanded in the immediate post-conver-
sion society. The early assimilation of the new feasts to the patterns of
chiefly sponsorship is well illustrated by a pair of historic exchanges
between the island's first two ordained priests, Hugo Hebala and Ben
Hageria, and their districts in the years 1927 and 1928. At this time there

Plate 10 Church day procession, Tirotongna village

were no European priests resident on Santa Isabel. The most recent, Rudolph Sprott, had died in 1924, and his successor, Richard Fallows, did not arrive until 1930. Located in Maringe and Hograno on opposite sides of the mountainous Cheke Holo area, these two indigenous priests had been working for years at establishing the church in their respective regions. Each became the most powerful religious/political leader in his area. As if to affirm their accomplishments in this transformative period, they organized a round of reciprocal feasting in which Hebala and Maringe hosted Hageria and Hograno one year, and the recipients responded in kind the next. In the process, at least two kinds of emergent identity materialized: that of the "Christian person," shared by both sides in the exchange, and that of the regional affiliations (Maringe, Hograno) that distinguished them. While interregional exchange was the norm of *diklo* feasts, these regions were larger than any that would have been mobilized in the past, encompassing nearly the entire Cheke Holo speaking population. In addition, people from other language groups, spanning the entire island of Santa Isabel, were also invited to participate in the Hebala/Hageria exchanges.

When people who participated in these feasts recalled them for me, they described them as sponsored by Hebala for Hageria, and by Hageria for Hebala, just as traditional *diklo* had been conceptualized as exchanges between chiefs acting as representatives of their followers. Descendants of Hageria retain written records of these events and refer to them explicitly as *diklo* feasts. A Maringe man described the first feast in 1927 as "made by Hugo Hebala, the first priest, and the rest of Maringe 'for' (*rahngi ni*) Ben Hageria, the second priest." The former is said to have "summoned" or "called" (*kilo*) the latter for a feast at Buala during Christmas time to mark the peace and friendship between them. In this way, the feasts were defined as both *diklo* and Christmas celebration (just as the annual feast for Matasi Iho is both an ancestor memorial and a marker of Pentecost, or Charlie's feast was both a Christmas feast and a testimony to ancestral ties in the Kolokofa region).

I recorded information about the feast sponsored by Hebala from Dudley Bale, a former Maringe priest who participated in the event as a young man. He described the feast as an expression of the "happiness" (*gle'a*) of Hebala, "our big man, the district priest of Maringe." Although the feast was for Hageria and the Hograno region, people from Bughotu, Gao and Kia were also invited, making it an island-wide activity. Preparations for the feast were coordinated among the Maringe villages, such that certain villages and leaders were responsible for organizing specific contributions. In addition, a significant amount of money had to be accumulated to purchase store-bought goods such as rice, canned meat, biscuits and cloth. Fifty years after the feast, Fr. Bale had no difficulty enumerating in detail the specific quantities of food and goods presented to the Hograno side. These included seven cows, ten shell armlets, fifty cases of canned meat, fifty biscuit tins, fifty bags of rice, 500 parcels of almond nuts and 300 parcels of fish.

These amounts accord remarkably well with Hograno people's written records of their feast which show that the following year the return exchange included eight cows, twelve shell armlets, 2,592 cans of meat, fifty biscuit tins, 170 bags of rice, and 300 parcels of almonds, in addition to unspecified amounts of tobacco, matches, pipes, coffee, tea and sugar. The return feast sponsored by Hageria in 1928 was held at Bibiru in Hograno. Estimates of attendance range from 1,000 to 3,000 people. Fr. Bale remembered that each village in his area sent a large canoe, and that all the major chiefs and catechists in the region attended. He also noted that district officer Hill from the government station in Bughotu was present. The scale of these exchanges make them among the largest (if not the largest) ever conducted in the Maringe and Hograno areas.

As part of his recollections about these feasts, Dudley Bale described an incident at the Buala celebration that illustrates some of the competitive impulses behind these interregional encounters, as well as the aura of power surrounding Hugo Hebala's leadership. As the story goes, a number of men attending from the Gao area heard several Kia men say that Gao canoe paddles were small, "like the tongue of a snake," and that it takes strong men to use the wide paddles preferred by Kia people. "So the Gao group wanted to fight by racing with canoes." They took up the challenge by going out in the lagoon in a plank-constructed canoe (*bi'a bina*) large enough for forty paddlers to demonstrate their paddling skills. Bale recalled that the paddlers carried axes and shields, which they had brought for dancing, not fighting. They proceeded to race twice across the lagoon, chanting as they went, with people lined up on shore clapping rhythmically and singing. "Some people told the Kia men to go out as well, but they were fearful of what Fr. Hebala's reaction would be." The Gao men had been paddling so vigorously that, when they returned to the wharf, the seat lashings in the canoe had become slack. Hugo Hebala is said to have chastised them, saying "Don't do that any more. We must love (*nahma*) each other." The Gao paddlers later told the Kia men: "We Gao can race with birds, and beat the birds that chase fish. We don't see you going faster than the birds."

The signs of strength in this story are clear. The event develops because of an outright challenge to the strength of the Gao men. Subsequently, in taking up the challenge, there are numerous indications of their strength: the size of the canoe, their axes and shields, the speed with which they paddle, the rhythmic chanting and the loosened seat-lashings. It is in this context of assertions and counter-assertions of strength that the dominant influence of Hugo Hebala is most apparent. In the retelling, the Kia men are said to refrain from engaging in competition because of their concern about the reaction of Hebala, who later exhorts the Gao men to cease their provocative behavior, for "we must love (*nahma*) each other." The use of *nahma* here, a cornerstone of Christian personhood, derives its meaning from the domestication of aggressive assertions of strength and competitiveness. The act of issuing a directive among strong men signals Hebala's own strength and authority; but the directive is, at the same time, a statement about solidarity. This story, and Hebala's role in it, are reminiscent of the story mentioned in the previous chapter about the local chief who refused to participate in a "last killing" against a rival group because of Soga's directive that killing should end. In both cases, the Christian leader is a peacemaker who asserts himself among "strong men" who would otherwise fight with one another. This image, reminiscent of the Knabu chief Matasi Iho among his warriors clamoring to attack the arriving missionary, is highly expressive of the social meanings of Christian identity and a core scenario in the employment of narratives of conversion to be examined in the following chapters.

The "Christian person"

The concurrent transformations in ritual practices and residence patterns took place in conjunction with the propagation of a moral idiom of the

Plate 11 Fr. David Leguhono and Fr. Dudley Bale with entourage fly the church flag

"new." At the heart of the conversion experience were messages about the meanings of Christianity for interpersonal relations and social conduct. These messages were (and continue to be) coded in images of the "Christian person" (*naikno Khilo'au*) and the "new life" (*nakahra majaghani*). As will be seen in narratives of Christian conversion, stories of the acquisition of Christian identity highlight its harmonious, generative, and "mana-ful" character. Building on existing ideals for relations within families and kin groups, the Christian themes of "peace" and "unity" at the societal level are reinforced by ideas about "love," "obedience" and the denial of hostility (and illicit sexuality) at the personal level.

Talk of unity and harmony is the stock-in-trade of orators who work at constructing models of common definition and purpose. Examples may be heard on almost any occasion of speechmaking, but especially those in which potentials for alternative definitions of competing interest exist. On one such feast occasion, Frederick Pado, the aging leader who had for years been the government headman in the Maringe area, spoke in such terms to a large gathering assembled for his village's church day celebration. Even though weak in body and voice, his audience, drawn from several neighboring villages, paid close attention as he exhorted them in the most general terms to cooperate, noting that acting separately or individually would weaken their efforts and diminish chances for success:

I want very much for these villages to be together. If you all are together (*fofodu*), you will be well. You will be able to make feasts, build houses, do well in traveling, meetings, discussion, in any of these things. If you are separate (*soasopa*) and speak separately, it will not be so . . . If that is your way then it is like your body, your speech and your manner become narrow and thin . . . One way is well for all of you. We mustn't take separate ways.

Here the speaker articulates collective solidarity (intervillage relations and cooperative activities) in terms of personal imagery. To "act separately" is likened to a person's body and speech becoming "narrow and thin." Talk of unity obtains greater moral force from ethnopsychological understandings about the personal and communal consequences of interpersonal conflict (White 1985a, 1990).

In Cheke Holo conceptions, characterizing behavior as "individualistic" or "acting separately" is one of the most negative judgments that may be verbalized about someone. In this view, to follow "one's own way" (*nogna sopa puhi*) is, by definition, to undervalue interpersonal relations which ought to be the bedrock of the moral community. The highly negative valence of "separate" behavior is perhaps most clearly expressed in the idiom used to describe "selfish" actions, *ghamu hnoto*, literally, "eats alone." In the small and tightly knit groups that characterize Isabel society, to "eat alone" is, by inference, to exclude others or at least to give priority to one's own needs over those of others. Here the metaphor of not sharing food reflects the densely loaded social and moral symbolism of food connected with the activities of food production and consumption. Some of the closest and most enduring social relations are constructed through practices of producing, exchanging and sharing food. These images of food sharing have also come to signify *kastom*, conceived as an indigenous valuing of sociability in contrast with the moneyed ways of Europeans and other island cultures.

Although much of the imagery of Christian morality is drawn through contrasts with the past, there are also contexts where quite different characterizations of the pre-Christian ethos emerge. When people talk about their own ancestors (as in Timothy's description of his ancestor-chief, Rekegau, in chapter 4) they frequently note continuities between ancestral ways and contemporary ideals. The speaker quoted above talking to the "church day" audience went on to draw a connection between the "golden rule" and indigenous moral ideals:

It is love (*nahma*) that I'm talking about. "Love other close friends the same as yourself," says the book [Bible]. That is the word . . . Otherwise you go and spoil things by disdaining the friends of others, sisters of others, kin of others . . . Love was already with our ancestors. They would say: "If you see their [others'] mother as your mother, their sister as your sister, their father as your father, their brother as your brother, then your palm will be wide. Everywhere you go, people will know you and love you."

In this passage the speaker rephrases the "golden rule" by casting it in terms of local metaphors of kinship which, along with related images of food and food sharing, are the most powerful idiom of solidarity and shared substance. Recall the similar rhetorical strategy voiced during the Togasalo remembrance of Matasi Iho (chapter 3) when images of descent were combined with more general metaphors of "life" associated with Christian peacemaking. The rhetorical extension of moral prescriptions otherwise contextualized among kin is more or less the same ideological move frequently put forward in Christian discourse: that is, expand the ideal of solidarity until it, ideally, has no contextual limits (cf. Hogbin 1958: 182). The attempt to state moral assumptions abstractly is one of the basic innovations of Christian dogma in societies characterized by more contextualized moral codes (cf. Leenhardt 1979; Read 1955; Shore 1982). However, even this innovation may be largely a matter of degree. Note that in the passage above the speaker presumes the salience of a kin-based morality among his ancestors, and suggests that they also made attempts to enlarge its sphere of relevance.

Other than urging people to cooperate so that they will be successful in their endeavors (as leaders seem to do everywhere), what is communicated in these rhetorics of solidarity? And how do they obtain persuasive force? On the one hand, answers may be sought in the interpretive models that give such characterizations meaning for Cheke Holo speakers. On the other hand, we may attend to the contexts and activities in which such voiced images work to shape relations and accomplish pragmatic ends. To begin with the interpretive questions, consider some of the things that the Cheke Holo language seems to "say" about local concepts of person, action and identity. Perhaps the most overriding aspect of linguistic meaning in this domain, and one that contrasts noticeably with English language concepts, is that the Cheke Holo language of persons is fundamentally *inter*personal and relational rather than about the distinctive attributes of individuals. In other words, indigenous understandings of persons are structured largely in terms of relations and contingencies between persons (White 1985a). The relational character of Cheke Holo views of social life has been widely noted in research on island ethnopsychologies (Lutz 1988; White and Kirkpatrick 1985).

Exploring some of the concepts that appear often in Christian discourse may serve to illustrate the manner in which understandings of the "new way" are built upon indigenous ideas about interpersonal relations. A term that may be heard often in Cheke Holo references to the "Christian person" is *nahma*, glossed above as "love." Although the English translation is problematic, the local salience of *nahma* (and the often-heard English/ Pidgin term *love*) is clear. When I asked a sample of Cheke Holo speakers to characterize their image of the "Christian person" in terms of a number of possible descriptive terms, *nahma* was the most frequently selected descriptor (White 1980b: 361). The "sample" I asked to make these characterizations consisted of twenty-nine middle-aged men; so the findings may represent a kind of normative orthodoxy for their generation (but I suspect they apply much more widely across genders and ages).

The range of meanings designated by the polysemous term *nahma* is suggestive. In addition to the sense of Christian concern or "brotherly love" and "kindness," the possible readings of *nahma* include "gifts" and "gift giving," "tame" and "taming," as well as "compromise," "pacify" or "achieve a settlement." The reading of *nahma* as "gift" points to practices of exchange and reciprocity that create the type of mutual obligation suggested by "love" as an interpersonal attitude. And the meaning of *nahma* as "taming" or "soothing" refers to the domestication of both animals and personal feelings. The latter sense reflects beliefs that unruly feelings, especially hidden anger toward others, commonly cause illness, injury or misfortune for self and/or others (White 1985a, 1990). Hence the *nahma* that describes harmonious interpersonal relations and the *nahma* that refers to emotional quietude both express facets of an ideal model of the person suited to maintaining personal (and community) well-being. These cultural understandings linking Christian identity, emotion and social process constitute an important motivational basis for adhering to the premises and prescriptions of the "new way" in so far as hostile acts and intentions (whether attributed to oneself or others) are seen to have highly undesirable repercussions (White 1985b).

In addition to characterizing the "Christian person" as "loving" Cheke Holo speakers describe the ideal type as "sympathetic" (*kokhoni di naikno*, literally, "sorry for people"), "humble" (*au faleghu*, literally, "stays behind"), "willing" (*sasa'a*) and "peaceful" (*au blagna*) (see White 1980b for details). Although each term signifies more complex understandings that cannot be captured with simple word-to-word translation, the juxtaposition of several terms commonly used to talk about "Christian persons" is suggestive of more elaborated understandings of the "good" that obtain their value in counterpoint with assumed potentials for hostility, conflict and divisiveness in daily life.

Images of the "Christian person" are constructed in the context of a "behavioral environment" populated with natural, spiritual and interpersonal forces seen as impinging upon the self (Hallowell 1967; Schwartz 1973). The most feared threats are those which remain hidden (malevolent spirits, sorcery, curses, gossip and unexpressed bad feelings), and so have been the object of concerted attempts at ritual expiation discussed throughout this chapter. People whom I asked what sorts of personal behavior are *least* appropriate for a "Christian person" focused not on overt acts of aggression or confrontation, but on covert forms of verbal attack such as gossiping, lying and cursing (White 1985b). The potential for suffering harm from these sorts of actions are conceptualized in metaphors of penetration and vulnerability, analogous to the conceptualization of spirit attack. With these potentials in the background, the social and ritual practices of Christianity are a means for constituting protective power or mana in the spheres of personal and collective experience. The rhetoric of solidarity gains moral force as it is externalized in talk and action aimed at minimizing the threats, seen and unseen, associated with interpersonal conflict and hostility. One of the formats in which conceptions of Christian identity are most consistently externalized are the local histories of conversion that symbolically reconstruct the origins of the church in moments of missionary encounter – narrative practices to be examined in the following chapters.

The Christianization of Santa Isabel, whether represented by Isabel people themselves or mission journals of the time, is generally depicted as a process of radical transformation. Missionary observers and local storytellers alike portray the epoch as an abrupt juncture, a fold in the course of social history marked by sharp changes in the ethos of everyday life. Yet, as this chapter has shown, significant strands of continuity run through the historiographic fold separating "old ways" and "new ways." It is one of the arguments of this book that local understandings of the "old" and the "new" are mutually constitutive, and that their evolving significance is worked out in representations of Christian identity. The foregoing discussion has considered several of the key social and ritual activities through which transformations of identity and community are accomplished. Whether the symbolism of churches and church services, or the activities of priests as moral guardians and feastgivers, Christian practices may be seen to obtain meaning and value through their assimilation to pre-existing indigenous models.

Among the important strands of continuity in images of the "new way" are concepts of person and identity associated with earlier constructions of shared place, common descent and chiefly leadership. Local conceptions of the person give Christian beliefs and practices much of their immediacy and relevance for people whose experience derives from life in small-scale (mostly) subsistence communities. Not surprisingly, local historiography tends to represent the strands of continuity in conversion history more explicitly than does missionary history. Analogous to the manner in which indigenous priests approach ancestral shrines as places to be "blessed" or "baptized" rather than destroyed, indigenous histories tell stories about the ancestor heroes who first incorporated the "new way" – some of whom already exhibited Christian characteristics. Having already encountered one example of the genre in the story about the Knabu chief Matasi Iho, the following two chapters examine more closely the manner in which conversion narratives constitute Christian identity for local communities today.

III *Narrating*

7

Becoming Christian: playing with history

On Maré, legend and even history are beginning to replace mythology.   *Maurice Leenhardt,* Do Kamo *(p. 119)*

Even though the social and ceremonial order instituted by Christianity has been in place for over seventy years, people young and old continue to locate themselves in the "new life" and to conceive of their identity in terms associated with oppositions of "old" and "new," heathen and Christian. Although the meaning and valorization of these categories is variable, they are repeatedly deployed in conversations and narratives in which people create reflexive images of who they are, where they've been, and where they are going. These oppositions persist not because they express timeless meanings but, to the contrary, because they may be adapted to changing circumstances, to the tasks of articulating identity and experience in small communities caught up in world events.

During the era of conversion to Christianity, and continuing today, Santa Isabel people have expressed desires to revitalize society in stories and symbols that contrast the "new" Christian life of the present with the "old" life of the past. The retelling of stories about raiding and kidnapping such as those told by James Nidi and Christian Odi represent the Maringe past as one of vulnerability, violence and victimization. The complement to these stories are others that people tell about how the past has been transformed – how the old became new, violence became peace, and so on. For those who have inherited this history, the story of transformation is regularly reconstituted in stories of Christianization such as Forest's and Josepa's reminiscences about their Knabu ancestors or the speeches at Charlie's Christmas feast.

For an historical event or epoch to become an emblem of community definition it must be incorporated in local modes of understanding and communication that recreate it as a subject of collective significance. As others have observed for more mundane sorts of personal recollection, the point of telling stories about past events is not simply to describe events, but to build a commentary about their social and moral significance for the narrator and his or her audience (Hill n.d.; Miller et al. 1990). This point is even more obvious when the events recalled are the object of collective remembrances that are repeated and even ritualized over time, as the events of conversion to Christianity have been in Santa Isabel. But the differences between stories of personal experience and accounts of collective history should not obscure the fact that in both cases meaning emerges from socially constructed narrative practice. Having already encountered a number of instances in which Cheke Holo people recall Christian conversion among their ancestors, this chapter and the one following inquire further into the processes that produce social meaning through recollections of shared history.

For any person or community, certain events tend to be retold over time such that they constitute meaningful or authoritative "histories." How have the events of Christian conversion in Santa Isabel obtained this type of significance such that they have been externalized repeatedly through time, to the point of obtaining a kind of mythic status? Two lines of response to this question need mentioning. On the one hand, "official" (collectively institutionalized) histories serve pragmatic ends and may work to sustain relations of dominance or power. On the other hand, for the past to remain "alive" as an object of felt concern or interest, it must speak to the hearts and minds of those who participate in its reconstruction. Because these aspects of local historicizing are not separate, I approach conversion narratives through public discourses that are at once culturally constituted and socially organized, playing upon understandings of persons and experience that have been glimpsed in previous discussion of models of chiefs and Christian persons.

While certainly not uniform across regions, generations or gender, the social meanings of Christianity are both widely shared and deeply felt throughout Santa Isabel society. One of the primary means for creating and propagating these meanings are narrative practices that regularly reproduce the drama of Christian conversion as shared history. Rather than look only inward at the minds of individuals to see how Christian identity is conceptualized and emotionalized, this chapter looks outward at socially produced representations that conjoin emotional meaning and sociopolitical significance. It is worth noting here that anthropological approaches to ritual have often looked to ritual symbols and practices as condensed expressions of (often unconscious) social and emotional meanings (e.g., Turner 1969). However, these approaches have most often viewed the ritual process as analytically separate from ordinary social life, as constituted in formalized and often mystified symbols whose collective significance may be decoded with penetrating analyses of hidden meanings. The historical narratives that I am concerned with are very much "betwixt and between" with respect to this separation of the ritual and the mundane. While certain stories have been subject to formalization and ritualization and genres of ritual drama or singing, others are replayed in ordinary conversation or in intermediate forms of speechmaking. While each form of representational practice colors the portrait of conversion produced, they may be shown to draw from similar understandings of persons, experience and history.

Whereas historical reflection pervades ordinary conversation and ceremonial activities, perhaps the most salient contexts for narrating shared history (*susurei*) are large feast occasions. For example, during the *diklo* feasts of old, collective histories were the subject of speeches, odes sung to important persons and ritualized comedy sketches. Formerly applied to the recitation of histories of descent, marriage and migration, these practices now often portray local histories of Christianization. This chapter and the one following consider several accounts of conversion constituted in different performative genres, beginning with an example of ritual comedy and going on to consider storytelling and singing.

Narrating conversion, constructing selves

Christian ideals in Santa Isabel exhibit an apparent irony: they are defined as symbolic departures from "old ways," but obtain meaning and value to the extent that they remain pragmatically continuous with them. Whereas colonial discourses such as the mission rhetoric of "old" and "new," "light" and "dark" have certainly shaped local patterns of thought (e.g., Keesing 1989), indigenous models exert their own hegemony in so far as Christian practices are assimilated to local concerns and meanings. Just as self-conscious notions of *kastom* are engendered in contexts of colonial experience, so local understandings of Christianity emerge in oppositions of *kastom* and Christianity, past and present. Of course, there is a distinct asymmetry in these relations since the latter are seen to supersede and transform the former. The seemingly static oppositions of "old" and "new," Christian and heathen in fact signal the dynamic significance of Christianity as a transformer of indigenous culture.

Religious conversion is, for the subject, an acknowledged transformation of the self. In the case of Santa Isabel, conversion is also regarded as a transformation of society, a communal experience that is collectively reproduced in historical narrative. In such a society, "new" religious symbols and practices become markers of a deliberate and self-conscious remaking of the person and community. In contrast with infants who are recruited directly into a religious identity at birth, conversion constitutes a change in which one set of beliefs and practices are overtly given up for another. Jules-Rosette (1975: 132) has described this aspect of conversion as ". . . . an experience that is rooted in both self and society. It involves a personally acknowledged transformation of self and a socially recognized display of change. In its social aspect, conversion resembles rites of passage in which the individual is acknowledged to move from one status and social environment to another." In the case of Santa Isabel, the "self" that is the subject of this acknowledged transformation is also a collective self; and the "rite of passage" is an historical epoch of community transition. As a transition involving movement and direction, a before and an after, conversion brings understandings about identity to the surface that might otherwise remain tacit and unrecognized. For this reason, the historical epoch in which a community converts to a new religion may readily become, in retrospect, an emblem of the present-day social order, somewhat analogous to the primordial events commonly depicted in creation mythology. Pursuing this analogy one step further, the agents of missionary change in conversion narratives (the missionaries and chiefs) become mythic culture heroes responsible for instituting the moral order as it is known today.

For the people of Santa Isabel, accounts of missionary contact are not abstract reports about a history that has become decoupled from the persons who recall it. Conversion narratives are statements about a past that leads unerringly to the lives of narrators and their audiences. Furthermore, these statements are not recorded in disembodied texts, but are enacted in socially situated performances, sometimes in ceremonial contexts, that make public declarations about identities being reproduced on the occasion of performance. Hence it becomes important to know something about the social situation in which history is remembered. Comparing portraits of conversion that emerge in distinct situations and genres exposes some of their context-specific significance associated with local traditions of place and ancestry as well as certain common themes underlying more general understandings of Christian identity.

The story of Christianization is now a part of the cultural heritage of every person in Santa Isabel. On one level, the image of the "Christian person" deployed in conversion narratives makes an important statement about the socio-religious unity of the entire island. (And note that it is not just Christianity, but Anglican Christianity that binds nearly all of the island's population to a common religious tradition.) However, when performed in ceremonial contexts, the narratives are not cast as general or universalistic statements about Christianity. Rather, they depict particular ancestors and missionaries as they encountered one another in the events of contact and conversion in a particular region. Speeches and songs performed during feasts are often presented as an ode to important persons – the ancestors and leaders of those who celebrate them. For many of today's older generation, their parents and grandparents were the key actors in those dramas, and are remembered as the figures who first adopted the "new way" of life. Thus, reconstructions of missionary history reaffirm the distinctiveness and importance of regional heritage, at the same time as they represent the common, unifying themes of Anglican Christianity. The result is a consistent ambiguity or tension between the text of generalized Christian identity and subtexts of regional particularism, rooted in definitions of lineage, clan and chiefly following. The latter stand for distinctive social boundaries just as surely as the image of the "Christian person" rhetorically transcends those same constructs.

As was apparent the first time the Knabu story was told to me, histories of early violence and Christian transformation are a prime topic for conversations with outsiders (such as an anthropologist) as well as for ceremonial enactments such as the Togasalo remembrance feast. It is notable that conversion narratives, which are *about* relations with the world outside localized communities, are often performed *for* audiences of outsiders. In this manner, the performance itself instantiates collective identity in relations between performers and audience – relations constitutive of the boundaries of community. Drawing attention to the audiences for historical recollection suggests one of the ways that the performance of conversion histories not only expresses but constitutes social reality.

Why are conversion narratives an effective vehicle for creating and sustaining understandings of self and identity? First of all, the conceptual backbone of narrative is temporal sequence; and temporal sequence is an elemental means for conceptualizing continuity and change. By connecting past and present, the temporal dimension of narrative creates a sense of continuity that is fundamental to the experience of the self (Hallowell 1967). Ironically, it is by virtue of representing difference or change that conversion narratives establish lines of connection with the past. Stories of change have a before and an after that may be used to constitute the present in terms of a critical moment of transition – a moment that temporally locates the juncture of "now" and "before."

Secondly, narrative exhibits a special capacity for representing human action in so far as behavior acquires meaning from temporally organized sequences of action and reaction (Gergen 1990). This quality is evident in conversion narratives that depict moments of historical contact and change in terms of persons, actions and interpersonal events. Narrative forms articulate abstract oppositions such as violence/peace, ignorance/knowledge or Christian/heathen as scenarios of action and reaction that have personal, social and moral significance. In this way, moments of transition obtain social meaning through the actions of persons linked to narrator and audience in terms of contemporary identities and ideals.

One of the rhetorical means through which Isabel people portray conversion as a sudden transition is through polarized metaphors that contrast the "present," the "new" and the "Christian" with the "past," the "old" and the "heathen." Characteristic of evangelical work nearly everywhere, the mission introduced and elaborated these dichotomous metaphors to conceptualize Christianization as a kind of life-giving moral regeneration. By conceiving of Christianity as bringing "light" where there was "darkness," and as "opening" what had been "closed," these metaphorical images express the significance of Christianity as a source of knowledge and as a harbinger of peace and nonviolence. Metaphors of darkness and light build upon well-established idioms of knowledge as "light" and "seeing" to characterize the Christian transition as one of knowledge acquisition. Thus, conversion is described as moving "out" into the "light" so that one may begin to "see" and "understand." In line with these connotations, the vernacular term for Christianity introduced in the Bughotu language by early missionaries is *Khilo'au* (or *Khilofajifla* in Cheke Holo, literally, "call out" [of darkness]). This term acquires its meaning from the image of emerging from "inside" (a dark enclosure) to acquire new knowledge "outside" (in the light). Similarly, the vernacular term for "heathen" borrowed from the Bughotu language is, literally, "dark mind" (*bongihehe*).

The other prominent theme in narrative portraits of conversion is *pacification*. In Santa Isabel, as in many parts of the Pacific, two concurrent transitions, from violence to peace and heathen to Christian, are so closely intertwined in local histories that one could not be constructed without the other. They are two facets of the same narrative, the same process of personal and societal transformation. The Isabel view that the suppression of warfare and violence is attributable to Christian teaching is widespread in the region (e.g., Guiart 1970). For example, Michael Young (1977: 132) writes of Goodenough Island in Papua that

... the demise of warfare and cannibalism and the advent of tafalolo (Christianity, Mission, Divine Service) are represented in oral tradition in a congruent or complementary set of basic terms. This is because they are viewed as constituting a simultaneous and indivisible process. The transformation wrought by the Methodist Mission in the realm of values and ideology, or so it is now believed, happened almost overnight.

Young here notes an important feature of local history-making: oral histories of conversion tend to depict change as total and sudden, happening "almost overnight." Others commenting on Melanesian historiographies have described the "episodic" character of models of change that construe the past in terms of a series of abrupt transitions (Errington 1974; McDowell 1985). Whether or not this is a general feature of historical memory in any particular society, representations of change as sudden and holistic are to be expected in the context of revitalization movements and conversion experiences guided by ideologies of a new era replacing an old. Throughout the Pacific Islands area local histories conceptualize the arrival of missionaries and conversion to Christianity in terms of disjunctive models that divide time into a "before" and a "now." The Pacific historian Malama Meleisea characterizes such a view in his comments about Samoan views of history: "The division of time into Before Christ (BC) and the Year of Our Lord (AD) began for us in 1830 with the arrival of the Gospel. We divide our history into the *pouliuli*, the time of darkness, and the *malama-lama*, the time of enlightenment" (1987: 144).

While such conceptions of the past do much to solidify images of radical change, they should not obscure other, parallel understandings that connect the past (even "times of darkness") with the present. Here it may be misleading to talk about local "historiography" as a single body of knowledge and practice that records history in consistent and uniform ways. A fuller understanding of the range of meanings and uses of history in any given community requires a closer look at naturally occurring dis-courses of remembrance across a variety of contexts and representational media. The remainder of this chapter and the one following pursue this directive through an investigation of portrayals of conversion in several Cheke Holo communities. The comedy sketch taken up below paints a portrait of dramatic change, emblazoned with contrasts of violence and peace, ignorance and knowledge. And yet even here the presumptions and contexts of the drama implicate numerous strands of sociocultural conti-nuity that are not only evident in, but essential to, the meanings that emerge from the performance.

Thukma

Along with singing and dancing, dramatic performances known as *thukma* are a frequent part of the entertainment at feast occasions. Like genres of comedic theater or ritual clowning everywhere, *thukma* skits use tropes of parody and caricature to represent events in terms that are both exagger-ated and funny (Handelman 1981). Similar forms of ritual comedy occur in many parts of the Solomons and the Pacific generally and have been adapted particularly to representing problems and themes at the interface of indigenous and colonial polities (e.g., Hereniko 1991; Sinavaiana n.d.). Historically, for example, numerous Solomon Islands communities re-played their experiences with the armies of foreign powers during World War II in these forms of village drama. The skits that I have seen in Santa Isabel are all concerned with the representation of past events, but the events depicted are highly diverse, including both recent and historic happenings. *Thukma* performances often re-enact recent events that lampoon the trials or misfortunes of particular people in the community. But they are also used to represent historical moments of considerable significance to the community. By far the most frequent subject of this latter type of performance are local histories of Christian conversion. Whereas plays that deal with recent events still fresh in memory are usually fleeting one-time performances, the conversion dramas deal with more remote events and are produced recurrently on occasions of collective importance such as village church days. In other words, the conversion dramas exhibit properties of ritualization.

The typical *thukma* play seizes upon a particular incident from daily life which has already received attention in circles of conversation and gossip. The *thukma* parodies events that may even have been serious or problematic by representing them in exaggerated and distorted forms. For example, in one of the skits that I watched the actors recreated an incident in which someone's domestic pig left to forage in the forest was shot by a man who thought he was stalking a wild pig. At the time of its occurrence, this incident was ripe for misunderstanding and conflict, but had been resolved amicably by the payment of compensation to the pig owner. Another skit portrayed the particularly painful misfortune of a villager who had been bitten by a centipede (which is one of the most severe afflictions the natural world of Santa Isabel has to offer). This also, of course, was not funny at the time. Centipede bites are widely feared for the intense pain that may last for several days with no effective antidote. In both skits, the persons involved in the real events watched with amusement along with the rest of the audience as their misfortunes were re-enacted in the clowning antics of *thukma* actors for all to see.

Numerous communities have adapted the *thukma* format, with its use of humor, hyperbole and caricature, to represent the mythic characters and events of conversion. For this subject, the genre's rhetoric of exaggeration accentuates contrasts in the appearance, demeanor and actions of Christians and heathens. Prototypic images of Christian and pre-Christian identity are brought to life in a series of interactive scenes that lead from an era of heathen violence to one of Christian peace. While the sketches differ from one region to another in the particular characters and events that make up conversion history, they converge in significant aspects of narrative structure and imagery of people.

During my first period of fieldwork I observed three skits about Christian conversion in different regions (including one from the neighboring island of Nggela) and recorded a description of a fourth. Then, during a second stay in Santa Isabel during 1984 I watched a repeat performance of one of those seen earlier. The skits I observed were enacted on separate occasions by people from different regions and language groups, spanning Anglican communities in Maringe, Bughotu and the neighboring island of Nggela. The Bughotu skit replayed the arrival of Bishop George Selwyn and the subsequent conversion of the famous Bughotu chief Soga; while the Nggela skit dealt with the work of the first indigenous catechist on that island, Alfred Popohe. It is the Maringe skit – a re-enactment of the flight of Buala village people from raiding headhunters, followed by their return as Christians – that is the subject of this chapter. The other Cheke Holo *thukma* that was described to me concerned the historic first encounter between the missionary Henry Welchman and the Hograno chief Figrima (the subject of several stories and a song taken up in the next chapter).

All of these skits exhibit a narrative structure that has much in common with the internal ordering of ordinary stories about conversion such as the Knabu legends. The dramas I witnessed show local ancestors accepting and learning the "new way" expressed particularly in transformations of violence and ignorance. *Thukma* performances develop these themes through narrative sequence (peace follows violence; understanding follows ignorance) and through interactive engagement (encounters between Christians and heathen in which the former pacify and instruct the latter). These transformations are depicted in two types of interactive scenario that are particularly well suited to portraying typifications of heathen aggressiveness and ignorance. These are (1) the moment of first contact between a missionary and an ancestor hero, such as between Walter Gagai and the Knabu chief Iho and (2) the process of teaching Christian neophytes the rudiments of prayer and hymn-singing, leading to baptism. Three of the four plays I recorded included both types of scene.

Thukma dramatizations of missionary contact reconstruct the process of Christianization along the same lines as the Knabu narrative that moved sequentially through episodes of approach, resistance and acceptance. As the following chapter will show, episodes of heathen resistance are critical to the meanings of conversion that emerge from these plays. These acts of resistance are constituted in the actions of heathen warriors whose first impulse, like that of Matasi Iho's armed men, is to threaten and attack. The approach of a Christian missionary creates an opportunity for amplifying this aggressiveness into humorous proportions. In the following skit, agonistic displays of warrior ferocity are the dramatic analog of the episode of resistance recalled in oral narratives such as the Knabu legend. Both portray the heathen "strong man" as impelled by violent urges. The prototype of the "strong man" is the ground against which the figure of the missionary is drawn as both brave and powerful. The latter's power is demonstrated most acutely by overcoming the immediate threats of violent attack posed by warriors. Three of the four plays mentioned above reconstruct first contacts between missionaries and pagan ancestors as an initial confrontation in which warriors dressed in loincloths and waving axes above their heads threaten to kill the visiting missionary. The skit discussed below projects similar images of pre-Christian violence through its own distinctive scene of attack.

In addition to their caricature of violent impulses, *thukma* skits commonly parody native ignorance or lack of knowledge of European ways. Contrasts between heathen ignorance and Christian knowledge are constituted in scenes of initial encounter and subsequent teaching. In recreating the events of first contact, the skits frequently show exaggerated native reactions of uncomprehending awe upon first encountering the unfamiliar accoutrements of Western culture, particularly clothing and trade goods. So, for example, the Bughotu skit about Bishop Selwyn's arrival began with re-enactment of the killing of the Catholic missionary Bishop Epalle. To embellish their performance, the actors borrowed what has become a standard Melanesian joke about early contact history: a European is killed and then cooked and eaten by cannibals who find the cuisine to be tough going when they get to his boots. Not having seen leather shoes before, they try to consume them and complain bitterly in the process. In another example of heathen ignorance of European culture, the skit about the chief Figrima showed him balking at smoking a pipe given him by Welchman because he thought it was like "eating fire" or "burning garden brush." To mention a final example from the skit performed by the Nggela people, the

Plate 12 Bughotu men re-enact greeting given to Bishop George Selwyn, Sepi village (July 7, 1975)

heathens are shown to react to the approaching catechist with a combination of aggression and awe. As the missionary comes near, one warrior cautiously moves close enough to touch his clothing, even crouching down and touching his long white vestments and uttering in hushed tones: "This is different from our clothing!"

The typification of heathen ignorance by aggressive warriors stunned by the most rudimentary Western goods is epitomized in scenes of Christian instruction that often follow in *thukma* skits. The attempts of mission catechists to teach heathens pronunciation, prayer and hymn-singing show neophyte pupils struggling against gross inabilities to mimic even the most elementary aspects of Christian practice. The depiction of faulty learning of simple tasks such as repeating the sound of a single letter or musical note is the type of exaggeration through which the *thukma* turns ordinary or serious events into something extraordinary and ludicrous.

Clowns everywhere are well known to trade upon emotionally and politically loaded topics that, in the context of clowning, are subject to inversion or burlesque caricature. For ordinary *thukma* plays, sexuality and bodily functions are a ready source of humorous play; for the "larger" topic of Christian conversion, aggression and ignorance are the social themes that receive the most consistent attention. But the humor and irony which are the hallmark of *thukma* plays reflect ambivalences surrounding topics that remain problematic in everyday life. Even though warfare has long since ended, worries about hidden hostilities and covert violence in forms such as gossip and sorcery are pervasive in Santa Isabel communities today. Furthermore, these concerns are framed particularly in terms of Christian values of harmony and restraint. By constructing images of violence and aggression in the exaggerated persona of the heathen warrior, the play makes the covert overt, taking real ambivalences and subjecting them to symbolic resolution through re-enactment of the conversion process and its hopeful transformation of "dark" passions.

In like manner, the patent asymmetries between Western technological power and *kastom* ways continue to be sources of ambivalent reflection in Santa Isabel today. The manifold disparities between indigenous and Western knowledge that intrude continually in modern contexts of education and development make the theme of early Christian instruction and native learning a parable for knowledge processes that still have social relevance. Such disparities are sometimes the subject of jokes that Isabel people make about the primitive quality of local ("native") technologies in comparison with Western ones. So, for example, laughing remarks about the crudeness of a log bridge or the impermanence of a thatched house run parallel to the hyperbolic images of ignorant heathen in *thukma* skits where they are attributed to an ancestral "other." Similar to the Navaho jokes about the "Whiteman" described by Basso (1979: 48), *thukma* caricatures of the heathen as both aggressive and unknowing project an image of the Other as a prototype of "ineffectively guided behavior, of social action gone haywire".

Bina boli

One of the most frequently performed skits about Christian conversion is one put on with some regularity by the people of Buala village. As noted earlier, Buala was in many ways the hub of Christianization for the Maringe region and is now the administrative center of the Santa Isabel provincial government. It was there that Hugo Hebala, the first Christian priest, established one of the first mission villages along the coast and evangelized the surrounding area during the first two decades of this century.

As often as once a year, the people of Buala re-enact the events leading to this wholesale conversion in a skit they refer to as *bina boli*. *Bina boli* or, literally, "migration by canoe," refers to the odyssey of ancestors of the Buala people who fled Maringe during the headhunting period and then returned as Christians to establish a mission center in Maringe. Unlike the Knabu people who also fled their ancestral lands for Bughotu but returned still practicing their traditional religion, the Buala group was converted while residing in Bughotu where the Melanesian Mission had established its headquarters. Hence, the Buala *bina boli* encompasses the migration to and from Bughotu, depicting both the headhunting that preceded it and the subsequent return by canoe to convert the surrounding Maringe population. A brief account of the Buala exodus and return is given below as a prelude to consideration of a *bina boli* performance.

Over one hundred years ago the people who lived near the shore of the Maringe Lagoon were decimated by headhunting raids such as those discussed in chapter 5. It seems that raids into the Maringe area escalated during the 1870s and 1880s, leading to widespread flight from the region. In addition to the stories about this time such as that by James Nidi (whose village sits on the edge of the Maringe Lagoon), various European traders made note of the violence. For example, in 1881 an agent aboard the labor recruiting vessel *Jessie Kelly* calling in at the lagoon wrote that he observed the "remains of a cannibal feast, about 10 people had been killed and eaten there . . . the hair yet clung to their skulls . . ." (Fiji Agent of General Immigration, No. 32, J. Gaggin, Journal: September 1, 1881). According to a mission account, there was an attack in about 1890 that killed more than one hundred inhabitants of the area (Melanesian Mission 1895 1(7): 9–10). It was this raid that led the ancestors of the Buala people to decide to flee to Bughotu where they sought refuge at a place called Lagheba at the very southeasterly end of the island. About fifty men, women and children under the leadership of a chief named Getu moved southward to live within the orbit of the (now Christian) Bughotu chief Soga. Within just a few years, Henry Welchman, living at his nearby mission station on the islet of Marana-Tabu, wrote that Getu was "anxious for a school" (Diary: April 11, 1894). So Welchman sent Hugo Hebala, trained at Norfolk Island, to build a school and instruct them. Within ten years all the Lagheba refugees were Christian, at which point (in 1905) Hebala and the Lagheba chief, now baptized John Selwyn Getu, led the colony back to their home in Maringe to resettle the area and begin evangelizing the surrounding region.

When the move was made, residents who had remained in the area granted Hebala and the mission two islands in the lagoon and a stretch of shoreline as an expression of their willingness to have the Christian group remain permanently. The first project was to build a church for this new hub of mission work. Eager to establish the Christian presence, Hebala and Getu asked Welchman to consecrate the new church building even before it was finished. With about two hundred Christians inside the building and both Christians and pagans observing from outside, Welchman presided over a ceremony to bless the new Buala church in 1906 (Wilson 1935: 80–1). Within three years, Welchman reported:

Buala has been growing rapidly. A number of heathen have come down from the hills at the back, and have made a settlement for themselves almost adjoining the Church compound . . . they were attracted by the friendly nature of the place. Many have joined the baptismal class which now numbers 70 . . . Hugo, the deacon, had done much missionary work with the bush folk, and two or three places are ready for teachers . . . *(Melanesian Mission 1908: 46–7)*

The descendants of Getu, Hebala and the other Lagheba colonists still reside at Buala. One way that they mark their distinctive heritage is through periodic performances of the *bina boli* skit. As is the case for all local histories of the Christian transformation, the Buala performers produce an account that is centered in their locale, with their ancestors as principal actors in the conversion drama. In this case, because of Hugo Hebala's missionary work, the boundaries of the region represented in the drama encompass potentially all of Maringe. Even though some of the teachers who contacted Maringe groups worked through other Christian villages (such as Walter Gagai going up to the Knabu from another coastal village, Baghovu), the *bina boli* skit establishes the Lagheba group as the harbingers of wholesale transformation.

As a village that now finds itself drawn more quickly and deeply into modern "development" activities than other Isabel communities, the function of *bina boli* as a ritualized statement of distinctive local heritage looms larger and larger. At the present time, Buala has a dual personality: it is both an administrative center for the provincial government and a village much like any other in Maringe. The village, with its rows of thatched houses along the lagoon shore, sits adjacent to Buala "station" – the cluster of architected offices and houses for civil servants that comprise the government center. Due to its proximity to the provincial center, Buala village is anything but typical. Many of its residents are in wage-earning jobs at the government station; and everyone benefits from the regular transport available from small ships and planes that connect Buala with the national capital, Honiara. (An offshore islet is the site of Santa Isabel's only airfield.)

Buala villagers, in addition to being relatively more involved in the incipient wage economy, are also the most involved in the many comings and goings of visiting dignitaries in both government and church. Buala residents frequently find themselves organizing festivities to welcome national politicians, church officials and the ambassadors of other nations as they first come ashore at Buala for tours of the island. The *bina boli* skit is frequently performed in the context of such welcomes – as a kind of distinctive local custom that may be displayed for important guests from outside the community. Since the topic of the skit concerns the historical origins of the community's involvement with Christianity and wider spheres of commerce, it seems appropriate that its performance for visiting representatives of church and government reconstitutes those very relations.

I have had occasion to watch two *bina boli* performances, one in 1975 and one in 1984. According to some, the *bina boli* performance is an annual event, although the timing will vary according to the occasions and opportunities that arise from one year to another. The skit is often performed as part of a larger feast or ceremonial event and is often directed toward an audience made up of Buala villagers, government workers from Buala station and visitors from outside the island. This was so in both of the performances I observed, although the significance of outsiders in the audience was more accentuated in 1984 when the skit was performed as part of a ceremonial welcome for one of the largest delegations of outside dignitaries to visit the village at one time. On that occasion, a Buala man who was one of the island's two members of the national parliament had invited a group of international representatives to tour the island. All based in Honiara, the group of visitors included the Australian and British High Commissioners, a proxy for the New Zealand High Commissioner, and the head of the South Pacific Forum Fisheries Agency.

The skit discussed below was performed on a Sunday in August of 1975. On this occasion, the *bina boli* was a focal element of the celebration, defined as a remembrance (*gatho fapulo*) of important ancestors and their role in Christian conversion, much like the Togasalo Pentecost feast and remembrance of Matasi Iho. The primary organizer was Nathaniel Hebala, Buala chief and one of several children of Hugo Hebala living in Buala. Although the rationale for the celebration was not explicitly identified with Hebala or his kindred (it was presented as a village activity), re-enacting the origins of Buala village in the context of his father's missionary activities reconstructed a genealogical and historical rationale for their prominence in the social world of the village. Accordingly, Hebala's position as chief and senior kinsman to many of the Buala residents was a key element in the mobilization of village households for the purpose of contributing to the feast. As the village most affected by the intrusion of the cash economy, Buala villagers have increasingly defined households as the primary locus of food production and consumption, with individual "families" rather than lineages or clans responsible for contributing to feast occasions. (Within the last ten years, the village has introduced a pattern referred to as "family meal" for village-wide commensal activities in which each household brings the food which it consumes at gatherings.)

On the day of this *bina boli*, the activities included a sequence of events much like any ceremonial occasion (which inevitably include feasting): an early morning Communion service in the church was followed later in the day by entertainment (the skit), "sharing" food and speechmaking. The *bina boli* was staged in one of the Buala hamlets where a wide, sandy plaza made a suitable stage for the performance. There was no explicit rationale for welcoming outside guests, but the presence of myself and wife Nancy (who had only just arrived) as well as others from Buala station constituted a small but noticeable outside presence among the Buala audience. After the play, everyone sat down to eat together and listen to accompanying speeches expected on such occasions. The distribution of food was not defined as an exchange between groups or "sides," but rather as an occasion for collective eating and speechmaking. Cooked food was contributed by most households and then redistributed and jointly consumed (this was prior to the "family meal" pattern), with additional shares of cooked fish and pork given to the notable outsiders to take away with them. The main speech during the feast was given by Nathaniel Hebala who spoke about the significance of the events portrayed in the skit and then encouraged younger villagers to ask questions of the older people about the history of the migration and conversion.

Underscoring the fact that outsiders and/or young people who may not share knowledge of local history make up an acknowledged part of the audience for these skits, someone usually assumes the role of narrator who gives a scene-by-scene commentary on the events portrayed. As was the case for other conversion skits I observed, here the role of narrator was taken by a local priest, Fr. Hugo Kmudu. (Like Nathaniel Hebala and many other Buala people, Fr. Kmudu is also descended from Hugo Hebala – as a grandson.) Other kinds of *thukma* performance about small and humorous events in the recent past usually do not have this kind of overt narration. The fact that the narrator on this occasion chose to speak in Solomons Pidgin suggests that his remarks were directed at least partly toward the various visitors and government workers from other islands who lacked knowledge of both local language and history.

Having an indigenous commentator/narrator informing the audience of the meaning of the performance might seem to obviate the need for any further interpretive work. Indeed, Fr. Kmudu even summarized the work's episodic structure, announcing to the audience that the play they were about to see would unfold in three "scenes." The two performances I witnessed were extremely close in narrative form, following the same sequence of scenes or episodes. Both the "script" and the main characters were the same from one version to another, although the actors who played the characters differed. The scenes in the *thukma* below are as follows: an attack scene in which raiders from the Western Solomons descend upon unsuspecting Maringe people; a return scene in which the Lagheba group led by Getu and Hebala paddle back to Maringe and make contact with people remaining there; and a final scene of Christian teaching and learning in which Maringe people are instructed and baptized. As each scene unfolds, the narrator offers further commentary, which I have appropriated for the account below.

The production lasted nearly forty-five minutes and involved about fifty performers. One scene even incorporated the lagoon into the production as those playing the part of the returning Lagheba party came ashore in three canoes, pulled up on an adjacent stretch of shoreline. The skit opens with about twenty-five men, women and children clustered together talking and cooking food. This group is obviously pre-Christian in appearance, clad only in waistcloths or loincloths with skin blackened with ash. As they occupy themselves with the mundane tasks of daily life, we see two lines of crouching armed warriors approach stealthily from a distance. The warriors, like the victims, are also dressed in loincloths, only they are distinctly more fierce in appearance. These "strong men," about fifteen in each line, carry axes, spears and shields. In addition to toting weapons, they have streaked their faces and bodies with white markings. The overall impression is one of single-minded absorption in the business of warfare. As the scene continues, the prototypic warrior comes to life in the violent movements and loud whoops that the attackers give out as they swoop down on their victims. The narrator introduces the scene as follows:

While they [the Maringe people] are staying in their village, we will eventually see the men from the west come in order to make war and fight. You know the way it was in the past. They came to attack people in Isabel. I think they started in the west and came until reaching Maringe . . . First they will look all around. Then the attack will come afterwards.

About ten suspenseful minutes elapse as the unsuspecting Maringe people chat among themselves and the warriors creep up on them unnoticed. Finally, the attackers descend upon the Maringe folk with a great uproar, brandishing their axes and shields, and shouting vociferously as the victims try to flee in panic. Pandemonium ensues as the attackers make threatening gestures and "kill" a number of villagers, chase others away, and carry off a number of children, presumably as kidnapped victims. One or two of the younger children appeared genuinely terrified by the attack. A young boy about five years old was swept up by an attacking warrior and carried off crying at the top of his lungs. (He apparently failed to keep in mind the Batesonian frame that said "this is play.")

In depicting the raiding and killing that led to the exodus of Maringe people, the attack stands for an historical epoch and a societal ethos in which Maringe ancestors suffered from the escalating violence of raiding and headhunting. The scene establishes a baseline representation of society prior to the introduction of Christianity that then frames the significance of conversion and pacification to come.

The next episode focuses on the return of Maringe people from Lagheba where they had been converted to Christianity. This scene shifts to the edge of the lagoon where three canoes filled with people returning from Lagheba come ashore. Their arrival is introduced by the narrator as follows:

Eventually the Lagheba people will return in canoes. Selwyn Getu and Hebala and all the big-men will come with their canoes and stop over there [points to the lagoon shoreline]. They are returning again to Maringe, the place where they were attacked earlier today. And they will be bringing the Church back with them. That's the meaning of this . . . Eventually we'll see the canoes come here. Because at that time this place was just bush. There were no houses or anything yet. So some people were just living all around here. But it was bush. There weren't any villages or houses . . .

The narrator goes on to say that on their way the migrating Lagheba group stopped at two places where they asked two local chiefs for permission to land at Buala. At that point, the three canoes paddle up to the land and people get out and wade ashore. The first on shore are the men playing John Selwyn Getu and Hugo Hebala. Hebala, the priest (at that time a catechist), is adorned with a large cross made from a coconut frond. But the depiction of their migration by canoe does not end here. These people, about twenty-five to thirty in number, then form a line and mimic paddling by walking in single file across the sand, making stroking motions with paddles and chanting a rhythmic canoe-paddling song as they go. The chant, led by women who are at the front of the line, lasts about ten minutes. They proceed toward a group of Maringe people gathered some forty or fifty yards from the shore (people who presumably had not migrated to Bughotu, but remained behind in their "heathen" state).

The indigenous group of about twenty-five men, women and children sits passively on the ground as the paddlers approach. Signaling their identity as ancestors still adhering to the "way before," more than half of the group perform a circle-dance (*gleghi*) of the type associated with pre-Christian dance styles. The festive tone of the *gleghi* notwithstanding, the dominant visual impression conveyed by this group of pre-Christian ancestors is one of impoverishment or primitiveness. All of those in the cluster of heathens appear disheveled with ash-blackened skin, very little clothing and few signs of material wealth. A local onlooker who assisted with the production intercedes in the narration to say that these people are suffering from "sickness" and "harsh weather" such as rainstorms. But despite their condition, the heathen group welcomes the Lagheba Christians amicably, offering them cooked food and greeting them with handshaking. (Even though handshaking was a custom introduced by the mission, it is appropriated at this point in the play as a way of expressing the receptive attitude of the Maringe group toward their kin who had fled years before.) The narrator describes the basis for this amicable greeting by referring to both groups as "the same people," implying that they share affiliations of place and/or ancestry:

A Maringe big man will welcome them again. Since they are the same people they [the heathens] want to come and welcome them [the Lagheba Christians] by giving them some food. And then they [the Christians] will give some of them a little bit of teaching and singing.

As the Lagheba people squat or kneel on the ground, the heathens walk up and shake hands amidst much chatter and repeated utterances of the Pidgin greeting "*kubai*" (the generic "goodbye" and "hello" uttered with handshaking at greeting and parting).

Significantly, this episode of return and encounter is enacted as an exchange. The offering of food constitutes relations between the two groups in an idiom of kinship and host–guest relations. The locals receive the Lagheba people as hosts would receive any guests, by offering them cooked food. But the food is reciprocated with "a little bit of teaching." Whereas in the past, at feasts food (cooked and uncooked) would be given to guests who would reciprocate with food and/or gifts, here the reciprocation comes in the form of ritual knowledge ("a little bit of teaching"). By framing this first encounter between Maringe Christians and non-Christians in this way, the social context of missionization is established as both egalitarian (shared ancestry) and hierarchical, with the dominance of the church established through its position as the source of new knowledge.

Following this greeting, the final scene turns to the efforts of the Lagheba group to spread Christian teaching through didactic instruction. This scene, like others in the same genre, parodies heathen ignorance by depicting their difficulty in learning the most elemental features of Western knowledge and Christian ritual. The scene unfolds in three parts, each one focusing on the efforts of a different catechist to impart Christian practice. Each of the three catechists is shown in turn teaching a different subject: first prayer, then the alphabet and finally hymn-singing. Each catechist, introduced by name, is one of those well known for their early evangelical work in the Maringe area. The narrator explains that this scene is concerned with Christian teaching, but notes that the heathens will have a difficult time learning because they are "very heathen" (in Pidgin, *hithen tumas*).

They are going to start giving teaching, prayer and service, hymn-singing and the like. At first they [the local group] won't understand because they are very heathen. But they will try hard and eventually it will go alright, I think. We don't know yet. The first one [catechist] we see, we call Bengire [Ben Ngapo].

The man who is playing Ben Ngapo then stands up and begins to lecture to the heathens seated on the ground around him. He tries to teach them prayer, *tarai*, by getting them to mimic the Lord's Prayer in the Bughotu language (the language formerly used for instruction and church service throughout Santa Isabel). He begins with the line *mama popo*, "father above," but that elicits only a jumble of discordant sounds as the heathens loudly mispronounce the phrase in their attempt to repeat it. So the teacher attempts to correct them in impatient tones, saying "not *papa, popo!*" and asks them to try again. After this line is repeated, the teacher goes on to a second phrase in the prayer and the same process of error correction ensues. Each attempt at correction evokes loud giggles and laughter from the audience, particularly from the children present. After completing the prayer, this portion of the scene concludes with the teacher leading the group through the entire prayer, line by line, affirming that they have finally gotten it right.

The second catechist is Wilson Doedoke played by Nathaniel Hebala. Like Ngapo before him, Doedoke stands up and begins to teach the students the alphabet. The same type of scenario used to teach prayer unfolds again as the teacher pronounces each letter of the alphabet and tries to get the students to repeat it correctly. The same sequence of trial-and-error rote learning repeats itself as each of the first three letters of the alphabet, "a," "b" and "c," is spoken by the teacher. Once again, the group of students initially mispronounces each letter with gross inaccuracy before finally getting it correct.

The third catechist portrayed is Steven Ko'ili. Played by Clement Felo, a man well known for his sense of humor, Ko'ili's task is to teach the heathen pupils how to sing hymns. Like the previous two catechists, he stands facing the group seated on the ground and tells them to listen as he sings in a falsetto voice "do–re–mi–fa–so–la–ti–do." By singing in a voice not his own he quickly draws laughter from the audience and hints at further foolishness to come. As he goes on to teach the elements of hymn-singing, he stands up and gesticulates with a reed as a conductor's baton. This scene starts out like the others with the students twice trying unsuccessfully to repeat the notes. But they then give up and spontaneously begin to sing a local song in well-practiced tones. The teacher says it sounds "number one" (very good) and encourages them to go ahead and sing even more loudly. As he directs and encourages their singing, his waistcloth falls off, revealing bare buttocks and a slim loincloth underneath, evoking an uproar of laughter from the audience.

At this point the skit is nearly complete, with only the finale remaining. The drama is brought to a close with the neophytes being baptized. Baptism is, of course, the culmination of the process of teaching and learning – the ritual certification of Christian identity. The narrator comments:

> Now we will see Hugo Hebala who will teach baptism. And eventually he will baptize one or two as well. And all the big-men will be baptized, too.

The actor portraying Hugo Hebala makes a token appearance, but does not prolong the baptism sequence. (The degree of elaboration of any one *thukma* scene depends upon the actors' skill in developing an idea into a dramatic and usually humorous event.) The skit I observed performed by people from Nggela also included a series of teaching episodes ending in baptism. However, on that occasion, the baptism scene was more elaborated, marked by an elated yell from the person receiving baptism. In that skit the narrator supplied the following interpretation of the convert's experience: "He has now received [baptism]. He comes to talk to the people [others not yet baptized]: 'My goodness! This is something really good. My body feels light!'" The Nggela actors thus portrayed baptism as a rite of passage into a new or wonderful state of the person marked by emotions of surprise and happiness.

Both the Buala and Nggela plays exhibit a common narrative structure that proceeds from first contact through teaching to baptism and the acquisition of Christian identity. And both skits end with the actors gathering together for a final enactment of contemporary Christian identity by exhibiting their skills as practiced singers of Christian hymns. At the conclusion of the *bina boli* skit, the actors join in a chorus singing a hymn in the Cheke Holo language. The loud and forceful singing of well-practiced hymns contrasts sharply with the tentative and erratic efforts of the Christian neophytes portrayed in the play. By shifting the temporal locus of activity from the era of conversion to the present, the final chorus completes the identification of actors and acted, merging in the identity of contemporary Christian persons.

With the completion of the skit, participants and audience disperse so that they can complete the preparation of food to be consumed at the feast marking the end of the day's activities. With the church "bell" ringing to signal that it is time to reassemble, about sixty people gather again on the margins of the plaza for eating and listening to speeches. As this is happening, Nathaniel Hebala and other Buala chiefs direct the distribution of food so that each household and each visitor is allotted the appropriate portion of fish, pork, chicken, rice, sweet potatoes and taro pudding. When this is finally completed, Fr. Kmudu says a prayer blessing the food, and everyone begins to eat. Consistent with his role as chief and leading organizer of the *bina boli*, Hebala is the first to stand and give a short speech about the significance of the occasion. Using the appropriate rhetoric for the sponsor of such an occasion, he makes a few self-deprecating remarks about the small amount of food which has been distributed, and then goes on to recite his version of the historical rationale for the occasion. Summarizing the skit's main theme, he talks generally about the arrival of Christianity in Maringe and refers to particular ancestors and chiefs involved in the migration, not the least of which is his own father, Hugo Hebala. By reviewing specific historical events and mentioning the names of ancestors of many of those present at the celebration, both the skit and the subsequent speechmaking reconstruct a version of missionary history that highlights the social distinctiveness of Buala in idioms of ancestry and place that work to reproduce significant dimensions of the contemporary social order. To quote (in translation) from the middle of Hebala's speech:

Today, we do this because all the Lagheba people ran away from this part of Maringe and stayed away twenty years or thirty years. Then they said: "Oh, I think Maringe is alright now." "I think you all should go back." I think Dr. Welchman may have said that to Getu and Hebala . . . Because Dr. Welchman said: "I think you, Getu, you take your people and go to Maringe, go to Buala. Because the fighting that was going on before is over now. The fighting is finished." . . . So starting at Lagheba they came to Buala. They came here before the church was here. That's all there is to it . . . Because the people of Maringe and Bughotu began at Lagheba and came here to start the church in Maringe. That's what this feast we have made is about . . . We do this *bina boli* because they started from Lagheba and came here . . . Getu and Hebala you all know, Beni, Boklo, Samu, all the big men, I forget now. All the big men of Bughotu brought the church here. That's all that this feast we are making now is about. We are just showing what they did in the past . . .

Hebala's remarks speak to issues often repeated in speechmaking on feast occasions. His review of key events in social history focuses particularly on past migrations and the persons (ancestors) who led them. Whereas those persons would at one time have been chiefs, today they are catechists and chiefs. Where genealogy, marriage and migration were the topics of historicizing narrative in the past, today mission history is. Following Hebala's speech, he and Fr. Kmudu (respectively, son and grandson of Hugo Hebala) encourage others present to ask questions and learn more about the events depicted in the play. Knowledge of the characters and events involved in the *bina boli* migration is by no means completely shared, especially among the younger generations. A brief question and answer period follows, with Hebala and Fr. Kmudu answering most of the questions – questions that focus largely on places and people. The first asks about the location of Lagheba, followed by a series of questions about the catechists portrayed in the skit, about who they were and where they worked.

By focusing on the conversion era, the *bina boli* skit recreates an historical transformation that links local communities with a wider network of Christian institutions that now extends throughout the entire island and outward to Anglican and Christian churches worldwide. In this sense, the play could be said to represent the acquisition of an identity that not only ties the people of Buala together, but links them with the rest of Santa Isabel and much of the world beyond. But note that this picture of Christian solidarity emerges from a story that is equally about regional distinctiveness. In counterpoint to these outward-looking, expansive meanings, the performance constitutes a social reality defined in localized idioms of descent and locale, affirming social relations and distinctions within the Maringe area and within Buala village itself. Just as the descendants of Matasi Iho at Togasalo "remember" their ancestor in narrative histories of conversion that become a kind of "charter myth" for the whole village, so the descendants of Hugo Hebala are the prime movers behind the Buala *bina boli* that reconstitutes relations of descent and village leadership in the context of celebrating collective history. Not only are these relations and identities symbolically represented in the text of the performance, they are constituted in the activities of the church service and the feast that bracket the performance. The leadership roles of the main organizer, Nathaniel Hebala, and the main commentator, Fr. Hugo Kmudu, are constructed in the entire organization of the event as a political and ritual process. These roles emerge particularly in the context of the feasting process and its

cooperative activities of preparing, distributing and consuming food –
activities that depend particularly upon relations of kinship and coresidence. Perhaps not unlike the earlier alliance of Hugo Hebala and Selwyn
Getu, Hugo Kmudu and Nathaniel Hebala form another priest–chief
alliance in organizing and articulating the purposes of collective
celebration.

The range of forms and occasions in which the people of Santa Isabel
communities seek to reconstruct the story of Christianization attests to the
meaningfulness of that story for people today. The following chapter turns
to several examples of conversion narrative in other regions and other
genres, particularly storytelling and singing. Here the cross-genre comparisons provide a perspective from which to tease out similarities and
differences among distinct varieties of historical discourse. Two general
lines of comparison may be pursued, corresponding to Jameson's characterization of two approaches to genre criticism as "the rivalry between old-
fashioned 'interpretation,' which still asks the text what it *means*, and the
newer kinds of analysis which . . . ask how it *works*" (1981: 108, emphasis in
original). Whether conversion history is represented in the form of a
conversational narrative, a speech or an enacted drama such as the *bina
boli*, we may approach it as both text and as socially situated performance.
When analyzed as symbolic representation, conversion histories as different as the Knabu legends and the Buala *bina boli* draw upon many of the
same concepts, metaphors and narrative forms. And, when situated in their
contexts of performance, whether in a conversation with a visitor or in an
elaborately produced drama, stories of Christian contact and conversion
consistently mediate localized identities and "outside" forces.

When reproduced within socially orchestrated contexts of remembrance
such as the Togasalo Pentecost celebration or the Buala *bina boli*, conversion stories obtain a kind of mythic status as emblems of collective identity.
While it is anthropological custom to regard myth and ritual as collective,
cyclical and planned (as opposed to more mundane practices that tend to be
individual, irregular and spontaneous), I have tried to resist treating
conversion stories as fixed forms of collective representation. Once discursive practices are reified as abstract, normative statements, they become
separated from their politicized and emotionalized contexts of production,
thus making problematic the rediscovery of their significance for either
individual experience or relations of power.

Even though they draw upon similar conceptual and narrative resources
for representing the Christian transformation, each performative genre
(such as stories, speeches, dramas and songs) offers a different set of
communicative possibilities for framing its message. For example, stories
and speeches such as that by Nathaniel Hebala may be performed as a kind

of straightforward "report" of historical events, whereas other forms such as *thukma* drama are told in ways that may parody or satirize their subject-matter. Like the self-deprecating humor sometimes expressed in stories about encounters with powerful outsiders (White 1989), the exaggerated caricature of the "heathen" in comedy skits obtains its emotional salience as the personification of multiple and possibly conflicting facets of the self. On the one hand, the category "heathen" constitutes a contrastive other to the Christian self – the locus of violent impulses that have been pacified or domesticated by conversion. On the other hand, however, the "heathen" represents an ancestral past and indigenous (*kastom*) ways that remain a central element of the local self in contrast with Western ways. The duality or multiplicity of these identifications (which are an everpresent aspect of everyday social reality) underlie the tropes of caricature and parody that are the hallmark of *thukma* images. The metapragmatic framing that calls attention to the artificial or exaggerated quality of these images depends upon a degree of self-consciousness, and of ambivalence, associated with multiple identities. Even though comedy skits have most fully developed the potential for self-commentary inherent in parody, "quieter" forms of conversion narrative also work to construct and evaluate images of self from the multiple meanings and valences of Christian identity.

8

Missionary encounters: narrating the self

In July of 1890 the missionary Henry Welchman decided to take his message personally to the notorious "bush" chief Figrima living in his mountain fort at Khakatio (chapter 5). It was to be an epic encounter, one that Welchman hoped would open the door to the conversion of a large population of Cheke Holo people living in the vicinity of the fort, and one that local oral historians recreate with some regularity in speeches, songs and plays. These indigenous accounts allow further comparisons of the concepts, metaphors and narrative practices through which Cheke Holo speaking people represent the origins of Christianity in their region. And, because Welchman himself recorded an account of these events in his diary, we have an unusual interpretive opportunity to compare latter-day indigenous recollections with the written notes of one of the principal participants. This chapter exploits that opportunity by juxtaposing these accounts to examine the internal "logic" of indigenous conversion histories. By comparing different local versions of these events, and identifying several points of contrast with Welchman's description, the analysis highlights the social and creative processes that shape historical narrative.

Previous chapters have considered several local histories of Christian contact and conversion. On the one hand, similarities in metaphorical imagery and narrative structure of stories about widely divergent events (as different as the Knabu story and the Buala *bina boli*) are suggestive of the force of sociocultural models in shaping representations of the past. On the other hand, differences among accounts of the "same" events may provide an additional perspective from which to view the influence of culture and context on social memory. As Fox (1980: 56) noted in his interpretation of two Rotinese historical narratives produced across a span of several decades, comparison "provides a valuable glimpse of the creative process by which supposedly immutable narratives are retold to maintain continuity with the past and yet account for changing circumstances of the present."

The story of Welchman's ascent to Khakatio and first encounter with Figrima is one of those pivotal tales that has been institutionalized through its retelling in a variety of formats and occasions. As mentioned in the previous chapter, the story has been the subject of at least one *thukma* play; and it continues to circulate in storytelling, speechmaking and singing. The discussion below begins by comparing two rather lengthy narratives told by Khakatio descendants, and then triangulates the comparison by analyzing Henry Welchman's diary account. The chapter concludes with consideration of a song that represents the conversion process in the *thautaru* genre of ritualized singing discussed earlier. This chapter takes a somewhat more textual tack than the previous chapter to pursue the interpretive possibilities offered by three rather elaborated narratives (the two stories and Welchman's diary) representing the moment of Christian contact as an interpersonal scenario.

Given that written records based on firsthand observation are likely to be afforded greater accuracy than oral histories retold over a period of decades, it is tempting to use the Welchman text as a kind of authoritative standard against which to compare the local accounts. But even though Welchman himself was one of the key actors in the conversion drama, his account is also produced in a set of social and cultural contexts specific to European missionaries of the time and does not provide any kind of neutral platform from which to view "what really happened." Welchman's diary record was also produced from memory (whether short-term or long-term), and is by definition a representation of his point of view, constrained by his own identity and status in the interaction. However, as a representation of certain basic features of the events in question, such as the manner in which he gained entry to the Khakatio fort, and the general details of when and how he first saw Figrima, it seems reasonable to regard the diary as a reliable source of information about actual events. Approached in this qualified way, Henry Welchman's story provides a foil with which to gauge further the cultural work done by conversion narratives in contemporary Santa Isabel.

Like the Knabu legend, the two accounts of the Welchman–Figrima encounter told in a storytelling mode both reconstruct historic events through the words and actions of central figures from the past. Applying styles of narrative performance common throughout Melanesia, narrators typically recreate events by adopting the voices of participants. Unlike the comedy skits, where mime, parody and exaggeration are the order of the day, here the rhetoric of enactment lends immediacy and veracity to accounts of past events by replaying them through the quoted speech of key actors. The personalization of spoken narrative also lends itself to the reproduction of images of behavior relevant to current understandings of person and interpersonal process.

The prototypic conversion story depicts a first encounter between a missionary and a well-known ancestor chief. The encounter scene focuses attention on the transformative roles of both missionary and chief as agents of change. Of particular interest is the mediating role of the chief who on the one hand personifies the past, but also becomes, in the missionary encounter, the one who first admits Christianity. In this manner narrative reproduces the model of the "chief" as one who regulates the boundaries of community, managing relations between "inside" and "outside." From this perspective, the image of "the chief" (*funei*) is drawn in a more complex way than the sharp dichotomous opposition of "Christian/heathen" would suggest. Recall that a key role in the Knabu story is played by the "good chief" Matasi Iho who, in his "sympathetic" ways, already manifested Christian ideals.

Before turning to the Welchman–Figrima narratives taken up below, I want to recall the story of Knabu conversion for purposes of comparison. Specifically, what can be said about the narrative structure of that legend as a sequence of scenes or episodes? If in fact it is appropriate to label the story a "conversion narrative," the central thematic development is the transition to Christianity. The narrator's elliptic remark in the middle of the story, "because of this, Christianity began to reach them [the Knabu]," frames the focal theme in this way. The story's dramatic tension builds through events of approach and resistance, with the climax coming after the missionary, Walter Gagai, has been threatened by aggressive warriors but spared by Iho and his wife.

For purposes of comparison and generalization, the narrative structure of the story may be represented as a sequence of core episodes as follows:

APPROACH→RESISTANCE→ACCEPTANCE

This episodic structure is apparent in most of the conversion histories I have recorded. Representing the conversion scenario this way reflects the more general form of stories everywhere which proceed by establishing a problem (here, heathen RESISTANCE) and attempting its resolution (ACCEPTANCE). The sequence shown above represents a kind of core scenario that is further expanded in the Knabu story by prefatory and concluding episodes that variously set the stage for contact and specify its consequences. The characterization of the pre-Christian Knabu as violent people feared by coastal Christians is an important stage-setting device that sets up inferences about Gagai's bravery and establishes his motive as that of bringing the message of peace.

Following the episode of acceptance, the Knabu narrative goes on to characterize the personal qualities of the chief, Iho, and then returns to the topic of the arrival of Christianity. The story is then taken one step further to mention the catechist, Wilson Bana, who subsequently worked as a teacher among the Knabu. The activity of teaching, often a final episode in conversion narrative, is the process through which people receive the new knowledge of Christianity prior to baptism and full participation in the "new way."

This schematic model of narrative structure may be used to compare the constitutive elements of different conversion stories. Although the historical circumstances of encounter may vary considerably from one locale to another, representations of those events in oral narrative show a remarkable convergence. Convergences in narrative structure suggest that mythic schemas which organize historical remembrance work to recreate social and emotional meanings as much as they function to "preserve" historic events. The cultural work done by conversion narratives is further highlighted by certain consistent differences between Henry Welchman's account of events and the (extensively similar) portrait that emerges from the indigenous narratives. To foreshadow briefly the results of this triangulation, all of the indigenous accounts (told by different narrators in different regions) include an important episode of resistance, whereas Welchman does not mention a single act of challenge in his rather less dramatic account of the episode.

Henry Welchman encounters Figrima in his mountain fort

One indication of the salience of conversion legends is that several informants volunteered them to me without being prompted, beginning with Forest's and Josepa's recollections of missionary contact among their Knabu ancestors. The descendants of Figrima and his followers who once gathered for protection around the fort at Khakatio are the inheritors of legends that recount the arrival of Christianity among their ancestors. Even though I did not have regular contact with these groups, the story of Henry Welchman's ascent was offered for recording during my first visit to two villages where descendants of the Khakatio population have since settled. (With conversion and pacification, people from Khakatio moved down to settlements on both sides of the mountainous interior, settling in villages in both the Maringe and Hograno regions.)

The primary objective of my first visit to one of these villages, Gnula-haghe, was to seek out the old man named Barnabas Sati to whom people had referred me as someone knowledgeable about matters of *kastom*. On my first visit, I spent half of one day sitting with Sati in his house and conversing (with someone to help with translation into Pidgin where necessary). But I had not got very far with my conversational agenda when Sati suggested that he tell the story of the arrival of Christianity among his ancestors. Although at that time I was not especially interested in the topic, I dutifully recorded the narrative, asked a few questions, and went on with my line of questioning about chiefs, traditional religious practices and other matters. His story, which I tape-recorded, is given below. It tells about the ascent of Dr. Henry Welchman with a group of men from Bughotu to make contact with Figrima at Khakatio. These events are of particular interest because of Figrima's prominent position of leadership during the head-hunting era (Naramana 1987; Whiteman 1983).

On another occasion, during a trek across the central mountains to the Hograno side of the island, I recorded another version of Welchman's first visit to Khakatio. Only this time I found the story preserved in writing – testimony to its value as a text that inscribes a significant part of local heritage. Fr. Ben Hageria, the second Isabel priest who engaged in the *diklo* exchange with Hugo Hebala in 1928 (chapter 6), recorded his version of the legendary contact and the subsequent history of conversion in writing. Hageria's son, Henry Kelimana, has kept possession of the text, and offered to read it out for recording during my stay with him at Kolomola village. Ben Hageria was one of Figrima's grandsons and one of the first two young men taken by Welchman from Khakatio for Christian schooling at the turn of the century. Hence, Hageria, author of the text, figures in his own narrative which sketches a longer history than just the events of first contact in 1890 (which make up the first episode). In addition to reading Hageria's history, Kelimana and his nephew, Richard Naramana, offered to perform a ceremonial song or *thautaru* that also commemorates the history of Christianization in their community of Khakatio descendants. The song had been composed a few months earlier for performance at a major feast honoring one of the most prominent Hograno chiefs. These two stories and the *thautaru* song are the subject of the remainder of this chapter.

Barnabas Sati, who has since passed away, was a descendant of one of the characters in his narrative – a man named Kofuthara who accompanied Welchman as guide on his trip to contact Figrima. Kofuthara is a significant actor in Sati's narrative, but also figures in the Hageria account as one of two named guides who "know the road to Khakatio." To summarize Sati's story, he tells of the Welchman party starting out from the coast and hiking up to Khakatio where they encounter Figrima and armed men gathered inside the fort. Figrima shouts: "I myself am at this door," implying that he is blocking the door; and he tells them to go away. However, after several challenges and replies. Welchman and his group are allowed to enter the fort. With Kofuthara playing a mediating role, Figrima is later given gifts of tobacco and food and convinced to try out the Christian ways advocated by Welchman. As Sati tells the story:

The doctor [Welchman] set out and came along that big river, climbing up. He followed the river up. He came up until he reached Sikopisu. Khakatio looked down on him coming up. There were chiefs in front and chiefs behind, with the Doctor walking in the middle. With his own sacred walking stick, the Doctor came climbing up. Figrima, the head of Khakatio, said to all the people who had gathered around: "They are coming up here, my children. Go up to the wall, my children," he [Figrima] said. So they went up to the wall with the closed gate. Figrima said: "I myself am at this door, children." All the people were gathered around with their axes, shields and spears. So then Figrima came to the base of the fort and shouted: "Why do you all come here? We don't want you to come!" he shouted at them . . . "No, leave off your shouting at the Whiteman. Stop that. He isn't doing anything. He is just coming up here," they (the men with Welchman) said. "No, you are lying. You are lying about that. It's your day [to meet your fate]. If you climbed up then it's your day" (i.e., "you've had it") . . . Henry Welchman then said, talking up toward the men looking down: "No, leave off [your shouting], we're just coming up to see you. We're not going to do anything to you." "No, you all are lying," said Figrima from the fort . . . Kofuthara then spoke up saying: "No, put down your axes, put down your shields, put down your spears. Why don't you go back to your house. The Whiteman isn't going to do anything. He's just come up to see you is all . . ." "Alright, let's go back, this doctor hasn't done anything." And they began to walk slowly toward their houses. Figrima went slowly toward his house. All the chiefs with their axes, shields and spears came, like Figrima himself, and sat down. The fort opened up and in came all the men, walking up. The first to come up to Figrima was Kofuthara. "Friend, chief," he said. "What?" "The Whiteman is coming." "Alright, go to the big house over there. You all take him to the big house over there, my children" . . .

Welchman then settles in the house indicated, and Kofuthara seeks out Figrima to request that he meet with Welchman. When Kofuthara offers him some tobacco, Figrima agrees. However, before he and his warriors go to see Welchman, Kofuthara asks them: "Put down your shields and axes. What are you going to do with those things? These men who have come aren't going to do anything." Having put down their weapons, Figrima and his men walk across the fort grounds and are introduced to Welchman by Kofuthara. The story of their encounter continues:

Figrima grasped the hand of the Doctor and the Doctor greeted him heartily. "Be seated, chief," he said, and Figrima sat down. "I have not come here, chief, to do anything to you. In Sepi, Bughotu, I heard that, 'He [Figrima] kills, he eats people, he kidnaps and he raids.' When I heard that about Khakatio, I thought, 'Alright, I'll visit Khakatio mountain. I'll go up to see this chief.' So I came up to you, not to do anything, not to do anything bad. The bad talk and the killing that you do are not my ways. I've come up with a seed in order to leave it with you, so that you will give up killing, so that you will give up kidnapping, so that you will give up eating people. It is in order to do these things that I have come up, chief. I'm not going to do anything. This seed is for leaving with you, in order to be fathers again, in order to be mothers again, in order to be friends again, in order to be kin, in order for you all to be together (*fofodu*) for the rest of your lives. That's why I have brought this seed to you. I haven't come to do anything else, chief," said the Doctor. "Now you answer back, chief," said the Doctor. "Alright, I will do this," Figrima said. "I will do this, it is like being born up (*kahra haghe*). I have killed, I have been aggressive (*faheaheta*), I have eaten people, and I have kidnapped, Doctor. But, if I do this it is like life coming up from this. You have come and revealed this and I will hold onto it. 'If you give up killing, if you give up cannibalism, if you give up kidnapping, you give up these things in order for you (all) to be united (*fofodu*).' Well! So this is the good way, that's what I say. Those were my bad ways, but now you come and reveal this! This must be the good way, I'll follow the way that you have made, chief," he [Figrima] said. "Yes, that is what I wanted you to get," smiled the Doctor. "Alright, sit down, chief," he said. Figrima sat down and rice, canned pork and biscuits were brought in, as well as a hatchet, a knife and cloth. "These are gifts for you, chief. I'm not trying to do anything [else], friend," said the Doctor.

Before comparing this story with the account of the same events left by Hageria, consider its similarity to the Knabu legend. Sati's story covers much the same range of events, with the moment of interpersonal encounter between missionary and chief a focal point of the narrative. Once again, the core structure of the story may be represented as a scenario of contact, resistance and acceptance. Where the Knabu legend constructed acts of resistance through the arrival of belligerent warriors threatening to kill Walter Gagai, resistance at Khakatio takes the shape of an extended exchange of accusation and denial, with Figrima taking the lead in rebuffing Welchman's approach by shouting at him to go away. Similar to the Knabu warriors clamoring to attack, Figrima's challenge is backed by people gathered at the fort gate with "axes, shields and spears" – portents of heathen violence. The subsequent interaction leading to the chief's acceptance of the Christian message, which is not elaborated in the Knabu legend, is here portrayed in some detail through quoted dialogue and interaction, especially gift-giving.

In addition to their similarity in episodic structure, both the Knabu and Khakatio narratives represent the events of resistance and acceptance in metaphors of "closed" and "open." In this story, the fort becomes a literal instantiation of the boundaries of pre-Christian society. The figurative closed space referred to in the Knabu legend is here, literally, opened to admit the missionary and his message. The fort is closed on first approach, but then opens as the act of resistance is overcome, with Welchman's entrance to the fort also marking the entrance of Christianity into Khakatio society.

Having postulated a model of narrative structure that organizes these local histories, it is possible to identify a point of difference where the same episode is repositioned at a different point in the sequence of events. Whereas the Knabu narrative began with a preamble about the "heathen state" of the Knabu feared by Christians along the coast because they "still kill, butcher and eat people," Sati does not begin his account with any such characterization. However, embedded *within* his story, at the point at which Welchman begins speaking to Figrima about his motives for coming up to the fort, he describes the state of violence that prompted him to come up with the Christian message. Welchman states that it was upon hearing that

"[Figrima] kills, eats people, kidnaps and raids" that he decided to climb up to Khakatio to see Figrima. His words closely echo the thoughts and motives attributed to Walter Gagai in the Knabu story. The parallel suggests that the characterization of violence in pre-Christian society recurs widely in conversion histories, and is an important element in their representation of the social meanings of Christianization.

In Sati's story, the conceptual counterpoints to heathen violence and death are the generative metaphors of life, kinship and solidarity associated with Christianity. As seen in the previous discussion of the Knabu legends, particularly in the context of feasttime speechmaking, metaphors of life encompass meanings of both pacification and birth-descent. Through the voice of Henry Welchman, Sati portrays the introduction of Christianity as a way of re-establishing solidarity and unity among kin, presumably divided and dispersed by the violence attributed to pagan society. Welchman says that putting an end to "killing, kidnapping and cannibalism" will make it possible for "fathers, mothers, friends and kin" to remain close together, united (*fofodu*). He offers Christianity as a "seed" that will "grow upward" (*kahra haghe* from *kahra*, "live, grow"). The image is one of increasing growth among families and lineages.

By recounting the contact–resistance–acceptance scenario through the details of the interpersonal encounter, Sati composes his actors through their styles of talk and action. The pre-Christian chief is exemplified by Figrima "shouting" threats at the intruders, commanding them to go away, while the ethos of pagan life is manifest in the everpresent "axes, shields and spears." As noted earlier, Figrima is here enacting the role of the chief as community protector and guardian. In this case he does so by literally regulating passage through the gate, attempting to keep the community closed to threatening forces from outside. The complementary Christian response is desire for rapprochement, first expressed by Kofuthara's request that those in the fort put down their axes, shields and spears. This same scenario, of armed warriors approached by Christians asking that they put down their weapons, is repeated once inside the gate when Kofuthara succeeds in getting the Khakatio men to disarm (only summarized above). Kofuthara's role here is reminiscent of the "good chief" Matasi Iho who, with his wife, restrained the aggressive impulses of his warriors to hear the Christian message. Here again, the narrator builds an account in which his ancestor manifests attributes of the Christian person in a context marked by the potential for heathen violence.

Hageria's history

Now consider the written history of these events left by Hageria. Only the first one-third of Hageria's account, the portion dealing with Welchman's first ascent to Khakatio and encounter with Figrima, is reviewed here. The remaining portion of the text describes a second trip by Welchman in which he takes away Hageria and one other boy for mission schooling.

Hageria's story begins when Welchman is told by the Bughotu chief Soga that there is a "big chief" in Hograno with "many, many heathen people." So Welchman decides to visit this chief (Figrima) and sets out with a catechist, two guides (Khana and Kofuthara) and several others. As they are going up the track, they are spotted by a party of Figrima's warriors ("strong men for killing"). Welchman asks his two guides to shout "teacher, teacher, peace, friends, not enemies," and then comes forward to pray. At this two of the Khakatio men say: "That man [Welchman] is weak, attack and kill him here!" But the catechist and Kofuthara reassert that they are friends. The potential attackers are startled when Welchman extends his hand to them. They shake hands with their left hand because they think they might "lose their power" (*sapu*) if they shake with the right. Welchman then asks the Khakatio men where they are from and who their chief is. At Welchman's request, the Khakatio men return to tell Figrima of his impending arrival. The story continues:

Takolo and Beata [two scouts in the hunting party] reached Figrima and said to him: "Chief, we met a man from Khololuka at Koloragu. We weren't able to do any of the diving for crayfish, hunting for pig or climbing for nuts that we set out to do. Khana and Kofuthara said that this man is a teacher of peace." So Figrima said: "Alright, you two blow the conch shell to signal all the children and people to come inside the fort." The two men signaled and all the people came up to the fort and the door to the fort was shut. Figrima then said: "You all don't let him [Welchman] come up to the fort. This man is weak, so the warriors should prepare to attack." When he reached the place Glelegona, Dr. Henry Welchman knelt to pray there. When he had finished praying, he stood up and climbed up next to the wall of the fort. He looked up and spoke: "Figrima, I want to come and see you now." "No!" said two lookouts to Dr. Welchman. Welchman said [again]: "No, Figrima, I want to come to see you." "No!" Figrima shouted. "Open the fort so I can come and see you," said Welchman. So Figrima said: "Alright, you all open the door, my children." With this, Dr. Henry Welchman said "thank you," walked up and went inside the fort at Khakatio . . .

Once inside the fort, it is the guide Khana who plays the role of go-between (rather than Kofuthara, as in Sati's story). Khana approaches Figrima at Welchman's request and offers him gifts. As in the earlier story, Figrima agrees to go see Welchman in one of the houses in the compound. The story characterizes Welchman's eagerness to see Figrima by noting that each time a Khakatio big-man approaches his house Welchman asks if it is Figrima. Then, when Figrima himself finally appears, Welchman says "Figrima, Figrima, Figrima." As they shake hands Figrima offers Welchman a gift of tobacco, and they begin to converse. Welchman begins:

"I have come here because I heard that you are the major guardian chief (*funei fothi*) of the Kaipito river and the fort at Khakatio. And you have many people here. That's what the chief Soga at Sepi told me, so I decided to come and see the chief, Figrima, to be together with him. So now I've arrived, chief Figrima. You are my friend now and I give you these gifts." His gifts of tobacco, cloth and a pipe make Figrima happy. With this, the doctor asks about all the people who live in the bush villages, the one thousand people at the head of the Kaipito river. Dr. Welchman says to Figrima: "Will you allow your people, for whom you are the guardian chief, to come inside (*ruma*) the teaching, my friend Figrima, in order for your people to live in peace (*phari keli*), in order for you all to have life (*kahra*)?" After which Figrima says to Dr. Henry Welchman: "Alright, I will allow my people to go inside the teaching of peace in order to live, as you say."

After this exchange, Welchman asks Figrima to let people come and watch and listen to his evening prayer. Those that do are then "amazed" at his long prayer robe and his eyeglasses, as well as the prayer he performs. This event is then followed (the next day?) by a feast sponsored by Figrima who offers Welchman a pig and baskets of taro to take on his trip back to the coast.

Hageria's narrative is organized around the same core scenario of approach–resistance–acceptance evident in the Knabu and Sati narratives. Here, as in the others, acts of resistance define the pre-Christian posture of Figrima and his followers toward the outsiders, and it is their resistance that lends particular meaning to the Christian approach and their ability to gain acceptance. One aspect that emerges clearly in Hageria's account that is only hinted at in Sati's story is the role of Christian mana or spiritual power in the missionary's success. In this version, Welchman twice stops to pray during his ascent: the first time just before Figrima's scouts say they should kill him, and the second just before he obtains entrance to the fort.[1] In both instances, Welchman inexplicably proceeds unharmed and unobstructed. He "subdues" the armed warriors simply by shaking their hands and saying that he has come as a friend. Indeed, the armed "strong men" acknowledge his power in their reluctance to shake hands with their right (axe) hand. In the second instance, Welchman manages to enter the fort after only a brief verbal exchange with Figrima, saying only "I want to come and see you." (Once again, the community is bounded by the fort, as Figrima calls his people inside so he can shut the door and keep Welchman outside.) The acts of prayer invoking spiritual power make all of this more understandable, given local views of Christian mana as a source of personal power evident in surprising or wondrous accomplishments. In Sati's narrative, Welchman's walking stick is an icon of his priestly mana. Referred to obliquely as his "own sacred walking stick," Isabel audiences would recognize this immediately as a symbol of spirit power.

Welchman's first prayer is followed immediately by the first act of resistance in which the Khakatio hunting party say they should attack and kill him. The entire approach sequence consists of acts of heathen resistance followed by (miraculous) Christian success in overcoming them. The demonstration of Christian mana in Welchman's ability to overcome heathen threats is underscored by the ironic remarks of the "strong men" that he is "weak" and therefore should be attacked. These remarks, coming early in the narrative, highlight the spiritual power that is invisible to the warriors. The hunters' perception that Welchman appears "weak" and so should be attacked is repeated by Figrima as the missionary approaches the fort. And here again the attribution of vulnerability is juxtaposed with an act of spiritual power as Welchman kneels to pray immediately after Figrima has commanded: "This man is weak so the warriors should prepare to attack." Hageria's description of this initial encounter mirrors closely Sati's narrative of the same event. Both scenes are composed of repeated requests for entry followed by loud and forceful rejection each time. Then, without elaboration, Figrima rather abruptly agrees to allow Welchman entrance after his third request.

The chief's command that the gate to the fort be opened indicates the end of resistance. The ensuing episode of acceptance is also similar to Sati's narrative in that Welchman elicits a receptive attitude through simple, direct talk about the "peace" and "life" offered by Christianity. When Welchman asks Figrima to accept Christianity, he asks the chief and his people to "come inside" (*ruma*) the new teaching, as if acquiring new knowledge (and identity) were like entering a dwelling. And, as in Sati's account, the creation of relations between Welchman and Figrima is constituted in an exchange of gifts. As noted earlier (chapter 6), the term for "gift" (*nahma*) is a richly polysemous word that also signifies the personal qualities of "kindness" and "love" identified with the "Christian person."

In addition to the parallels between the two versions of the Welchman–Figrima encounter, there is some discrepancy in the roles attributed to Kofuthara. Even though Hageria's account mentions him as one of the two guides, and as one of the two men who confronted the Khakatio hunting party to persuade them not to attack Welchman, he is not mentioned during the approach and entrance to the fort. Once inside the fort, Welchman asks the other guide, Khana, to go and ask Figrima if Welchman may come to see him. Consistent with the use of conversion narratives to project regional and lineage identities through the actions of one's ancestors, it is not surprising that Sati would depict his ancestor, Kofuthara, in a prominent role. Similarly, Hageria, a grandson of Figrima, focuses more on the chief himself, and does not dwell on Figrima's "killing, cannibalism and kidnapping" as much as the other version.

The remainder of Hageria's history tells of the subsequent process of conversion among the Khakatio people and their entrance into Christian life. This begins with Welchman's second trip in which he takes away the two boys for schooling, and follows with their return and teaching, leading to Welchman's baptism of Figrima as "Abraham" in 1903. At the end of the account, both Figrima and Hageria have come to represent Christian ancestors – as Christian chief and Christian priest, respectively.

Comparing the Sati and Hageria representations of the Khakatio encounter illuminates the uses of historical narrative in fashioning social realities, whether defined in terms of localized identities or generalized concepts of the "Christian person." The cultural work done by conversion stories may be further examined by comparing the local narratives with the account of the "same" events left by Henry Welchman. Adding this third account, of one who was himself a participant, adds yet another vantage point from which to examine narrative history comparatively, as a creative, semiotic process.

Henry Welchman's diary

Henry Welchman recorded a fairly detailed account of his ascent to Khakatio from his station in Bughotu. The trip took five days, from Tuesday, July 29, 1890 to Saturday, August 2, 1890, including two nights in the Khakatio fort. While there are numerous points of convergence, differences between Welchman's record of the events surrounding his encounter with Figrima and the two local accounts are illuminating. The major point of divergence between the European written record and the indigenous histories is the fact that Welchman does not mention any hostile acts of resistance by the Khakatio people during his approach to the fort. When he describes his entrance to the fort, he refers only to the physical difficulty of getting through a narrow, steep passage, and makes no mention of any opposition from within. While there may indeed have been fearful and hostile responses from the Khakatio people, Welchman either did not notice or did not record them. In any case, my purpose in this comparison is not to establish the "actual" events of 1890, but rather to explore the processes that represent and valorize their significance in contemporary society. In this regard, it is significant that local constructions of these events *systematically* formulate acts of resistance that occupy a critical place in the process of narrative recollection. Without an episode of resistance, the actions of central actors such as Welchman and Figrima would not take on the significance they do as models of Christian and ancestral identity.

The relevant portions of Welchman's account of his approach (including contact with the Khakatio hunting party) and entrance to the fort are given below:

July 30, 1890 ... About noon while we were in some bush we suddenly faced a native, whose face certainly depicted astonishment & alarm. A few hurried words from our guide, & he turned around & ran off followed by the two guides, leaving me to follow the path which was fairly plain there. Then we heard a great shouting and calling, & the boys told me we had come upon a party of Uta men fishing. Soon emerging from the stream we saw them about twenty in number sitting in great wonderment at our appearance. Kana explained our mission, & we sat down that they might leisurely inspect us, & I made one man shake hands with me. We only stayed a few minutes & when they were pretty sure we meant no harm to anyone we continued our march ... At length we emerged on a bare spot at the top of which stood Figirima's [*sic*] village, or rather his castle. As far as I could see the ground was quite bare for a hundred yards away from the wall of logs which hung outwards from the interior & the gate, itself very narrow, was approached by a narrow path up a steep ascent. We had just left a path cut through the rock the bottom of which was a trough the width of one foot & helped in the more perpendicular parts with shallow holes cut for steps. At the gateway were two huge logs set on end, but loose & these sufficed to gain admission to the fort some 8 or 10 feet above us. A bundle of reeds on either side served as a hold (when the logs were mounted) to pull myself onto the very gate & then as plenty of boys were about the rest was easy. The houses are close to the door and to one another. We had to wait awhile till Kana got leave from his brother to go into his house & we were soon all safely collected inside. Very tired, but in grand spirits at our success. Some dry clothes made me quite happy. It was not quite five o'clock, & we have walked for nine hours.

While preparing food I received a message from Figirima to say that if I had come to trade or if I had come to talk, I was to go see him as he could not come down to the house I was in ...

Given that certain aspects of Welchman's diary show a remarkable convergence with the indigenous histories (such as the reference to hand-shaking with the party of scouts), the absence of other elements that are not only mentioned but are central to the local narratives is especially noticeable. The fact that the most dramatic, focal episode of the indigenous histories (the moment of encounter when Welchman confronts and over-comes Figrima's resistance) is absent from Welchman's diary is worthy of interpretive comment. Since missionary accounts of the time would them-selves be likely to amplify acts of heathen resistance that had been overcome through prayer and persistence, it is unlikely that Welchman would have failed to note acts of hostility directed at him, particularly one as dramatic as the chief he had come to see shouting at him to go away. Not only was he not denied entrance to the fort, but the gate was not barred or closed in any way. (It may be that Welchman's guides had already arranged unob-structed access, just as the guide Khana arranged for them to occupy a relative's house once inside.)

There is another silence in Welchman's diary that is consistent with this interpretation of the local histories. Whereas the indigenous accounts refer to Welchman praying at critical moments of encounter on his way up to

Khakatio, he himself does not mention praying until he is inside the fort. Although Welchman did, as always, say morning prayers before setting off on his ascent, there is no indication of praying at any point during his approach to the fort. If indeed Christian prayer evokes the mana or power that ultimately explains Welchman's ability to overcome heathen resistance, then it is understandable that prayer and resistance are coupled in the local narratives, even if absent from Welchman's account.

Continuing in his more matter-of-fact diary mode of reporting, Welchman does not mention that he talked about heathen violence in his conversations with Figrima. If this subject was a topic of their exchange, he did not record it. He writes of being summoned to Figrima's house where he and his party sit on one side with the Khakatio people on the other and an interpreter in the middle (Figrima is out of their view, behind a screen):

> ... The conversation was carried on through Philip [Parako, a Bughotu man] who put my Mota into Bughotu while a Kakatio man translated that into Uta [Cheke Holo]. Figirima wanted to know what we had come for. I told him we had come to see him, the chief of Uta & to make friends with him. He said he was glad to see us that he thought it kind of us to come so far along such a bad road & he would like to be friends with us. I told him that if he liked to come with us I would take him to pay a visit to Soga [the Bughotu chief] & that the boat should bring him back to Ravihi. At this I heard a great deal of very loud, energetic and nervous spitting, & at length he said that I had startled him by the suggestion but that he would think of it. Then I asked him to send us some boys to Bugotu to be taught to which he replied that he had heard a good report of Christianity & would like to know more & that by & bye he would pay Soga a visit & make enquiries. Then he said that we were to rest at Kakatio all the next day and not to return till the following morning – a great compliment as they don't care about visitors making long stays. With that the conference ended and we returned to get our food ...

In this first of three conversational encounters with Figrima, Welchman did not make face-to-face contact with the chief. As he reports the exchange, it noticeably lacks the sort of ideological discussion of the "bad ways" of heathen society (such as "killing, cannibalism and kidnapping") or even of the "peace" and "life" offered by Christianity which is prominent in the local reconstructions of their dialogue. Rather, Welchman makes a simple appeal to be friends with Figrima, suggests he visit Soga, and requests "some boys" for Christian teaching. As described, the dialogue is pragmatic and direct. The request to take away some young men for schooling, which appears to be one of the important topics of conversation, is omitted from the two local accounts (although Hageria wrote that this was negotiated during a second, later trip made by Welchman to Khakatio).

Welchman's second audience with Figrima, in which he does make face-to-face contact, appears to be concerned largely with gift-exchange and trading:

Thursday, July 31, 1890 We were up betimes & had prayers, & soon after were sent for again. I prepared a present for the chief and took some trade. We entered his house & sat down in solemn silence on our separate sides. In a few minutes much to my astonishment out came Figirima, bouncing up in a nervous sort of way & stood beside me, shyly holding out his hand. He was quite trembling with excitement. I told him how glad I was to see him, & we sat down side by side on the log. Then I told him I had brought him a present, & he retired behind the screen, I had seen my last of him. I gave him some tobacco, some cloth & a big knife with an interval between each present & a little speech. When this was over he & I had a little trade, he handing the things over the screen & taking back in the same way. He said he had not many things to sell of Uta manufacture, & these were mostly lime boxes and net bags. When I had enough of these, he said he had nothing else, & the trade was over.

This encounter between Welchman and Figrima, the day after Welchman's arrival, resembles the indigenous accounts that also describe the two men greeting one another, shaking hands and sitting down to talk. And, just as the local accounts refer prominently to the exchange of gifts, Welchman describes giving Figrima tobacco, cloth and a knife "with a little speech" between each, and then receiving "lime boxes and net bags" in return.

In the third and final encounter Welchman describes Figrima presenting him with more substantial gifts of food. No doubt this is the reason Figrima told Welchman he would have to remain at Khakatio the next day. So, the day after his arrival, Welchman describes receiving a pig and baskets of food. As would be customary in such a feast-exchange, the sponsor, Figrima, is said to have made a speech about the meaning of the event as a sign of his new friendship with Welchman.[2]

Towards afternoon another summons came, so up we went again, to hear the chief's last words. He made quite a long speech, ornamented with emphatic expectoration, from behind his screen & to the effect "I am glad you have been to see me & that I have spoken to a white man, & now I want you to tell the enemy & all the world that you are my friend and that this peace is yours. I want to pay Soga a visit, but at present I have not enough things to take with me to make a suitable present & it is hard work for me to go as I have no canoes & my people do not know how to paddle. When I have got my things together I will go to Bugotu & Soga shall tell me all about Christianity. Then I will send you some boys. You have come a long way on a bad road to see me & I shall not forget it. I wanted to give you some things of Uta but they are not many & they are poor, so I have told them to tie up a pig for you & it is outside waiting for you. Now go back to your house & rest & tomorrow you will set out on your return." I told him that if he would like to send men to Bugotu I would take four with me in the boat & he said he would think of it. That being over we went out & I asked leave to go round the vanua ("grounds").

In describing this last encounter, Welchman does tell us that "peace" was a topic addressed by Figrima in his speech. Figrima's presentation of a pig and baskets of food, together with his accompanying speech urging Welchman to "tell the enemy & all the world that you are my friend and that this peace is yours . . ." suggests that Figrima perceived the missionary's visit as an opportunity to form a strategic alliance that would prove useful in defending against "the enemy."[3] His talk echoes the reasoning of Goregita, another Cheke Holo chief cited in the previous chapter who wished to have a catechist in his community because that would, he thought, keep raiders away. Furthermore, his remarks point to the importance of Soga as a central figure in the propagation of Christianity in Santa Isabel. Figrima's comments that ". . . he had heard a good report of Christianity & would like to know more & that by & bye he would pay Soga a visit & make enquiries" indicate that Soga's reputation as a Christian chief was already established among language groups outside his own at the time of this encounter (1890).

Implicit in Welchman's account here, and throughout his diary, is the chief-centered approach to conversion that typified mission work in Santa Isabel, as it did in many places in the Pacific. In Welchman's notes, Figrima is the key to community conversion, as he is in the indigenous accounts. There is, however, a significant difference between the indigenous and European accounts. In the local histories, Welchman emerges as an even more heroic figure than in his own description. It is he who, through prayer and mana, overcomes substantial dangers posed by the war-like Figrima and his men. Welchman's elevated status is signaled in other, small details of the narratives. For example, on the rather telling point of who goes to see whom once Welchman is inside the fort, the indigenous histories recall Figrima visiting Welchman, whereas Welchman himself writes explicitly that he was "summoned" to the chief's house which he describes as the largest house in the fort compound. By recalling that it was Figrima who came to see Welchman in the house where he was taken upon entering the fort, the two local narratives have inverted the direction of movement to bring it in line with the assumption that a higher-status person typically receives someone of lesser importance. By transposing the positions of Welchman and Figrima in the encounter scenario, the narratives have transformed potentially discordant information so that it "makes sense." In current conceptions of persons and identity, Christianity is the greatest source of knowledge and mana, so it makes sense that the renowned missionary priest, Welchman, would receive the chief, Figrima.

The elevated status of Welchman, the Englishman, would seem to pose a challenge to locally centered structures of power and prestige, such as those often constituted in histories of descent and chiefly leadership. It is here, I suggest, that the roles of mediating agents, such as Ben Hageria who is both ancestor and priest (and ultimately even Figrima after he becomes a Christian chief), are especially significant. In so far as conversion stories represent the mythic exploits of Christian ancestors, they symbolically recreate the transformation through which Christian ideology and power were first incorporated in local communities. The inherent fluidity in these multiple identities is momentarily fixed in the retelling of narrative. Consider now the manner in which this symbolic incorporation is reconstructed through another kind of historical practice, that of *thautaru* singing.

An ode to Christian ancestors

Many large feasts include a type of ritualized singing that, as discussed earlier (chapter 3), is a particularly emotive genre of remembrance used to recall a past that links sponsors and guests participating in the feast. Like the *thukma* skits discussed in the preceding chapter, *thautaru* songs performed during public gatherings have also been adapted to tell the stories of Christian conversion. The remainder of this chapter examines one such *thautaru* composed for a feast honoring one of the most prominent Hograno chiefs, a man named Wilson Sikapu who was the senior government headman for Hograno during his time, and related to Figrima and Hageria. The song recites, in poetic fashion, the Christian transformation of Khakatio represented more discursively in the narratives of Banabas Sati and Ben Hageria. However, rather than relying upon scenes of interpersonal engagement and quoted dialogue to portray moments of contact and transformation, the song represents the Christian transition in a series of metaphoric polarities and allusions.

There is a long Cheke Holo tradition of composing and performing *thautaru* songs for the purpose of honoring important ancestors, either living or deceased. *Thautaru* are composed specifically for the occasion of their performance, as a kind of gift to be directed toward one or more designated recipients. Their melodies are text-oriented, with little embellishment or ornamentation to distract from the lyrics. They are usually performed by an unaccompanied chorus of about five to ten people, with one lead singer who initiates each line, prompting the chorus to join in. The slow rhythmic cadence of *thautaru* with heavy stress on the offbeat gives them the subdued emotional tone of a lament.[4]

The most frequent contexts for *thautaru* singing today are the feast exchanges between sons and fathers described earlier (chapter 3). The singing (*taru*) on these occasions usually evokes weeping and expressions of nostalgia for the father–son relationship. As noted before, these exchanges, termed *faghamu thaego* (literally, "feeding the caregiver"), involve the presentation of significant quantities of food and other goods from son (and his lineage) to father (and his lineage). By making this exchange the son ritually establishes rights to the father's property such as coconut trees (but not land) that would not otherwise follow according to matrilineal descent. In addition to enacting this economic transaction, these feasts mark a significant moment in the life-cycle, a symbolic end to the parent–child relation of dependency. *Thautaru* lyrics often elaborate this theme by reviewing the father's years of caring and sacrifice for the child. Listeners, especially the father, frequently cry as they hear the singers recall the father's devotion to the tasks of childrearing. The emotions evident on these occasions are described as feelings of "sorrow" (*natahni*, from *tahni*, "cry") and "sympathy/compassion" (*kokhoni*) associated with feelings of loss associated with the symbolic termination of the strongly nurturant relationship between father and son.

The nostalgic tone and intensity of *thautaru* songs performed in this context appear to carry over to other occasions when similar songs invoke the names of the ancestors and chiefs of a wider collectivity, as in the case of a village church day or Christmas feast. Enactments of *thautaru* in these contexts symbolically extend emotions engendered in close, family relations to a wider field of social relations and identities. Hence the discourse of sung remembrance works to instantiate felt images of ("good") ancestral chiefs as also nurturant and "sympathetic," like a metaphoric father to less powerful followers or descendants. By representing the collective past, whether of family, lineage or region, the songs create a history of common experience that is imbued with the sentiments of familial solidarity. The composition of each new song affords an opportunity to pick out historical events and personages and weave them into a presentation for a particular person or group.

The *thautaru* below was composed by Hageria's son, Henry Kelimana, for a large Christmas feast in 1974 honoring Wilson Sikapu who was one of the foremost Hograno chiefs during the middle of this century. The *thautaru* expresses the social significance of the occasion by praising the aging chief Sikapu and marking the rise of new leaders (the feast's sponsors). The story of conversion to Christianity and the story of a line of leadership mutually constitute one another in the song's lyrics. The first two-thirds of the *thautaru* consists of a lyrical social history of conversion in the Khakatio area. The remainder is concerned more directly with paying tribute to Sikapu.[5]

1	*Tuani ngau sia ku'e*	It is true, grandfather
2	*Tuani ngau sia mama*	It is true, father
3	*Ka au di tifa na*	In the old life
4	*Figrima Kapokahra*	Figrima, Kapokahra
5	*Goregita ghe Da'a*	Goregita and Da'a
6	*Thoa o Khakatio*	They lived in Khakatio fort
7	*Thoa o Gighila*	They lived in Gighila fort
8	*Neke khame hneta di re*	In their right hands were
9	*U khila greoreo aro*	These axes and shields

10	*Ihoi mama ido na*	They didn't know father and mother
11	*Lehe kahra keha na*	Another's life cut short
12	*Sesekai keha na*	Another kidnapped
13	*Me snakre mei ni nga*	Then they let him come
14	*Dr. Welchman*	Dr. Welchman
15	*Ne tali fajifladi*	Led them out
16	*Hageria, Thagragita*	Hageria and Thagragita
17	*Me lao faghamudi nga*	They fed them [i.e. taught them]
18	*Me lao fako'udi nga*	They gave them drink
19	*Au nga me lao*	And so they stayed on
20	*Me snakre fapulodi nga*	Then they were allowed to return
21	*Ka thoa o Khakatio*	To the Khakatio fort
22	*Ka thogele Piplitoni*	To Piplitoni mountain
23	*Me salo fodu di nga*	Then they gathered together
24	*U khila grere'o re*	The axes and shields
25	*Igne phari keli*	This is peace [they taught]
26	*Igne farihriu na*	This is the teaching [of life]
27	*Eghu ia ba ku'e re*	This is the way grandfathers
28	*Eghu ia ba kave re*	This is the way grandmothers
29	*Ghu me tusu rahngi di*	So they handed over to them
30	*Farihriu phari keli*	The teaching of peace
31	*Au blagna nga me mei*	Then peaceful life arrived
32	*Me filo dei nigho nga*	Then they found you
33	*Igne khame hneta di re*	This is the right hand of
34	*Figrima, Goregita*	Figrima and Goregita
35	*Me tusu ari ni nga*	And so you were given
36	*Mama ku'e Hageria*	By father and grandfather Hageria
37	*Nolaghi phari keli*	The power (mana) to make peace
38	*Nolaghi kinakapru*	The power (mana) to gather people
39	*Tughudi kusu phadaghi ra*	Replaces the sacrificial cutting
40	*Tughudi fa'aknu ra*	Replaces the killing
41	*Tughudi chari leghu ra*	Replaces the revenge raiding
42	*Tughudi sesekai ra*	Replaces the kidnapping
43	*Ghu me fodu poge khapru*	So you gathered people together
44	*Ghu me fodu kilo velepuhi*	Together you called for catechists
45	*Ghu me fodu kilo prisi*	Together you called for priests
46	*ka finogha kmakmanai ra*	During these many past years
47	*Me jifla koko nigho*	But they had departed from you

48	*Prisi velepuhi ra*	Those priests and teachers
49	*Funei Kilo'au ra*	Those Christian chiefs
50	*Ao la me poge khapru*	Yet [alone] you gathered people
51	*Ao la roghe ugra*	You organized fishing
52	*Me ghile thoke nogna*	Until we reach
53	*La narane gognaro gne*	This very day
54	*Ne gatho nou di iagho*	You must have thought of
55	*Nou prisi tifeiro ra*	Your priests of the past
56	*Velepuhi tifeiro ra*	Your teachers in the past
57	*Nou funei tifeiro ra*	Your chiefs in the past
58	*Mala blakno teu nigho ra*	Those who worked and supported you
59	*Gehati gne neu nu*	But as for us
60	*Fagrougronu keha na*	Others uncertain with mixed feelings
61	*Sopa cheke keha na*	While others disunited in their talk
62	*Ghu nomai rahngi nigho*	Not working together with you
63	*Funei velepuhi ra*	The chiefs and teachers today
64	*Ghu nigho neu ia ku'e*	Have done this for you grandfather
65	*Na aro te edi re*	Perhaps this will be our way
66	*Ke legumu iagho na*	After you [have gone]
67	*Ghu neu ghehati gne*	These are our thoughts
68	*Io dere*	Io dere

This *thautaru* performed in context accomplishes many things pertinent to the specific relations among performers and recipient(s), between composer and audience. Much of this is beyond the scope of this chapter, and the information available to me during my brief visit to Kolomola village where it was composed. In this discussion, coming on the heels of the longer narratives, I want to focus primarily on those aspects of the song that represent the Christian transformation.

The first two-thirds of the song [ll. 1–42] is concerned with depicting Christianization as a replacement of heathen practices by Christian ones. Like the narratives of missionary contact already discussed, the song builds upon presupposed oppositions of Christian and heathen to construct its story of change. The lyrics presume (and reproduce) the same base of historical knowledge as the stories, centering also upon the heroic figures of the conversion drama. However, where the stories focus on the episode of initial contact, leading the listener through interpersonal episodes of approach, resistance, and acceptance, the song represents collective transformation through a series of metaphoric oppositions, contrasting pre-Christian violence with Christian mana, peace and solidarity.

As the song progresses, the focal actors change from famous chiefs (associated with famous forts) to Christian leaders, catechists and priests (ll. 44–5), marking the move from heathen violence to Christian peace. And the cultural operators that accomplish this transformation are, put simply, "teaching" (knowledge) and "mana" (power). The reference to "axes and shields" in line 9, followed by mention of premature death and kidnapping, is the same stage-setting rhetoric used to characterize heathen society in the previous narratives. Images of prior violence and death frame the advent of Christianity as a generative source of peace and life, ending raiding and institutionalized violence. Following reference to Welchman's visit and the exit of Hageria and Thagragita (ll. 14–16), the subsequent work of conversion is portrayed as a process of teaching, beginning with the instruction of Hageria and Thagragita (expressed metaphorically as giving them food and drink, ll. 17–18), and continuing with their return to gather up the instruments of war (axes and shields) and teach their ancestors and relatives (ll. 23–6).

The transformative effects of Christian teaching are then depicted as "replacing" (*tughu di*) violent ways with Christian peace and solidarity (ll. 37–42). Here, as in the stories, the violence of pre-Christian society is manifest in a litany of "ritual sacrifice," "killing," "raiding" and "kidnapping." The successors to these practices are "peace" (*phari keli* and *au blagna* "calm, peaceful") and solidarity or "togetherness" (*fodu*, also *kinakapru*, "gather together"). These themes create images of society consonant with the "Christian person" construct and its idealization of interpersonal harmony and passivity. The song suggests that behind the themes of peace and solidarity lie the generative powers of Christian mana (*nolaghi*). Similar to the implication of the previous narratives that Welchman's success in overcoming heathen resistance was due to Christian mana and prayer, this song attributes change to the "mana of peace" and the "mana of solidarity" (ll. 37–8). And, as mentioned above, the changes are accomplished through teaching, beginning with Hageria and Thagragita who are the mediators of Christian knowledge among their people. The song describes their return and their work imparting the teaching of peace with lyrics that recall the didactic instruction of Christian ancestors in the teaching scene of the Buala *bina boli*: "Like this, grandfathers"; "Like this, grandmothers" (ll. 27–8).

In addition to generalized references to unnamed ancestors, the song focuses on several prominent leaders of the past, both chiefs and priests. As discussed in chapter 4, local models of the "chief" are particularly dense with social meaning, such that allusions to chiefs past and present evoke identities constituted in unstated relations of kinship, locale and chiefly following. The *thautaru* makes use of such allusions to contextualize the story of Christianization in the social world of feast participants, at the same time as it reconstitutes the "chief" as a sociohistorical category. Just as Forest Vokho began his telling of the Knabu legend with reference to Matasi Iho as one of several major chiefs at the time of missionary contact, this *thautaru* opens by referring to the three most renowned chiefs in this area at the time of Welchman's ascent (Figrima, Goregita and Da'a), as well as to the forts identified with two of them (Figrima at Khakatio, and Goregita at Gighila). By reiterating the names it does, the song locates the listener in a particular epoch of historical time and a particular region of social space. With the stage firmly set in the locale where the song was composed and performed, the initial move toward transformation then begins with the introduction of the agents of conversion: Welchman and the two catechists Hageria and Thagragita.

The song is explicit in its representation of a line of leadership constructed as a historical succession that begins with Figrima and descends through Hageria (l. 36) to Sikapu, the recipient of the *thautaru* (ll. 32–8). This "succession" is described as a kind of personal transaction, a "handing over" of power between Hageria and Sikapu, who is depicted as receiving Hageria's power to make peace and "gather people together." In this manner the *thautaru* works to validate leadership status by linking it with historical and genealogical antecedents. The social reality of chiefly status is to a large degree constituted in the activities of producing feast occasions and their accompanying oratory. To the various oral genres of historical representation we must now add written history. The perspective on Hograno leadership put forward in the *thautaru* has also been written up and published by Richard Naramana (sister's son of the composer) in his own studies of culture and history in the Hograno region (Naramana 1987). In his writings (which he shared with me in handwritten form in 1975), Naramana charts a sequence of chiefly power for the region as consisting of three separate lines of succession leading to Goregita, Figrima and Da'a. These lines then converge at the moment of conversion in the person of the "Rev. Ben Hageria" who, in 1928, is followed by Wilson Sikapu for the period 1928–74 (Naramana 1987: 44). The latter part of the *thautaru* suggests that, after Sikapu's leadership, his followers (the singers and others present) may fall into uncertainty and disunity. The song is not explicit about who follows Sikapu in this historic succession, but in an ironic mode characteristic of feast occasions, the sponsors call attention to their role through a rhetoric of self-denigration at the end of the song.

Portrayals of the Christian transformation in legends, songs and ritual drama rely on widely shared models and motifs to bring Christian and heathen into face-to-face encounters. A fundamental ambiguity in these stories, and one essential to their usefulness, is their ability to construct identities that are at once general, forged in common experiences of colonialism and Christianity, and specific, rooted in the particular traditions of localized collectivities and histories.

Comparison of several narratives across regions and across variants of the "same" history yields a picture of convergence that suggests the operation of shared models of persons, causality, and the past. Evidence from other parts of coastal Melanesia indicate that these models may have wide generality beyond the shores of Santa Isabel. For example, in asking Goodenough islanders how the first prominent missionary came to work in their region, Michael Young elicited an account which he called a "veritable charter myth of the local Mission" (1977: 143). As in the Knabu and Khakatio legends, the missionary reasons that "Oh, it is bad that war still continues on Goodenough" and decides to visit there to stop people from "killing and eating one another." Like the stories above, the Goodenough legend also unfolds as a scenario of approach, resistance and acceptance. The missionary approaches in the face of threats posed by men who "took up their clubs, spears and slings to kill him." On Goodenough as in Santa Isabel, the first acceptance of Christianity is reconstructed in terms of pacification, of getting people to "set aside their things of war." The central portion of the Goodenough Island legend reported by Young (1977: 143) is reproduced below to show its parallel with the thematic structure and imagery of the Isabel narratives. After an initial response by many who fled into the bush at the sight of the missionary, Dr. Bromilaw:

They took up their clubs, spears and slings, meaning to kill him. But he raised one hand to his nose and the other to his navel and grasped them, saying: "Peace! I come for peace!" So already many respected him, and they set aside their things of war. Many bowed in prayer as he sang and prayed to God that the men here might stop killing and eating one another. He came here because men were eating each other. And he stopped them.

One interpretation of these areal commonalities is that they reflect the internalization of categories introduced by European missionaries. Almost everywhere in the Pacific, oppositions of pre-Christian violence versus Christian peace were used by evangelists to publicize and rationalize their work. In this interpretation, the similarities result from the ideological hegemony of a pan-Pacific missionary enterprise. But Christian ideology has not been simply passively recorded on Pacific minds like a tape-recorder left running in the background of a Western conversation. It is instead actively interpreted in local contexts and put to use within culturally constituted spheres of interest and activity. This chapter has detailed some of the activities that reproduce histories of conversion as a discourse of identity that creates socioemotional meaning at the same time as it works to recenter power in chiefly histories. Conversion narratives renew localized identities by historicizing traditions of descent and chiefly leadership and placing them "at the heart" of emergent realities.

A key ingredient in the success of the Melanesian Mission in Santa Isabel was the ability of local communities to appropriate Christian symbols and still reconstruct the conversion experience as one that was generated from within. Although Christian teaching is often portrayed in local histories as originating outside these communities, the agents of transformation are for the most part Christian chiefs, teachers and priests who are the ancestors of those recalling the history.[6] As agents of the "new way," early chiefs and priests could espouse new moral and ritual practices at the same time as they anchored these ideas in microtraditions of ancestry, place and chiefship.

In essence, chiefs and their new counterparts were mediators – mediators of symbolic realities as well as relations of power. Just as people in Santa Isabel tell stories of change through the agency of renowned leaders of the past, so the history of colonization on the island may be reconstructed as a "genealogy" of contending realities centered upon chiefly big-men. It is this story that the following chapters take up, culminating in the 1975 ceremony to install a paramount chief that was itself framed in terms of conversion history. The rather remarkable ongoing attempt to institute a position of chiefly power for the entire island is rationalized and supported by the propagation of an island-wide conversion narrative – one that centers the history of Santa Isabel Christianity upon the conversion of the Bughotu chief Soga and his subsequent rise to a position of "paramount" influence. It is my argument that, to the extent that this story works for people in various parts of the island, it is understood in terms of locally situated variants such as those considered here.

IV *Revitalizing*

9

Collisions and convergence

The Christianization of Santa Isabel transformed the fabric of social and political life at the same time as it introduced new religious practices. Much of this was accomplished through new types of big-men working within the mission sphere, including Christian chiefs, catechists and priests. Into this emergent Christian society with its village-based communities, Christian chiefs and chiefly catechists came a new presence: government. Beginning with the incorporation of Santa Isabel within the sphere of the British Solomon Islands Protectorate in 1899, and accelerating with the establishment of a government office on the island in 1918, the colonial administration based at Tulagi in neighboring Nggela became an increasingly intrusive force in local affairs.

Here, as with missionization, the government presence was felt through the agency of local leaders: at first government-appointed chiefs and then headmen, councilors and, today, "members" of the provincial assembly. Through all of this, the "chief" remained a central figure even as the field of power and meaning in village life was increasingly differentiated by processes of colonization and Christianization. In their former roles as feastgiver, alliance-maker and warrior, chiefs had mediated relations among localized followings, personifying the vitality and integrity of their regions. It was perhaps inevitable, then, that chiefs would become the focus for indigenous efforts at managing the exogenous forces of change – efforts that are evident in a series of attempts to redefine and readjust sociopolitical realities.

The cultural-historical account of colonization and response developed in this chapter provides a framework for contextualizing the next chapter's discussion of the latest efforts at renewal: the installation of a new paramount chief and creation of a "system of chiefs." Having already examined understandings of chiefly leadership that emerge in a variety of forms and contexts, this chapter explores the institutional forces that have shaped and reshaped the meanings of "the chief" through history. As a prelude to the ensuing discussion of the paramount chief, the chapter concludes with a brief analysis of contemporary images of "chiefs" in relation to the new big-men of church and government.

"Our own chiefs should rule us"

Where the Melanesian Mission was firmly established missionaries often played an active role in supporting local leaders to function authoritatively in the social and political contexts of the new mission society. Even before Welchman began work on Isabel, and twelve years before the island was incorporated within the British Protectorate, the Melanesian Mission priest J.H. Plant initiated a number of large meetings on Nggela with participants invited from Anglican communities on neighboring islands to discuss political organization, settle disputes and levy fines (Melanesian Mission 1887: 56). These meetings, attended by Soga and other Bughotu leaders (catechists and chiefs alike), were called an island "parliament" by Plant.[1] The 1888 "parliament" was an elaborate affair, complete with fireworks:

A parliament was held during the Bishop's stay at Belaga, at which all the chiefs excepting Dikea were present; even Lipa of Olevuga, the most powerful of all the heathen chiefs, was persuaded by the Bishop to come. The teachers were all present, and the day opened with the Holy Communion. Matins, with a Confirmation, followed; and then the meeting under the great trees. Laws and regulations were passed for the restraint of immorality and the punishment of trespasses; there was also a consultation over the prohibitive dowers required for a daughter. The Bishop was further requested to represent to the authorities the wrong that was done by traders carrying off boys without the consent of their parents. The whole passed off most satisfactorily, and a great feast followed, at which 300 baskets full of food were discussed [*sic*]. Fireworks by Mr. Plant closed the evening.   *(Armstrong 1900: 268)*

Fifty years later, another Melanesian Mission priest, Richard Fallowes, inspired local attempts to institute a similar type of political forum, which he also called "parliament." But whereas Mr. Plant had begun his parliament prior to the formation of a British Protectorate, Fallowes' efforts quickly ran up against the colonial regime that had been in place for forty years.

Activities such as the Plant meetings on Nggela contributed to the evolving status of catechists as much more than ritual specialists. In some cases, catechists seem to have continued some of the same coercive measures employed by early Christian chiefs. After he was appointed Resident Commissioner, Charles Woodford worried about the hegemony of church power in many areas, writing that there was a "necessity for taking measures to prevent the mission usurping the authority that should be expected of the Government alone" (Woodford to Thurston, September

7, 1896, cited in Jackson 1975: 73–4). On Santa Isabel, Henry Welchman worked at building a network of catechists as village leaders, but was also instrumental in supporting Christian chiefs and creating the status of "paramount chief." He looked to the new colonial administration as an ally to buttress the sagging authority of the chiefs. At Soga's death in 1898, it was apparent that no traditional leader could wield the kind of influence that Soga had in enforcing the new moral order. In remarks that reflect his role in encouraging the paramount chief idea. Welchman counseled the Bughotu chiefs about their selection of a successor:

I called all the chiefs together and a great many of the people came as well. I pointed out to them the mischief that occurred when there were a number of petty chiefs without a head, and also the good that had resulted in Bugotu from Soga's single and strong rule and I asked them to settle then and there, before they separated, what they intended to do.   *(Wilson 1935: 44)*

A year later in 1899, Welchman was still concerned about this and again "urged them to settle among themselves who should be the leader and the sole judge for Bugotu" (the term "Bugotu" is ambiguous here, but at that time was used to refer to all of Santa Isabel) (Wilson 1935: 57). When those present selected Eric Notere as their successor chief, Welchman commented: "The next step will be to have the election confirmed by the Resident Commissioner, and then I hope we may look for a return to the more law-abiding days of Soga" (Melanesian Mission 1901: 142).

Santa Isabel had already been within the British Protectorate for two years when Woodford visited the island to stage a flag-raising ceremony in Vulavu village in 1901. On that occasion he also appointed Soga's successor, Eric Notere, "chief of Bugotu," thus lending the government's voice to the emerging discourse of *kastom* in which the status of chiefs was externalized in dialogues between Isabel communities and outsiders. Although Eric Notere succeeded Monilaws Soga as the acknowledged "chief of Bugotu" until his death in 1909, he is generally not remembered as having been "paramount chief" as Soga was.

Early government "chiefs" (as they were called circa 1900 – "headmen" came later) had very few duties. The colonial administration appears to have played only a minor role in island affairs during these years. When Notere requested a detachment of police to assist with his work as headman, Woodford turned him down, advising that he give orders to a few "trusted men" to help with arrests or punishment (letter from Woodford to Notere, June 3, 1903: WPHC 426/21). In these early years, the government did not even show much interest in collecting legal fines. But Notere, now oriented toward the seat of the Protectorate as the center of political power, saw Woodford as the ultimate recipient of fines and compensations paid for local infractions. When he had accumulated a certain amount of money from his work as government "chief," he took it to the Resident Commissioner. Woodford, however, returned the money, saying that Notere should use it for the benefit of his people. Notere then consulted Welchman who advised him to use the money to buy medical supplies.[2]

Even though only a background presence, the government's authority was presupposed in the act of recognizing the "chiefs" who would represent Isabel communities in their dealings with the outside world. Notere's successor, Lonsdale (Bojahofi) Soga, was both officially recognized by the Resident Commissioner and blessed by Bishop Wilson (N.S. Heffernan to Acting Resident Commissioner, April 21, 1921: WPHC 4/II/18,426/1921). Lonsdale Soga's time as Bughotu headman (1911 until 1920) seems to have been one of minimal government involvement, with continued development of the mission-based social order.

It was on Santa Isabel that the Melanesian Mission most deserved the appellation "true architect of the British Solomon Island Protectorate" (Morrell 1960: 349). This was so because the Melanesian Mission was by this time not just an organization of European missionaries but, at the local level, consisted of indigenous leaders of great power and talent such as Monilaws Soga and Hugo Hebala. After fifteen years of an official, if

Plate 13 Chief at Sepi village, 1906, possibly Lonsdale Bojahofi

distant, colonial presence on Isabel, the Acting Resident Commissioner wrote to the British High Commissioner in Fiji saying that "the island of Ysabel has received next to no Government supervision, the natives are quiet and peacebal [*sic*], everyone being under the control of the Melanesian Mission" (WPHC 4/II/8/1915). This absent rule by the colonial government was, however, about to change.

In January of 1918 the first district officer, N.S. Heffernan, was assigned to Santa Isabel and took up residence along with a small detachment of police at Tunabuli (now Tataba) in Bughotu.[3] At about the same time, official but unpaid headmen were appointed without salary to work in the Kia and Maringe areas as well. Until 1920, the primary duties of the headmen were to act as "magistrates" in arbitration. Their recourse to coercive sanctions, including jail sentences and police enforcement, distinguished headmen from chiefs and catechists who also acted as arbiters in dispute settlement. In 1920, the introduction of an annual tax of one pound per man quickly focused growing resentment against the increasing government presence.

The tax requirement was probably most burdensome for the villages in the Maringe and Hograno areas where people had been least involved in trade and cash cropping.[4] The development of disparities between regional economies probably contributed to local frictions generated by the principal government headman, a Bughotu man named Walter Notere who used his position to wield expansive powers throughout the entire island. Unlike Monilaws Soga, who also aspired to unprecedented island-wide influence, Notere's activities were not framed by a narrative of Christian conversion. His message was one of taxation and enforcement of a new system of rules for public work and living standards. He is remembered by many of the older people in the Maringe area as a man who was feared for his liberal use of punitive sanctions against those who violated these rules. The sanctions available to him as headman included arrest and imprisonment for evading tax or work duties, and burning houses for "sanitary" infringements.

While the tax requirements and punitive measures were greeted with some consternation, the underlying dislocation of chiefly (and priestly) power was even more disturbing. Predictably, it was the men who occupied positions of leadership in the established mission order, the catechists, who most actively resisted these new developments. The imposition of government rules by the new district officer, Heffernan, and his principal district headman, Notere, elicited an organized response from a group of young catechists who attempted to have Heffernan withdrawn. Perhaps hoping for a return to the earlier form of indirect rule from the capital at Tulagi (Nggela), four Isabel catechists (including Japhet Hamutagi and two prominent Cheke Holo men, Stephen Talu and Eric Gnhokro) wrote out their complaints and asked Bishop John Steward to forward a written translation to the Resident Commissioner.

In addition to complaints about the hardships created by the taxation of people who had no regular source of cash income, the catechists' statement referred to new rules and punitive measures that had been abruptly imposed. The list of stated injustices included (1) taking land and materials without payment for building the government station at Tataba, (2) fining or imprisoning thirteen persons for various offenses, (3) burning thirty-seven houses in eight villages for sanitary violations, (4) requiring public work on the road for the government station and fining delinquent villages (up to a total of ten pounds for some Maringe villages) and (5) innumerable fines for dogs.

More important than their list of specific complaints was the catechists' attack on the idea of a district office on Santa Isabel. In no uncertain terms, they hoped to repel the intrusion of an unknown "White Officer" into local affairs. Following their list of grievances, the catechists articulated a pleaful request to have this new irritant removed:

These are the things he [Heffernan] has done to us and in all his actions at the present time and when we see his behaviour we have decided that we do not want him to stay here because the owners of the land have not agreed to his living here. We have written this not to ask you [the Bishop] to do anything for us but it is our fixed desire that he should no longer remain among us of Bogotu [*sic*] and we cannot change our minds forever. This also, if it be possible that this White Officer leave us and go away, we do not wish any other white man to take his place for we have already made trial of the White man dwelling among us and all Government laws seem unfair to us. But we wish that our own chiefs should rule us as did Lonsdale Soga formerly. We recognize Our Governor of the British Solomon Islands him alone who lives at Tulagi [the Resident Commissioner].

(Bishop Steward to Resident Commissioner, January 3, 1921: WPHC 426/1921)

This statement suggests that the catechists were aware of the political seachange that was taking place in the events of 1918–20. These changes were on a collision course with established structures of meaning and power in the village-centered and island-centered mission society. Note that the white man is rejected "because *the owners of the land* have not agreed to his living here" and because "we wish that *our own chiefs should rule us* as did Lonsdale Soga formerly." The catechists' plea for a revival of official recognition of chiefly leadership strikes a chord that has been a recurrent theme in Isabel history to the present.

When queried by his superiors about these complaints, Heffernan replied that the matter was largely a fabrication of the four catechists who were reacting to threats to the "political influence of the Teachers (catechists) . . . who had to be consulted in every action, civil or criminal" (letter from D.O.

Heffernan to Acting Resident Commissioner, February 14, 1921: WPHC 426/1921). Walter Notere, the government headman who was himself the object of some of these complaints, also produced a written defense of the government position. In his letter he went on a counter-attack against the catechists, claiming that two of them had said, "we two only we will make the Government to get off" (*ibid.*).

An investigation of the complaints against Heffernan found that he had exercised almost no supervision of the headmen working under him. Upon arrival he had centralized government authority in the hands of district headmen by giving them the sole power to exact fines in arbitration, whereas previously chiefs had also been able to impose government fines. He was reprimanded for not keeping closer watch on the exploitation of this power by ambitious headmen. Other complaints, however, were given short shrift. For example, on the matter of burning houses, the report noted: "The burning of houses was a sanitary measure and appears to be the usual practice throughout the Protectorate in order to compel natives to replace insanitary buildings" (letter from Resident Commissioner to High Commissioner, Fiji, April 28, 1921: WPHC 426/1921).

Heffernan remained at his post until 1925. After that, no district officer was stationed on Santa Isabel for the next three years. None ever learned an Isabel language, relying instead on Solomons Pidgin, learned by Isabel men working on plantations or trading ships (MacQuarrie 1946; Fowler 1959; Isabel District Reports 1934–40, and district officer diaries: WPHC F14/1). Government headmen in the regions of Bughotu, Maringe and Kia were given formal recognition in 1923 with a scheme to form three subdistricts with two paid headmen, Walter Notere of Bughotu with Edmund Bako of Kia under him, and one unpaid for Maringe (WPHC MP 660/1923). In Maringe, Frederick Pado was appointed as headman, succeeding John Selwyn Getu, the chief who had led the Labheba refugees back to Buala with Hugo Hebala in 1905. In 1934 the Maringe headman Pado began receiving a government wage of eighteen pounds per year (BSIP 1/3, F14/8). After the death of Notere in 1935, Bako of Kia later became the senior Isabel headman, a position he kept for about twenty years.

The administration scheme also called for the recognition of "village constables" who later became known as "village headmen." Village headmen were expected to assist with the collection of taxes, organize work on the weekly government work day (Friday) and hear disputes, sometimes dealt with during visits by the district officer. By designating one day a week as its day, government made itself felt through the rhythms of daily life. Yet selection of village headmen was often arbitrary and unconnected with existing assumptions about power and political stature. Not finding any formalized, "hereditary" chieftainships on Santa Isabel, it was easy to assume, as one colonial officer did, that "the absence of any hereditary chiefs, although disadvantageous in many ways, permits of the choice of District and Village Headmen on their merits" (Ysabel District Annual Report 1939: BSIP 1/3, F14/7). "Merits" in such cases tended to consist of knowledge of the *lingua franca*, Pidgin, and experience with European trade or labor practices. As a result, the headman's authority was often limited to specific contexts such as Fridays or visits by the district officer. Nonetheless, the formation of this network of government leaders, linked as they were to the "big-men" resident in colonial offices, worked to erode further the prestige and influence of local chiefs.

Even though highly contextualized, many of the government headmen, especially the regional appointees, rose to positions of considerable prominence in the new conjunction of colonial, mission and indigenous realities. Some of the government headmen turned out to be aspiring leaders of a more general sort who could parley their work experience and status with government into even greater prestige. Competence in Pidgin and experience on ships or plantations were signs of knowledge and ability valued in the world being opened up by increased contacts with Europeans of all sorts. These were regarded as important elements in the reputations of twentieth-century big-men who needed to manage relations with an increasingly complex outside world. Combining their new-found government status with activity in more traditional arenas of local political life (feastgiving, dispute mediation, economic pursuits), each of the regional headmen mentioned above – Notere, Bako and Pado (and later Wilson Sikapu in Hograno) – emerged as major figures in island politics during the 1930s.

Fallowes and the church chiefs

It was into this context, of an expanding government administration making inroads into the social order consolidated over thirty to forty years of missionization, that the next influential European priest arrived. In 1929, the English priest Richard Fallowes took up residence on Santa Isabel where he would live on and off for the next ten years. He was the first European missionary to establish the kind of extensive influence that Welchman had during his time thirty years earlier. Like Welchman, Fallowes perceived the erosion of authority of local chiefs as a weakening of the moral order desired by the church. But the situation which Fallowes encountered in 1930 was quite different from that which Welchman had hoped for with the arrival of Charles Woodford in 1901. In Fallowes' eyes, the government presence threatened the influence of both chiefs and church alike. In a letter to the author in 1975, Fallowes recalled his view of the situation at that time: "The District Officer & the Govt. Headman [Walter

Notere] were indifferent or hostile to missions and made for a Govt. versus Mission situation" (letter to the author, October 2, 1975).

With insight which most district officers seemed to lack, Fallowes soon learned that there is a semblance of chiefly descent in Santa Isabel, and that these individuals were largely ignored by the administration. He referred to these leaders as "hereditary chiefs" and reasoned that giving them formal status within the mission would enhance their prestige at the same time as it would reinforce the influence of the mission in village affairs. Within a year of his arrival, Fallowes introduced a new leadership status, "church chief" (*funei Khilo'au* in Cheke Holo; *vunagi Kilo'au* in Bughotu), to be held by one man in each village. At the same time, he also attempted to revive the paramount chief status which had lain dormant since Monilaws Soga was elevated to that position with the backing of Henry Welchman. Fallowes recognized and supported a Bughotu man, Lonsdale Gado, as the next paramount chief. Gado was widely respected in his area, and had been educated at the prestigious Norfolk Island school of the Melanesian Mission. Furthermore, Gado was a prominent Bughotu chief who could claim the title of Soga as a descendant of Monilaws Soga. In aspiring to this position through his association with Fallowes and the island-wide effort to create a system of church chiefs, Gado became the church counterpart of the senior government headman Walter Notere. Given the rather unique situation in Santa Isabel of one church (Anglican) and one government for the entire island, the status of Gado and Notere constituted comparable positions of island-wide leadership, representing the separate but parallel institutions of church and state. Furthermore, each of these positions was linked to parallel (and at times intersecting) networks of village-level leaders (church chiefs and headmen).

Fallowes' conception of the church chief status was borrowed from the Anglican notion of a "church warden" with duties such as tending the village church. And, analogous to the government workday on Friday, Saturday was designated as the mission's day for villagers to perform church-related work directed by the church chief.[5] In describing his view of the role of church chiefs, Fallowes mentions the more specific duties as those of a "church warden," but alludes to their broader functions as well:

My purpose primarily was to strengthen the church in each village by encouraging each community to choose the most influential member other than the Govt. Chiefs to act as Church wardens & be responsible for the material assets of the Church such as buildings. The teachers would continue taking services and teaching in schools but have the backing of the church warden's greater influence in the community.

(Letter to the author, October 2, 1975)

Clearly, there was more going on in this broad movement to institute church chiefs than providing for the upkeep of village churches. Indications of a larger agenda, involving a self-conscious remaking of models of leadership, emerged during the 1930s as many communities adopted the church-chief idea with much enthusiasm in the evolving colonial context.

The invention of church chiefs and the revitalization of the paramount chief proved to be timely innovations that were readily accepted because they extended existing ideas about chiefs. Specifically, they tended to reintegrate aspects of the model of the "chief" that were strained by the process of colonization. Men already recognized as chiefs by virtue of their personal reputation and activity in feastmaking and dispute-settling were here ritually initiated as representatives of the moral and spiritual authority of the church, thus giving them new legitimacy within the context of colonial institutions. In practice the integration achieved by this ritual move could be even greater since many of the church chiefs were already catechists or government headmen. At least fifteen villages (or about one-third of the villages on the island) had church chiefs who were also village headmen. Where Europeans in mission and administration envisioned specialization, local communities sought creative forms of reintegration (albeit with opportunities for competitive rivalry as well).

Fallowes understood the importance of ritual for creating and validating the new church-chief status. Since the essential innovation of the church-chief idea was the notion of combining chiefly stature with the moral and spiritual authority of the church, what better way to demonstrate this linkage than through a church blessing enacted by the head priest, Fallowes himself? Fallowes thus undertook to institute the network of church chiefs by blessing leading chiefs during the church services he conducted while touring the island. In each village he would hold a Communion service to bless the designated chief, and then give him a signed "license" certifying that he was now the church chief for that place.

A particularly elaborate celebration was held to install Lonsdale Gado as paramount chief. A large feast with an accompanying church service was held at Sepi village in Bughotu and attended by catechists and chiefs from all around the island. The focus of that occasion was the church service in which Fallowes blessed Gado as the paramount chief. Fallowes saw his association with Gado as lending him support to build his influence as a chief and church leader, countering what he regarded as the disproportionate influence of the senior government headman, Walter Notere:

I took it upon myself to get his claims more fully recognized and this was not difficult as the village chiefs were fed up with the usurpation of power by Walter Notere. As the time went on Lonsdale Gado excited himself & with the encouragement of the "Great White Chief" became more and more recognized as the successor of the great Soga.   *(Letter to the author, May 9, 1976)*

Note the implication of Fallowes' recollection that, as time went on, Gado became "more and more recognized" as paramount chief. The installation of Gado as paramount chief did not mark an endpoint, an act of occupying an existing status so much as a moment in a process that might, over time, constitute itself through Gado's actions in conjunction with Fallowes. The ritual of recognition did not bestow a title that carried with it a set of pre-existing rights and powers, but rather marked an opportunity to recreate a dormant social category – one that might meld significant aspects of church and *kastom*.

Fallowes undertook an island tour in 1931 in which he conducted installation ceremonies for church chiefs in nearly every village. Lonsdale Gado accompanied Fallowes on the tour, just as Monilaws Soga had traveled with Welchman throughout Isabel and to other islands, and had risen in stature as a result. Fallowes wrote about the 1931 tour in his diary: "In every village we had a 'vagtuwale' [Mota for 'meeting'] in the evening. I and Soga [Lonsdale Gado] spoke to the people on the authority given to the Church Chiefs and urged the people to respect and obey them. In every village, the Church Chief, elected by the people, was given his license in church at the mass" (Diary: November 7, 1931). The "license" referred to by Fallowes was a certificate which he had drawn up as a formal documentation of the new status. These certificates made a strong impression, even lending the church chiefs one of their colloquial names, "ticket man" (*mae tikiti*).[6]

Not long after Fallowes' tour to install the church chiefs, Gado organized a meeting attended by chiefs and catechists from all areas of the island in which eight men were selected as "district church chiefs" to work in at least five distinct regions. The notion of "district church chief" constituted a church counterpart to the government district headman. In some ways, these men did what prominent local leaders had always done: circulate through their regions, speaking at feasts and meetings, settling disputes and coordinating collective projects. But now they did so with the ritual validation and "mana" of the church. In the case of church chiefs who were already catechists, the new status could work "in the other direction" to call attention to the person's chiefly identity with broader, organizational roles to play.

Over forty years later, Fallowes remembered distinctly the impact made by these more active church leaders. He attributed their success and influence to their personal abilities and "mana": "Some of these Church Chiefs were men of outstanding 'mana' & among them was Japhet Hamutagi of Regi brother of Walter Gagai the priest, & they took upon themselves to travel beyond their own village to encourage Church Chiefs in other villages" (letter to the author: October 2, 1975). It is more than coincidental that the example of a church chief of great mana was also a catechist. By the 1930s, extraordinary mana was attributed only to persons identified with church knowledge and ritual. The cultural beauty of the church chief idea was that it ritually opened access to institutional sources of power for community leaders not otherwise positioned to draw upon them. And the idea worked in converse ways for catechists such as Japhet Hamutagi for whom it signified links to tradition that could be opposed to the growing government apparatus. Significantly, Hamutagi, mentioned by Fallowes as a church chief of "outstanding mana," was one of the four young catechists who had signed the petition in 1920 to rid the island of the government district officer.

Introduction of the church-chief status did not so much form new roles for catechists and Christian chiefs as it created a category that combined and legitimated old ones within the contemporary matrix of mission and government institutions. This period saw church leaders active in dealing with a wide range of social and moral issues in the villages, including adultery, sorcery and acts of aggression. Adultery emerged as a particularly controversial topic in the uncertain relations between government and church during this time. Given the deep involvement of the mission in the regulation of sexual conduct, it was inevitable that adultery would become a contested site for implementing church and government authority.[7]

Most Maringe communities during the 1930s appear to have drawn upon both mission and government resources as alternative modes of dealing with moral and political quandaries. One man who was both headman and church chief during that time stated that he resolved these ambiguities as follows: "In the case of adultery if the husband and wife are cross and wish to go to Court I will take them to the Government but if they are not cross and do not want Court then I ask the Mission to fix it up" (March 3, 1933: BSIP F479/33). His statement is not unlike the attitudes of contemporary villagers such as Kesa and Bilo (chapter 4) who argue about the role of village chiefs and traditional means of talking through interpersonal conflicts, as opposed to government courts that tend to be regarded as more impersonal and harsh. Court is generally resorted to only after the failure of traditional means aimed at repairing relations rather than apportioning penalties or fines (White 1990).

In the face-to-face arenas of village politics, the voices of moral authority speak not from positions of formal status, but from identities and reputations that are continually created out of social practice, especially speech practices that demonstrate particular forms of cultural knowledge and ability. Prior to church and government these voices were by definition those of "chiefs." In the 1930s until the present the most influential voices are those of persons who construct leadership status from any number or combination of identities ranging from "chief" to "priest" or "headman." Position within colonial (and postcolonial) institutions is just one component of personal reputation, but it is a vital component for big-men (and their communities) today who wish to create and sustain recognition across regions, islands and even nations. While the new institutions could be used to define domains of exclusive action, many communities worked out pragmatic ways of incorporating both government and church in their affairs despite areas of ambiguity. When I asked the retired Maringe district headman Frederick Pado how he had handled court cases during the Fallowes period, he recalled that he and the district church chief, Japhet Hamutagi, simply divided up disputes according to convenience. He would take some and Hamutagi would take some.

With people using all of these various means of managing local disputes, there were inevitable areas of uncertainty. Wilfred Fowler, a district officer posted on Santa Isabel during Fallowes' time, recalled a question from his police constable: "Every village has a mission headman now . . . Some say mission headman is number one in the place and some say Government headman is number one . . . People are asking who is boss, King George or Archbishop?" (Fowler 1959: 40). Not surprisingly, the senior government headman, Walter Notere, reacted particularly sharply to what he saw as the mission's incursion into the government's role in adjudication. Notere was, it may be recalled, the same headman against whom complaints were lodged during the Heffernan incident. And, as mentioned earlier, some of the church chiefs whom Notere accused of subverting the government were the very same catechists who had filed the complaints against the government ten years earlier.

Notere applied the full weight of government sanctions, backed up by police, to restrain the activities of church chiefs. On one occasion he had a Maringe catechist arrested for resisting the appointment of a village headman. A resident of that village today remembers the catechist saying to Notere that the village already had a church chief, so "How many chiefs do we need?" The arrested man is said to have spent time in jail as a result of his remarks. In his diary during this time, Fallowes described an incident in which Notere brought charges against a district church chief for "belittling the work of the govt." Fallowes attributed this charge to "a long standing feud and jealousy" between the two men (Diary: March 1, 1932).[8]

Notere, as senior headman, was particularly resentful of the church chiefs who traveled widely as "district church chiefs." He spelled out his frustrations about these "mission headmen" in a written complaint submitted to the Resident Commissioner in 1933. He began his complaint by referring to the decision of a former district officer to allow these mission leaders to adjudicate adultery cases:

The result of this is that the mission had grown in power and the government has accordingly lost grip [*sic*]. The mission headmen are now fixing up practically the whole of the ordinary business and the only things dealt with by the Government are matters which are really serious. There is very little serious crime amongst my people and so the mission is practically running everything ... These Mission Headmen are spoiling everything and I wish that they might be prevented from running all about. It is not so bad where the Mission Headman remains in his own place but when people like Gado, Selo, Poni, Napo and Hamutagi start to go all about to other places and fix up business it is spoiling everything.

(*Commandant Armed Constabulary to Resident Commissioner, March 5, 1933:*
BSIP F43/14)

In his submission to the authorities, Notere also said that he was displeased with those individuals who had accepted both headman and church-chief status. He listed a number of such people, saying, "I want to take all these people before the Court for not doing their work properly" (*ibid.*). A subsequent investigation of these complaints produced a statement sympathetic with Notere's position, instructing headmen to resume their jurisdiction in adultery cases, but recommending no other action.

It was not long after these disputes came to a head in these court cases that the apparent conflict between mission and government subsided with the withdrawal of two of the principal actors, Notere and Fallowes. Fallowes, who had become increasingly unstable during his five years resident on Isabel, suffered a mental breakdown and left the Solomons. With the death of Walter Notere a few months later, this chapter in Santa Isabel colonial history came to a close. But the problems and contradictions associated with the colonial intrusion did not subside. Subsequent attempts at reformulating social reality in the colonial context were soon to follow.

The parliament and *Maasina* Rule movements

The activities spawned during Fallowes' first years in Santa Isabel planted the seeds for later, more dramatic developments after his return to the Protectorate in 1938. The creation of a network of church chiefs, together with the renewal of the paramount chief status, contributed to a remarkable inter-island movement that articulated some of the first collective strivings toward political autonomy in the prewar Solomons. With Fallowes as a kind of charismatic catalyst, Santa Isabel leaders, together with those of other islands, orchestrated a series of meetings moving from island to island that overtly questioned the British regime (Belshaw 1950; Hilliard 1974: 113–16). Even though these meetings were brought to an abrupt end with the expulsion of Fallowes, they constituted an important precedent for the much larger *Maasina* Rule movement that posed a major challenge to colonial authority after World War II (Laracy 1983).

From the time of his first arrival on Santa Isabel, Fallowes and Lonsdale Gado, the aspiring paramount chief, had been engaged in organizing a number of large meetings at which leaders of all sorts gathered to discuss the important social and cultural issues of the day. Fallowes described one such meeting at Sepi village in 1932 as "the largest meeting I have seen on Ysabel." He noted that "Church & Govt. chiefs were present almost in toto with a goodly number of teachers. We counted nine launches in the harbor . . ." (Diary: August 31, 1932). At this point in the island's social history, indigenous leaders were vigorously involved in seeking an expanded involvement in the cash economy, reflected in an increase in coconut plantings and trade stores during the 1930s. And, after Fallowes' tours to install church chiefs around the island ritually, local leaders were also raising self-conscious questions about the role of *kastom* and "traditional chiefs" in colonial society, just as the earlier group of catechists had asserted: "Our own chiefs should rule us." The fact that the large meetings organized by Fallowes and Gado included the full range of local leaders, including government headmen, church chiefs and catechists ("teachers"), reflects the continuing relevance of the more integrated model of chiefly leadership, regardless of the separation of church and state into distinct spheres of institutional authority.

The larger and more visible meetings that followed Fallowes' return to Santa Isabel in 1938 can be read as direct descendants of earlier meetings such as that described above, and even of the mission "parliaments" organized by the Reverend J.H. Plant at the turn of the century. The primary difference was that, in the context of an expansive colonial administration bent on collecting taxes and enforcing new legal codes, the dilemmas of power and powerlessness were now articulated in anticolonial sentiments and demands for autonomous political institutions. Fallowes used his command of the Bughotu language to discuss people's frustrations with the colonial situation, including poor returns from taxes, inadequate education and health care, and inequities in wages and prices. In doing so, he acted as a catalyst for growing discontent with the colonial apparatus and the slow pace of socioeconomic change. Even more important than the particular grievances was the attempt to fashion a discourse capable of voicing indigenous concerns in the colonial arena. During 1938 and 1939 the groundrules for political discussion became the overt subject of interest as big-men of all types responded to the call for a new institution (a "parliament") through which to deal with the colonial authorities. Fallowes, ever the entrepreneur of new knowledge, reviewed the political history of Britain for his Isabel friends and introduced them to the idea of parliament as a model for organizing and directing political discussion. Thus emerged a series of three meetings, known variously as "Parliament," "Chair and Rule" (Belshaw 1950), and the "Fallowes movement" (Hilliard 1974). The size of these gatherings grew from one meeting to the next as the site moved from one island to another: first Santa Isabel, then Savo and finally Nggela, on the colonial administration's doorstep.

Within a few months after his return, Fallowes and Gado had organized the first meeting at Vulavu village in Bughotu. With Fallowes acting as adviser, the meeting constituted itself by designating those present as "delegates" and electing a "Speaker" to preside over the meeting. An elaborately carved wooden chair was introduced as the seat for the Speaker – hence the rather mystical, cult-like name given to the movement by some Europeans, "Chair and Rule" (Belshaw 1950). The district officer on Santa Isabel reported that, in discussion with him, Fallowes asserted that "neither Government nor Mission was furthering the natives' interests and they were being exploited . . . He particularly stressed the lack of educational and medical facilities" (District officer Isabel to Resident Commissioner, March 6, 1939: BSIP F43/14).

The second meeting of parliament, held on Savo on April 29 and 30, 1939, was an even larger gathering, drawing participants from Isabel, Nggela, Guadalcanal and Malaita. Some of the Isabel men who were at that meeting remember that Fallowes was received by the gathering with tremendous enthusiasm marked by hearty clapping. The delegates on Savo then proceeded to draw up a list of requests to present to the High Commissioner, Sir Harry Luke, who was to visit the Solomons in June, 1939 on his first official visit (see Laracy 1983, Appendix B). The Savo gathering decided to hold a third meeting on Nggela in June. So, on June 12–13, 1939 the third (and as it turned out, final) parliament convened at Halavo on Nggela.

The administration was viewing these meetings with increasing alarm and, a few days after the Nggela meeting, summoned a number of the leaders to an interview with the High Commissioner. Fallowes himself was summoned for the following day. The list of "requests" and the written statement from John Pidoke were all the evidence the High Commissioner required for roundly chastising Fallowes and ordering that he desist all political activity and leave the Protectorate by the first available ship, prohibited from returning for at least two years. Fallowes departed before the end of July.

The concerns expressed in the parliament meetings continued to be expressed after Fallowes' departure, and resurfaced in even more strident form during the postwar *Maasina* Rule movement discussed below. When the Resident Commissioner toured Santa Isabel in 1940, the year after

Fallowes had been deported, he received some of the same specific requests voiced in the parliament meetings, including the need for a "technical school" and complaints about high taxes. More importantly, he was also asked about the possibilities of establishing a "Native Parliament." He took note of these topics in his comments on a meeting with village leaders in Bughotu: "Elders were not very clear what they wanted, but [their point] finally resolved itself into permitting Elders and people to take a more active part in the government of the District. It was explained that such a system cannot possibly be introduced until it is seen that the people are capable of dealing with their own petty disputes" (BSIP 1/III, F22/12). It was this sort of exclusionary response, uninformed by local knowledge, that fueled the *Maasina* Rule movement and led to even more assertive calls for rejection of the colonial apparatus. In this instance, the official involved suggested that "native courts" be legitimized, giving an official nod to an ongoing practice.

Village "courts" had, from the earliest years of colonial presence, established themselves in practice, with or without European supervision. During the period of the Fallowes' movement, a district officer observed that village meetings were held by chiefs to deal with disputes and infractions, and that these were frequently attended by government headmen. He saw this as "a purely native development" which represented the emergence of "native arbitration courts": "The District Headmen, apart from their strictly official duties, frequently sit with elders to discuss local matters and out of these meetings native arbitration courts have gradually grown. The latter's great attraction is that they are a purely native development and of such an informal nature as to be well within the comprehension of the people" (Ysabel District Annual Report, 1939: BSIP 14/7). But these practices were not easily accommodated in the formal structures of colonial government. An official in Tulagi commented that the above report was "misleading" since these "courts . . . have no legal sanctions, their decisions cannot be enforced." Despite these inconsistent attitudes within the government, local courts continued to function, constituting the same sort of forum for local dispute settlement that had occupied chiefs, headmen and church chiefs for a decade. Lonsdale Gado, for example, used the incipient courts to perform the work that chiefs had always performed by listening, talking, mediating and settling disputes among those in his area. The year following the last Parliament meeting, the district officer noted that a Bughotu court headed by Gado was being "conducted with admirable results . . . A respectable body of law is being built up . . ." (Isabel District Quarterly Report, September 30, 1940: BSIP 28/40).

These developments were overtaken by the onset of World War II which saw the British administration abruptly withdraw in the face of the Japanese advance into the Solomons in 1942, followed by a massive American counter-offensive that engulfed the archipelago in two years of intensive fighting. But wartime experiences further stirred the political imagination of people who remembered the Fallowes meetings, leading many to receive news eagerly of the new *Maasina* Rule (*maasina*, "brother") movement that spread rapidly throughout the central Solomons in 1947.

Maasina Rule or "Marching Rule" has been written about extensively as one of the most significant anticolonial movements anywhere in the Pacific, and I will not repeat a general description here (see Worsley 1968: 170; Keesing 1978; Laracy 1983). The expressed goals of *Maasina* Rule were much like those articulated during the prewar parliament meetings: create autonomous political institutions, control taxes and wages, build schools and clinics, and promote economic improvement. A Malaita man who was a *Maasina* Rule leader recalls attending the 1939 parliament meeting on Nggela and being influenced by its message "to choose some people to represent you as chiefs. Chiefs who will be in charge in your districts . . ." (Keesing 1980: 103).

Generally anticolonial in ideology and millenial in fervor, the movement had somewhat different meanings and spawned different activities in the various regions where it took hold. Its origins and center were in Malaita, but it spread throughout the islands of Guadalcanal, Nggela and, briefly, Santa Isabel. On Santa Isabel the movement was cast in a distinctly Christian idiom, and was linked to the Fallowes movement more consistently and overtly than elsewhere. Although *Maasina* Rule on Santa Isabel did not lead to the formation of new villages or leadership positions as it did on Malaita, its combination of colonial challenge with visions of wartime wealth was received with an enthusiasm that one man likened to "lighting a match to kerosene." The fire, however, quickly burned itself out. Due to the arrest of its leaders, and to the power of certain big-men, especially the government headmen, who did not join, *Maasina* Rule on Santa Isabel consisted of just a few large meetings over a period of several weeks in 1947.

The *Maasina* Rule message was brought to Santa Isabel by a Cheke Holo man from Hograno named Brown Zalamana. Zalamana was a mission trained teacher and catechist who had worked as a chaplain's assistant on a nearby American base during the war. After the war he had been posted to teach at a mission school on Guadalcanal where he participated in *Maasina* Rule meetings organized by the war hero and movement leader Jacob Vouza. When Zalamana landed on Santa Isabel, he went first to his home area in Hograno and met with the senior Isabel priest, Ben Hageria. Hageria expressed enthusiastic support for *Maasina* Rule and offered

Zalamana the history of British parliament he had written down in the Bughotu language from Fallowes' teaching. The history became a validating text supporting the goals of the Isabel movement. When Zalamana later testified in court during the trial of movement leaders by the British authorities, he was explicit about his perception of the links between Fallowes' teaching and *Maasina* Rule doctrine:

> When I was asked to explain on Gela about Marching Rule, I thought that it must be the same as what Mr. Fallowes had explained before . . . this Marching Rule wanted taxes to be used by the people, which Mr. Fallowes wanted . . . Mr. Fallowes had wanted to help the Solomon Islanders before and give us a Parliament but the Government had sent him back to England . . . Marching Rule was taken from his teachings.
>
> *(High Court Records, Rex v. Bobongi & others, January 1948: WPHC, J.C. 37/197)*

Given the pervasive significance of the church in Isabel society, it was inevitable that the movement's ideology would be given a Christian reading (cf. Peterson 1965–6). Zalamana had been educated at mission schools, had served in the indigenous missionary order of the Melanesian Brotherhood, had been in training as a deacon and had worked with an American priest during his Labour Corps service. When he held *Maasina* Rule meetings in Santa Isabel, he held them in village churches, and began with a ceremonial procession, much like church services. Zalamana himself appeared at these occasions clad in catechist robes given him by the American priest. And in his speeches he frequently quoted from the Bible to augment the message he had picked up from Vouza and the Guadalcanal leaders.

Although Zalamana was arrested, tried and sentenced to four years in prison for his involvement with the "seditious" movement, he and others point to the subsequent emergence of more autonomous political institutions as a fulfillment of many of the goals of *Maasina* Rule. The push for political change after the war led the administration to introduce a plan for local government councils on each major island. In 1948, the year after the *Maasina* Rule activity in Santa Isabel, the government headmen formed the first "native council" by selecting ten leaders from around the island, with the three leading headmen from Kia, Maringe and Bughotu serving as president and two vice-presidents (BSIP 1/III, F14/27/2). (Popular elections for councilors were introduced in the 1950s.) The council plan called for the councilors to have village counterparts known as "committees" (Pidgin, *komiti*). One or more men from each village would be chosen by consensus to take responsibility for organizing government work, overseeing tax collection, taking care of official visitors and the like. The participation of the district headmen (Edmund Bako of Kia, Frederick Pado of Maringe and Lonsdale Gado of Bughotu) ensured that the new council would be a prestigious, if little understood, body. As an example of the shifting uses of status in the colonial structures, Gado was by this time regarded as the senior Bughotu headman, with his status as "paramount chief" apparently fallen into disuse in the absence of Fallowes. On the government council Gado served under Edmund Bako, his mother's brother and the council president. And, as a final statement of the continuity between *Maasina* Rule and the government council, Zalamana himself was later elected to the latter body for three terms over a period of twelve years.

Of models and men

In the rationalized and bureaucratized discourse of modern political institutions, linked as they are to distant state and international horizons, leadership status is seen to inhere in offices or positions distinct from the people who occupy them. In sociological parlance, status and power are based on "universalistic" rather than "particularistic" premises. In this view, the colonial history of Santa Isabel consists of a process of imposition whereby Western institutions of church and state have gradually displaced or transformed chiefly polities centered in localized and personalized histories of collective experience. The argument put forward here (and one that has become a consistent theme of recent works in Pacific history) is that such a history misses the creative force of culture in shaping sociopolitical reality out of the dynamic interplay of indigenous and colonial elements. Social meaning and political power are not fixed structures, but rather emerge from multiple realities contending for legitimacy. Achieving legitimacy (never complete or permanent) depends upon the ability to produce (rather than simply invoke) meaning in the discursive practices that define collective identity and value.

Given the traditional significance of chiefs as mediators (in both a semiotic and a political sense), chiefs and their modernizing counterparts in church and government have been the contested ground upon which forces of change seek to inscribe their realities. As the events described in this chapter should make clear, colonization and missionization in Santa Isabel were anything but a unilinear or mechanical unfolding of institutional structures with predetermined significance for local actors. Whereas an array of new leadership statuses were introduced to administer the orthodoxies of church and state in villages removed from centers of colonial power, the individuals charged with doing so did not so much "occupy" ready-made statuses as they actively used them to build personal reputations and create new discourses of power. These creative uses of colonial categories are evident in the numerous ways that local leaders have combined statuses in the institutions of both church and state. Examples of such innovative uses include the many villagers who were appointed as both "government headman" and "mission headman" (church chief) during Fallowes' time, Lonsdale Gado who went from being a catechist to paramount chief and then government magistrate and councilor, and Brown Zalamana who was catechist, *Maasina* Rule leader and member of the government council.

Attempts to combine statuses in the separate spheres of church and government suggest that local leaders often aspire to broader, more integrated types of leadership reminiscent of the "chief" who, through a variety of roles and activities, could become an important symbol of regional identity. Whereas the distinct roles of traditional priest or warrior represented potentials for specialization, the most visible leaders tended to personify forms of power and prominence that subsumed and incorporated these potentials. Hence, while the (colonial) institutions of mission and government have tended to splinter and shift the centers of power and legitimacy away from localized polities, big-men of every persuasion nonetheless continue to validate their status within the social and historical space of small communities where chiefly practices such as feast-making and history-making constitute understandings of shared interest and experience.

This chapter has outlined a series of organized efforts to resist or redefine the intrusion of government in local communities, noting that, in different ways, they each attempted to renew or reinvent forms of chiefly leadership. In each of several movements (the Heffernan incident, the church chiefs, the 1938 parliament, *Maasina* Rule), a discourse of chiefs was invoked in attempts to realign political realities and cultural models. In my interpretation, these movements have sought a symbolic and practical reintegration of aspects of social life made problematic by the dislocation of power from local life and by the institutional splitting of political and moral-spiritual dimensions of the person into separate spheres of church and state. In the remainder of this chapter and the one following, I explore further the hypothesis that talk of "chiefs" in these contexts constitutes a discourse for reintegrating and recentering sociopolitical realities. In other words, efforts to renew the model of the "chief" through the invention of church chiefs and the paramount chief work to recenter meanings displaced from localized constructs of ancestry, place and chiefly leadership.

I suggested previously (chapter 4) that categories of leadership status do not simply designate positions, but also evoke broader understandings of person and social action. In addition to opening up claims to specialized knowledge and authority, statuses such as "priest" or "councilor" represent behavioral prototypes organized in terms of cultural concepts of person and interaction. Like Cheke Holo images of the "Christian person" discussed in chapter 6, types of big-men are associated with specific varieties of social activity and moral agency. To pursue this idea, I conducted a brief lexical "experiment" examining the composition of such images for a range of leader types (White 1980b). The results are suggestive of the differentiation of social meaning into spheres of church and government evident in the history of institutional splitting discussed in this chapter. The portrait of status images that emerges offers a telling glimpse of the significance of the "chief" as an intregrative symbol mediating polarized images of church and government.

In order to assess the cognitive organization of these images, I asked twenty-five adult men to characterize ten different status types in terms of personal or social dispositions such as "strong," "humble," etc.[9] I asked each informant to characterize the "way" or "manner" (*puhi*) of each type by selecting attributes from a given set of Cheke Holo terms. I then analyzed the responses to examine what sorts of images are associated with each type of leader, and which differentiate them one from another. In this discussion, I focus briefly on the implicit similarities and differences among status types based on the social meanings they evoke. Keeping in mind that the adult male "sample" is likely to produce a picture of normative (adult male) orthodoxy, and that this sort of lexical representation can only be suggestive or heuristic, the results give a graphic portrait of some of the conceptual tensions hypothesized as concomitants of colonization.

The similarity between any two status images may be represented in visual form by assessing the degree of overlap in the characteristics attributed to them. Figure 2 shows the results of this sort of analysis, depicting relations among statuses such that the most similar ones are shown closer together and encircled within lines forming clusters showing degrees of similarity.[10] The pattern of convergence and divergence among the ten categories indicates that the contrast between church and government images is an important dimension in local perceptions. Even though the similarities are derived from descriptions of personal characteristics, the clusterings correspond closely with institutional roles and boundaries. At the broadest level, the diagram shows two large groupings anchored in the overall contrast of church and government types.

The main exception to this interpretation is the positioning of the chiefly statuses of chief, church chief and paramount chief such that they are all proximal to each other and span the two large clusters.[11] Even though the paramount chief and the other two chiefs are separated by cluster lines, the paramount chief is closer to the chief and church chief than any of the other statuses.[12] This "shadow" cluster of chiefly statuses hints at the persistence of a model of "the chief" that spans the polarized images of church and government. The fact that the chief categories appear somewhat uncomfortable in the dichotomous configuration of the diagram is significant and will be taken up further below. For the moment, note that the church chief position created by Richard Fallowes more than sixty years ago as a way of formalizing the role of village chiefs in church work appears to be modeled on conceptions of the chief. Both are bundled closely together in the similarity diagram. And the proximity of the church chief to the headman status also reflects the rationale for the former as a "mission headman," a church counterpart to government headmen.

The duality of figure 2 seems to represent an ideological distillation of the colonial process that has seen the introduction of a succession of new types of big-men with specialized roles in church and government. However, the diagram is derived from person descriptions rather than direct judgments of institutional affiliation. Looking briefly at the specific personal and inter-personal attributes that underlie these bifurcated images shows more clearly their link to models and contexts of chiefly action. By contrastively analyzing the pattern of attributions, it is possible to tease out the characteristics that most differentiate these polarized images.[13]

The terms that emerge from this analysis overlap in meaning themselves, forming interpersonal themes such that church leaders are distinguished by

Figure 2 Perceived similarities among ten leader categories

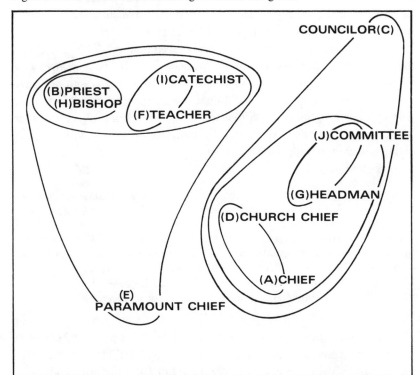

traits of interpersonal solidarity and Christian mana; and government-type leaders carve out those aspects of the "chief" associated with directive speech activity typical of contexts such as disputes, meetings, feasts and collective work (see White 1980b: 360). The typical government-type big-man is one who "discusses," "commands" and "mediates." In contrast, church leaders personify spiritual authority, mana, and the Christian ideals of cooperative, compliant behavior ("humble," "kind") and its emotional concomitants ("peaceful," "untroubled"). In communities where power and influence are built up through speaking and command of moral rhetoric, and where the most potent forms of moral authority are associated with spiritual transactions, compartmentalizing these different kinds of agency in separate institutional spheres has tended to fracture existing models of leadership.

This rather compact analysis suggests that the statuses of new big-men introduced through colonization obtain at least some of their meaning from local concepts of person and chiefly practice. Because leader categories entail typifications of ideal behavior, they often enter into the social and moral "negotiations" of daily events. For example, recall the discussion between Kesa and Bilo cited in chapter 4 in which the two men argue about the contemporary role and relevance of traditional chiefs in resolving disputes. Consider briefly an additional example, taken also from a village meeting where people were airing small grievances.

In the passage below a man invokes idealized images of the "catechist" and "chief" to evaluate his neighbor's misbehavior. The speaker, an elderly man, is voicing his concern about a fellow villager (Maikali) who, contrary to local norms, had hit several children to punish them for rowdy behavior. The speaker amplifies the seriousness of these actions by noting that Maikali is a "catechist" (*velepuhi*). In doing so, he alludes to the "good chief" and church leader who should exemplify ideals that are the antithesis of anger and aggression:

I have something to say to Maikali. One evening some time ago there was crying at Oha's [house]. So I left my house to go over to Maikali. I said to him, "Man, you're always hitting children. And you were using a reed to hit with" . . . "Catechists are not supposed to hit anyone, not supposed to be mean to children. They should care for them like chiefs with a good manner. All you're doing is what my children do to each other." That's what I said on that evening. I was really angry with you, Maikali, because you are a catechist and should teach people about not hitting anyone. We are not supposed to hit others. How are you who were fighting going to teach people?

In this conversation, the speaker uses models of catechists and chiefs to evaluate aggressive actions as contrary to shared ideals. The speaker states his case by drawing an analogy between adult/child relations and those between chief and follower. The asymmetries point to an even greater need for temperance and a posture of "sympathy." As discussed in chapter 4, the model of the "chief" (the "chief with a good manner") represents the domestication of acknowledged potentials for domination and aggression. By reminding listeners that the transgressor is a catechist, the speaker underscores the incongruity between his actions and his role as a teacher of Christian ways.

The characteristic that most differentiates church and government big-men is "mana" (*nolaghi*) – an attribute associated almost entirely with church leaders and the paramount chief. As already seen, the history of missionization is replete with examples of "men of mana" such as Hugo Hebala and Eric Gnhokro who personify Christian spiritual power. The association of mana with the image of church leaders as peaceful and kind reflects an ideology that associates spiritual power and well-being with adherence to moral strictures, particularly those pertaining to interpersonal harmony. Since spirits (both Christian and pre-Christian) are regarded as moral guardians who may punish or withdraw protection because of moral transgressions, the priest, the "man of mana," is ideally one who is "clear" (untroubled, peaceful) of interpersonal entanglements (see Keesing 1985).

By contrast, the images of government-type leaders appear to derive from their prominence in activities of talk and debate about matters of community importance. It is through forceful and knowledgeable talk in contexts of collective action such as feasts, meetings and disputes that chiefs typically influence people and events. The role of chiefs as arbiters of the social order is one of the areas of social life most affected by the presence of government on the island, especially through its introduction of an external authority for dealing with conflict and punishing serious offenders. The activities of councilors, headmen and justices are distinguished by the fact that they may speak with legal authority supported by recourse to coercive sanctions. The characterization of government leaders as "strong men" suggests that they are heir to the image of the "strong" chief of the past who could have enemies or offenders killed if he wished. Whereas coercive measures on an intergroup scale formerly involved organized raiding and killing, today's "strong men" may call upon police and the courts.

The colonial intrusion in the everyday life of Santa Isabel villages progressively narrowed the status and power of "chiefs" (but not necessarily of the local men who moved into syncretic, creolized statuses in church and/or government). Rather, the major cultural consequence of the rise of government in the well-established mission society was the fragmentation of models of leadership. The model of the chief is not simply that of a political actor, but of a person who embodies collective identity and history in a wide variety of practices and contexts. As discussed in chapter 4, the "good chief" is one whose personal reputation exemplifies relations of solidarity within the community, and who ideally moderates the chiefly strength or dominance expressed in intergroup relations. In contrast, government institutions create images of dominance not tempered by a shared history of mutual involvement.

The revival of the paramount chief and the invention of church chiefs in the 1930s constitute a kind of ritual and practical patching-together of a dissonant field of colonial experience. These renewals of the model of the "chief" mediate or bridge the polarized spheres of church and government. The cognitive data represented in figure 2 reflect the mediating significance of chiefly statuses in so far as they condense elements of meaning characteristic of *both* of the two opposed status clusters. For example, the image of the paramount chief consists of the Christian qualities of "kind," "sympathetic" and "mana" as well as attributes typically associated with chiefs and government leaders such as "discusser," "mediator" and "strong." These statuses appear to renew images of the "chief" by infusing them with the moral and spiritual power of the church. The latest effort to revive the status of the paramount chief by installing the Bishop of Santa Isabel appears to do just that by ritually reintegrating chiefly leadership and church power – a speculation taken up in detail in the following chapter.

Historically, the Heffernan incident in 1921, the parliament movement in 1938 and *Maasina* Rule in 1947 all articulated desires to create autonomous political institutions, institute "native courts" and legitimize or redefine various aspects of *kastom*. These desires reflect concerns about the dislocation of power and meaning once centered in localized constructs of ancestry, place and the practice of chiefs. In the previous discussion of local histories of conversion I argued that these narratives, similar in conceptualization across many different regions, work to reproduce these localized identities, while still incorporating new forms of knowledge and power through Christian conversion. This chapter has explored institutional forces of colonization that have tended to fragment these models throughout this century. While these problems have at times been coded in oppositions of "native" and "European" or "black" and "white," their persistence in the postcolonial era indicates that these issues do not disappear with national independence. The emergence of a renewed effort to revive the status of the paramount chief in 1975 on the eve of independence, a harbinger of another epoch of attempted revitalization, testifies to that.

10

The paramount chief: rites of renewal

Given the prior history of the idea of the paramount chief, originating in the era of conversion and appearing sporadically during the colonial years, the most recent attempt to revive it offers an opportunity to observe cultural processes of long duration "up close." The ceremony to install a new paramount chief at Sepi village in 1975 breathed new life into the symbol, but on the surface offered no new powers or duties to the man installed, Dudley Tuti. Like his uncle, Lonsdale Gado, it would be up to him to "make something of it," to seize the moment, as it were. Although formally outside of government, Tuti was already "paramount" among local leaders in terms of personal reputation and influence. What, then, was the significance of the events of 1975 for those who so enthusiastically produced them?

The Sepi ceremony was both a crescendo of ritual activity and a prelude for events to come. As ritual, the event reconstituted a master narrative of Christian origins – one that resembles the various regional conversion stories discussed previously, but also encompasses them by offering an account of island-wide conversion focused on the person of the first major Christian chief. Part of ongoing political processes at that moment in time, the ceremony was the culmination of efforts to renew the category of the paramount chief, and also the beginning of another epoch of attempted revitalization – an era in which Dudley Tuti would be at the center of moves to reinvigorate traditional leadership (chiefs) generally. In 1975, with the Church of Melanesia becoming independent, the national independence only three years away, old problems and new possibilities conjoined to produce a remarkable ritual event in the form of the Sepi celebration. As seen in the previous chapter, the paramount chief occupies a particularly strategic, mediating position in the field of social meaning created by images of big-men, new and old. Hence, Tuti's instantiation of the category can be examined as a process of reconstituting understandings of chiefship in the contemporary context.

The story of Soga, the "great warrior chief" who first embraced Christianity and then turned evangelist helping to convert the entire island, offers an historical rationale for an emergent island-wide identity – for being "Isabel." Ascriptions of such an identity are superordinate to the various linguistic and regional groupings on the island, but coordinate with the more abstract unities implied by the island's status as a province (or diocese) in government and church (the latter because of the island's Anglican homogeneity). While this emergent sense of island identity may be somewhat abstract or remote for many, the availability of a Christian origin myth for nearly the entire island offers a powerful source of cultural meaning that is symbolically connected with more localized constructions. The Sepi ceremony capitalized on these connections in its attempt to inscribe an updated model of common Christianity (and *kastom*) in public memory.

In the Soga story, and in its ritual reproduction, relations between *kastom* and Christianity are redefined and revitalized through the enactment of a story of original transformation. The story, of course, does not consist of an indelible 100-year-old script. It is a narrative of the times, like the conversion narratives that circulate within localized regions, a history created of and for contemporary society (cf. Lindstrom 1982b: 317). In fact, since the history of Soga is only dimly known by many people, the regional histories provide models for creating an island-wide "charter myth" with new generative possibilities.

The paramount chief in (post) colonial discourse
To the Westerner accustomed to dividing "tradition" and "history" or "indigenous" and "foreign," the paramount chief and the church chief may appear as cultural paradoxes. Most Santa Isabel people, however, readily acknowledge that these statuses are creations of colonial history and nonetheless regard them as standardbearers of *kastom*, of the traditional in contemporary political discourse. The difference stems in part from indigenous views of chiefs as mediators who have always been agents of and for the incorporation of new knowledge and power. If there is irony here, it is that the notion of "paramount" is deliberately expansive, connoting a chief above chiefs, while created in contexts of colonization and nationalization that have so far diminished sources of chiefly power and prestige.

The meanings and realities of the paramount chief have been different in each of its historical manifestations. If there is a common thread running throughout, it is that the paramount chief has combined elements of the model of the "chief" with the moral and spiritual authority of the church. The person recognized as paramount chief has in each case been supported and encouraged by the principal figure of church leadership. In this most recent manifestation, the paramount chief *is* that figure himself.

Chiefs such as Soga and Figrima, already recognized as dominant "strong men" by the time they identified themselves with the "new way," had a one-time opportunity to draw upon sources of power and influence garnered from both traditional and Christian arenas. In a sense, they embodied both the "old" and the "new," and derived prestige from both. As chiefs and as converts to the new religion, the early Christian chiefs drew upon continuities with the past to transform the present. They could use identities and reputations centered in local universes of descent and regional history to engage in dealings with other parts of the island and beyond.

Prior to conversion, Soga (and his predecessor Bera) had formed alliances and raided on the neighboring island of Savo. In 1890 he visited there with Welchman aboard the mission ship *Southern Cross* and (according to Welchman) announced to the Savo leaders: "I am the only chief in Bugotu, & when I say a thing it is done; you are all 'little' men. So you can't agree among yourselves" (Welchman, Diary: September 9, 1890). Demonstrations or assertions of chiefly status have the greatest performative effect in the context of intergroup relations where a leader's significance as representative of collective identity may be cast as a unity in contrast with outside groups or places. Hence it is in addressing the people of another island, Savo, that Soga represents himself as the "only chief in Bugotu [Isabel]."

The relationship between Richard Fallowes and Lonsdale Gado was, in certain respects, parallel to that of Welchman and Monilaws Soga. But, forty years after Monilaws Soga, there were major differences. Rather than drawing on the extensive fund of power and influence that inhered in the status of chief as Monilaws Soga had done, revival of the paramount chief in the 1930s was aimed at bolstering the sagging position of chiefs in local politics. But in this case the reality may never have been fully established, as Gado's position in local leadership was eclipsed by the Kia chief Edmund Bako who became president of the first "Native Council." Indeed, the partial, tenuous nature of this and other manifestations of the paramount chief on Santa Isabel is evident in the highly variable knowledge of its history among people on the island today.

Because of the paramount chief ceremony held in 1975 the topic was again under discussion during the time I first worked on the island. In the course of asking about this, I was told by a number of people that they simply did not know about such things, but that others with more knowledge of history presumably did. Those who did offer accounts of the succession of paramount chiefs usually placed Tuti as either the fourth or fifth person to hold the title. The only individuals about whom there was universal agreement were the first (Monilaws Soga) and the last (Tuti). For example, one young Hograno man said he thought that there were three previous paramount chiefs: Monilaws Soga followed by the two most prominent headmen and successive presidents of the government council, Edmund Bako and Frederick Pado. Tuti himself does not mention Lonsdale Gado, but sees himself as successor to Edmund Bako who died in 1960 (cf., Zeva 1983: 135). Others did not mention the headmen, but rather pointed to Lonsdale Gado and either one or two others (usually Manua Soga, a maternal uncle [once removed] of Lonsdale Gado, and before him Lonsdale Bojahofi [also called Soga Bojahofi and Lonsdale Soga], a son of Monilaws Soga, the first paramount chief).

Just as the particular instances of the paramount chief have varied with each historical epoch, so one finds today wide variation in local understandings of the status. Most importantly, there is disagreement about the validity of the notion of a single chief for the entire island. It is apparent that the story of the paramount chief is subject to diverse readings and writings. Some of this diversity plays upon the ambivalences that derive from the problematics of dominance associated with the model of the "chief." As discussed earlier (chapter 4), chiefly status in Santa Isabel is a site of potential disagreement and contention, particularly "around the edges" as the boundaries and limits of chiefly power collide across descent-based followings. Not surprisingly, then, the notion of a paramount chief – a single chief for the entire island – has evoked its share of critical commentary seeking to qualify or challenge its extent. For example, in the course of writing about chiefly traditions in his area of Hograno, Richard Naramana (1987: 45) turned from listing the genealogy of Hograno chiefs to giving his view of the power and relevance of the Bughotu chief Soga in the Hograno region:

As for Soga, he was one of the chiefs of his own tribe not the chief of Ysabel, as mentioned in some history books. It was only through the influence of christianity [*sic*] which he helped exert over other chiefs that made him famous. Had he not been the first converted chief, people would never believe that Soga was chief.

Note that Naramana is well aware of dissonant versions of the Soga story, referring to the account circulating "in some history books" by way of offering his as a corrective. His comments are testimony to the force of the paramount chief idea as an emergent reality that had to be reckoned with (at least circa 1975 when Naramana first wrote the above) by anyone articulating localized lines of chiefly power.

Others in the Hograno area have reconstructed Soga's historical role in terms of alliance with the known chiefs of that region. Fr. Cecil Meimana, a retired priest living in Hograno in 1975, told me about a large feast staged on the Hograno coast by the three chiefs Figrima, Da'a and Goregita for the purpose of ceremonially recognizing Soga as the chief who would guard against invasion from the sea (*bara fotho ni raru*, "close off the seaward direction"). They, for their part, would protect the area from approach across the mountains. In his narrative, the Bughotu chief and the Cheke Holo chiefs are on equal terms, with the latter taking the initiative to bestow the guardian status upon Soga ritually. Referring to Soga as Soga Bojahofi who, as noted above, was one of Monilaws Soga's sons (even the names of the various Sogas are a matter of variation), Fr. Meimana told of Soga and his retinue coming ashore bearing a flag, with the inland people heaping up their weapons on the beach as a sign of peace. The three Cheke Holo chiefs then ceremonially tied a porpoise teeth bracelet on Soga's wrist to acknowledge (*fakhegra*, "stand") his status in this alliance.

Whatever the historical particulars may be, the paramount chief idea is a generative concept, a focal point for formulating understandings of *kastom*, history and social relations – understandings that may be revised (and challenged) according to the circumstances in which they are applied. Just as the 1930s revival of the paramount chief took on different purposes and meanings than the first Soga, so the contemporary instantiation in the person of Dudley Tuti constitutes a further transformation. In this instance, the presence of an individual, in the person of Dudley Tuti, who uniquely combined elements of ancestry, status and personal reputation that made him a leader of paramount influence throughout all of Isabel society was an essential ingredient. And, like previous revivals of the paramount chief status, the impetus for the latest episode did not originate entirely inside the island polity (if we may for the moment isolate such an entity). This moment in social history saw leaders at the national level preparing for independence voicing a concern for the position of chiefs in postcolonial society. These interests combined with the presence of Dudley Tuti to crystallize the forces that ultimately produced the ceremonial installation at Sepi village.

1975 was the year of self-government for the Solomon Islands, three years prior to the country's independence. In preparing for that event, local leaders from every island group elected to the Protectorate's governing council began talking about the development of national political institutions. One of the themes in their talk was the importance of tradition or *kastom* in formulating a postcolonial political system. The position of chiefs in local societies was at that time, and continues to be, a central symbol of tradition in the rhetoric of national development. Although no Melanesian islands in the Solomons have traditions of paramount chieftainship that encompass the entire island, "chiefs" and "paramount chiefs" were recurrent topics raised in the pre-independence deliberations of the governing council. (Usually what is meant in these discussions of "paramount chiefs" is a chief who stands above village-level chiefs for a particular region or language group.) One of the two Santa Isabel members of the Governing Council from Tuti's home village of Kia, Willie Betu, recognized the possibilities for renewing the Isabel paramount chief and began formulating and circulating his ideas about how to do so.

When I arrived in the Solomons late in 1974 I heard about the paramount chief idea even before setting foot on Santa Isabel. While in Honiara I visited Betu in his office and learned of his efforts to develop a plan for reinstituting a "system of chiefs," headed by a paramount chief. He had written his views of these institutions in a paper prepared for the "Ysabel Council and Ysabel Regional Diocese." He said that he wrote the paper to stimulate discussion on ways of legitimizing the role of chiefs within the modern system of government. His interest in this topic had been inspired by national-level discussions in the governing council. At the opening of Betu's paper, he cited "recommendation 33" from "Paper No. 89 of the Governing Council Select Committee on Constitutional Development, 1972": "That in the proposed review of government a function should be found for chiefs in local government bodies; consideration should be given to according chiefs some form of recognition; consideration should be given to holding an annual conference of Elders."

Cognizant of Santa Isabel's unique history, Betu in his paper acknowledged the origins of the paramount chief idea in mission society. He wrote: "There were many chiefs, but no paramount chief until Christianity came." However, he offered a plan for regularizing the position in the contemporary situation. Three "great chiefs" representing each of the three major clans on the island would be selected (by consensus?), and these chiefs would then select a paramount chief from among themselves. Betu went on in his paper to list eleven recommendations for implementing such a system, including having these chiefs sit on the Isabel council with the paramount chief as co-chairman. While the idea of three clan chiefs has never taken hold, other recommendations, such as including chiefs in council meetings, were eventually instituted after independence. And one of his recommendations was true to the mark in both time and place: "That the paramount chief's elevation ceremony . . . take place at Sepi next year . . ."

Betu put his plan forward as a basis for further discussions of the paramount chief idea – discussions that had been going on for a couple of years. Responding to this, members of the Isabel council (and others such as Richard Naramana mentioned earlier) undertook their own historical investigations to determine for themselves the validity of the paramount chief status. When treated as an object of deliberation in this way, it is apparent that the idea of the paramount chief is contested ground, a site for constructing and validating understandings of culture, history and power. The ability to externalize (or contain) those understandings is itself constitutive of the realities of paramount chiefship. In this case, the government council for Santa Isabel, the primary body of government administration for the island, discussed and debated the idea of instituting a paramount chief as part of district government – the government which *they* represented. The councilors aired various opinions in their deliberations but eventually decided to reject the idea in one of their meetings in 1974, and again at a meeting I attended in January 1975 (see chapter 1). These discussions were influenced largely by a number of young, educated men who were elected to the Council because of their Western knowledge and command of skills that allow them to function well within the system of modern, bureaucratic government. They expressed little interest in reviving the syncretic notion of paramount chiefship. Their refusal was reminiscent of the split between church and government that had surfaced several times before as individual big-men sought exclusionary rights to certain types of power within the new colonial society.

However, just six months after the meeting in which the councilors rejected the notion, Dudley Tuti was installed as paramount chief in one of the largest feast celebrations ever to be held on the island. What are the reasons for the success of the initiative of Betu and others despite some "official" opposition? Once again, the church played a key role, providing the institutional framework for planning and organizing the installation event. But more important than this was the reputation and persona of Dudley Tuti himself, and the resonance between the reconstructed status of paramount chief and cultural models of the person, history and community. A brief look at Tuti's life gives some sense of the wider cultural significance of his personal reputation.

Tuti

In 1933, when Dudley Tuti was a young boy about fifteen years old, Richard Fallowes visited his home village of Kia to recruit two boys for mission education. Fallowes wanted to find boys of chiefly descent as part of his effort to strengthen the church by linking it with local structures of power.[1] When he asked Kia elders to select the appropriate youngsters, they chose Tuti and one other boy. On the basis of descent, the Kia leaders could not have selected a boy with a more prominent chiefly heritage. Tuti's mother's brother was Lonsdale Gado, the man supported by Fallowes as paramount chief; and his mother's mother's brother was Edmund Bako, the district headman who later became senior government headman and president of the first government council.[2] Furthermore, this entire lineage is said to share common ancestry with Monilaws Soga, the first paramount chief.

The following year, Tuti was sent to the mission school at Siota on

Nggela, and shortly thereafter to Veranaoso on Guadalcanal at the time that English language instruction was first introduced. This was but the beginning of a long process of formal education for Tuti who went on to secondary school at Tiote in Hawkes Bay, New Zealand for three years between 1942 and 1945. Upon returning to Santa Isabel from this experience, Tuti found himself at the center of local efforts led by Bako and the other members of the new government council to develop a secular school on the island (an interest which had been expressed repeatedly since the early 1930s, and then amplified by the Fallowes movement and *Maasina* Rule). He subsequently was made the first head of a locally initiated "junior" school (post-primary) that was the first school run autonomously from church or government anywhere in the Solomon Islands (see Fox 1958: 236). And this was at the very time that Zalamana and other *Maasina* Rule leaders were vociferously calling for improved secular schools.

Dudley Tuti's educational star, however, was still rising. In 1950 he went on to study for the priesthood at St. John's College in Auckland where he was ordained in 1954. After two more years as headmaster of the Anglican Vureas school in Ambae, Vanuatu, he finally returned to Santa Isabel in 1956. Even though he had been away from the island for most of the preceding twenty years, his ancestry, his status as a priest and his previous work starting the junior school had already established Tuti's credentials as a major figure in island life.

Tuti returned to take up the job of district priest for his home region of Kia, and, even more importantly, the job of Rural Dean for the entire island. His work as Rural Dean gave him the opportunity to have personal contact with people in every village on the island. As the senior priest he would tour the whole island each year, visiting each village for an overnight stay and church service. Traveling by canoe, these tours could take up to three months. In each place he would conduct a Communion service and, equally importantly, lead an evening village meeting to discuss the full spectrum of local and worldly affairs. As the best-known Isabel man to have spent so much time overseas and attained the highest levels of Western education, Tuti was regarded as the same type of oracular source of new knowledge as Fallowes, Zalamana and others. Like Hugo Hebala and other chiefly priests before him, he involved himself in all aspects of community life, addressing social, political and economic concerns, in addition to his ritual roles as spiritual leader.

These activities placed Tuti at the interface of indigenous and Western cultures, as a person who articulated and directed developing ideas about modernity and how to participate in it. As part of this developing discourse of modernity, Tuti took the lead in examining the place of many traditional practices in contemporary Isabel society. Many of the issues which Tuti recalls talking about had been topics of discussion for decades, and some are still debated today. These included the desirability of maintaining the practice of exogamous marriage and the appropriateness of the large feasts which continue to mark important social and ceremonial occasions. Like some of his priestly predecessors, Tuti also devoted attention to the lingering problems of dangerous ancestor spirits and continuing concerns with sorcery. As a priest, he, like Hugo Hebala and Eric Gnhokro, undertook processions on several occasions to pray at the sites of old shrines or spirit habitats. He also supported Fr. Gnhokro's efforts to eradicate sorcery and malevolent spirits ritually.

In addition to dealing with such matters as marriage and the traditional spirit world, which fall squarely within the domain of the church, Tuti's involvement in community affairs extended to issues of migration, land and economic development. Continuing a major theme in mission history (chapter 6), Tuti urged people in small settlements to form larger villages which would be more accessible to the routes of transportation and communication, thus facilitating "development" and the work of church and government. Residential histories in the Maringe area show that the years around 1960 when Tuti was most actively encouraging residential consolidation were in fact a period of renewed village amalgamation. He also took a leading role in the difficult economic issues of the day, including acting as a mediator in land disputes and, during the 1970s, as an organizer and supporter of the first island-wide commercial enterprise, the Isabel Development Company (IDC).

After seven years as a district priest, Tuti was ordained in 1963 as one of the first two Solomon Islands bishops in the Melanesian Mission. The appointment as bishop (a position he filled for nineteen years until retirement in 1982) made Tuti the most visible representative of Santa Isabel in the context of relations with others outside of the island – whether elsewhere in the Solomons or beyond. In 1988 Dudley Tuti, the paramount chief and retired bishop, added knighthood to his distinguished list of honors and titles, having been awarded the K.B.E. by the Queen of England. At the time of the paramount chief ceremony, and still today, people in the Maringe area who have no genealogical or regional connection with Tuti nonetheless regard him as the most prestigious representative of the island as a whole. Recognizing him as paramount chief was one way of dramatically projecting a distinctly Santa Isabel Christian identity, distilled from an inventive, but nonetheless culturally constituted, heritage of *kastom* and missionary history.

The Sepi ceremony
When I arrived in Santa Isabel in January, I encountered occasional speculation about the appropriateness and desirability of the paramount chief notion. One chief in Buala who had listened in on the council meeting

where the matter was debated thought that perhaps appointing (or electing) three chiefs from each subdistrict might work, but that there was no real precedent for a single island-wide chief, noting that even the first Soga did not travel over the whole island until Welchman arrived. But these particulars did not seem of great concern to others who discussed the paramount chief idea not in the abstract, but in terms of Dudley Tuti, the person – of granting the paramount chieftainship to "the bishop." On this there was general enthusiasm.

While people around the island during this time may have had differing views of the desirability of installing a "paramount chief," nearly everyone agreed that Tuti was the only person appropriate for the position. This could be put even more strongly: Were it not for the presence of a person capable of combining the elements of ancestry, accomplishment and reputation that Tuti did, the status would probably not have been realized at that moment. In addition to the significance and prestige associated with his position as bishop, the island-wide discourse of Christian identity, supported and propagated by the institutions of the church, was essential for creating the rationale for the installation ceremony. In addition, the organizational resources of the church made possible the logistically complicated planning and implementation of the ceremony.

A meeting of the Isabel "church council," a body coordinate with the government council, first formulated the plan for the installation ceremony during a meeting at Nareabu village in Maringe in 1974. Willie Betu had submitted his document both to this body and to the government council. Here the response was quite different from that of the young councilors. At the church meeting, attended by representatives of subdistrict church councils from all around the island, some of the most influential elders spoke in favor of the idea. One of the main items on the agenda of the Nareabu meeting was to plan a celebration of the independence of the Church of Melanesia. In the context of that discussion participants decided to combine celebration of church independence with a ceremony to install a paramount chief. Following Betu's suggestion, it was decided to hold the celebration at Sepi village. When I asked later what had transpired at the meeting, I was told that two aging but respected big-men had been particularly influential: Frederick Pado, the retired district headman, and Fr. Eric Gnhokro, the priest with miraculous powers (and one of the catechists who had tried to have the first district officer removed in 1921). Since the Nareabu gathering was a church meeting, Tuti was there presiding over the discussions. Those present said that he fended off attempts to designate him as the candidate at that time, saying that there were others who might be acceptable. But no other names were ever seriously raised.

After the Nareabu meetings, with a place and date set for the paramount chief ceremony, the topic was discussed in village meetings around the island. Here again the local church groups (subdistrict councils) were an important forum for coordinating regional participation. Local-level planning was conducted largely through these councils (of which there were six in 1975) composed of two representatives (usually catechists) from each village. In May 1975, just two months before the ceremony, the east Maringe church council convened a meeting in Kologaru village, the village of Frederick Pado. Even though the elderly Pado could no longer travel far from his house, his voice continued to carry a great deal of weight in regional affairs. At this meeting, held outside with village leaders seated in the shade by the side of the sea, both Pado and Tuti spoke to the significance of the upcoming celebration. Pado, then in his eighties, stood with difficulty to address the assembled group who listened attentively to his weakened voice. He spoke only briefly, but when referring to the purpose of the ceremony enunciated the views of many (indeed such chiefly pronouncements tend to *become* the views of many):

> ... I am thinking about our gathering at Sepi. One meaning is to make the bishop of the whole Diocese here in Bughotu [Santa Isabel], to seat him as the chief for all around Bughotu [Santa Isabel] ... But this is not something small, not a game. This is like something that leads the way, that guides like the church, like the way of the church that first reached us ...

Pado here constructs the purpose quite specifically: "... to make the *bishop* . . . chief for all around Bugotu." His remarks reveal the common perception of the paramount chief as inextricably tied to the church and to Bishop Dudley Tuti in particular. Furthermore, he does not simply refer to Tuti as the bishop, but to the "bishop of the whole Diocese," thus highlighting the structural homology that will follow from having a single bishop *and* a single paramount chief for the whole island. He also locates the installation in the context of the arrival of the church and the "way of the church that first reached us." By invoking the era of conversion, Pado here touches upon conversion histories in general, and the Soga myth in particular, as historical validation for the proposal.

Tuti also spoke to this group about the dual purpose of the Sepi ceremony as celebrating both church independence and the recognition of a paramount chief. However, his remarks frame the paramount chief event in a way somewhat different from Pado's speech. Instead of emphasizing the connection with the church (particularly through him, the bishop), Tuti referred to the initiatives at the national level, to the governing council in Honiara. Speaking somewhat coyly, he spoke as if no one had yet been finally designated to be the paramount chief. This posture is consistent, perhaps, with the image of the "good chief" who "puts himself behind" others and does not aspire to "make himself high." Speaking in Pidgin, Tuti articulated the rationale as follows:

... The governing council [in Honiara] have thought about this for a long time ... They want to include some chiefs in the government for governing the country ... And every island will choose one or two or three, according to their custom ... that's our idea for holding [the ceremony] at Sepi. Although we [you and I] have not found who will be the paramount chief, this might be the work of the church and all the people in the council [members of the church council such as those present]; and especially all the people are for finding out who will be the paramount chief. In our system according to our custom, we do not have an election ... for finding out who will be the paramount chief, we should follow our own way, follow our custom ...

Here Tuti assumes the voice that would be expected of him as a representative of Santa Isabel knowledgeable of events and issues in the wider national arena. He locates the origins of the idea in that larger context by ascribing it to an initiative of the governing council. The Isabel event is thus part of a mandate to put up paramount chief(s) on every island "according to their custom." Whereas Pado found meaning for the idea in the church and its history, Tuti (who does not neglect this aspect) finds its legitimacy in relation to both modern government and *kastom*.

After Pado and Tuti had spoken about the overall meaning and purpose of the Sepi event, those assembled turned to the business of laying plans for their contributions. It was decided at this meeting that each village in the Maringe district would contribute two baskets of sweet potatoes and six dollars in cash (to be used to purchase four pigs). In addition to contributions of food and money, men and women from each district rehearsed songs, dances and *thukma* skits to perform as part of the celebration. Each of the other regions made similar contributions, except for the host area of Bughotu where preparations were more extensive.

In addition to its historic association with Soga, Sepi was chosen as the village to host the ceremony because it is a central point in the diocese, which includes the islands of Nggela, Savo and the Russell Islands. Sepi, recall, was the place where Welchman sought to find a successor to Soga; and also the place where Fallowes presided over a ceremony to install Lonsdale Gado (Tuti's mother's brother) as paramount chief. Every household in Bughotu was supposed to contribute one basket of sweet potatoes, and each village was to purchase an item of European food, such as a bag of rice or cooking oil. Residents of Sepi and Vulavu villages worked for two months prior to the celebration making preparations to host the guests who would spend at least one night in their villages. They constructed a large number of temporary shelters and built a new house for the paramount chief with the name "Soga" woven into the plaitwork of the front wall.

The extent of popular support for the installation of Tuti as paramount chief was evident in the scale of the ceremony and the degree of participation in preparations for the event. I estimated that about 2,000 people attended the celebration. (The Solomon Islands Broadcasting Service later reported twice that number in reporting the event on national radio.) The fact that the event was also an occasion for locally celebrating the independence of the Church of Melanesia legitimized the mobilization of church resources for the occasion. Such a large and complex event could only have been organized through church or government infrastructure. For example, the church helped solve the formidable logistical problems of transportation on an island where there are no roads by making its ships available for ferrying people and supplies back and forth to Sepi. In addition, funds were provided to charter most of the other small boats which normally travel the Isabel waters – boats owned by the government and by the Isabel Development Company.

On Monday, July 7, people began arriving at Sepi from all parts of Santa Isabel and from neighboring islands. Each time a boatload of visitors came ashore, they were greeted by the people of Sepi and nearby villages with the familiar welcoming ritual of handshaking. On this occasion, the hosts formed a long greeting line near the shore and welcomed the guests who walked along in single file, shaking each person's hand in turn. Later in the afternoon the church ship *Southern Cross* arrived carrying the bishop and other dignitaries from Honiara, including Archbishop-elect John Palmer, Bishop Leonard Alufurai of Malaita, Willie Betu and a number of others, including several Europeans. Even the wealthy Chinese businessman who at that time owned most of the large commercial plantations on the island made a cameo appearance by landing offshore in his private seaplane (briefly distracting audience attention from the festivities which were going on at that point). The participants and audience from other islands and countries were essential to the definition of the situation as one that would recognize a leader for the whole island – an identity that depends upon the inter-island context for its relational validity.

After most of the dignitaries and guests had arrived, an evening church service was held in a somewhat overcrowded village church. Following the service and a distribution of food for everyone's evening meal, people gathered by lamplight in the open village ground to watch a *thukma* skit performed for everyone's entertainment. People from Sepi and Vulavu villages had prepared a skit depicting the events of first contact with missionaries in their area and the subsequent conversion of the Bughotu chief Soga (who resided at Sepi village). Since Bughotu was the area first contacted and converted by missionaries, its story is also one that can be used to construct an account of shared history for the entire island. In presenting their conversion history, just as the Buala people do in their *bina boli* skit, the Bughotu performers enacted an historical drama that was simultaneously local and island-wide in significance.

The play the actors had prepared for this occasion ran through the full gamut of first missionary experiences with a succession of three scenes depicting (1) the killing of the Catholic Bishop Epalle on their shores, followed by (2) the later arrival of Bishop George Selwyn of the Melanesian Mission, and finally (3) the conversion of Soga by Bishop John Selwyn. The parallel with the *bina boli* scenario is clear: an episode of violence, followed by acceptance and finally conversion. Among the more clever props for the drama were sailing "ships" made of long poles lashed together and carried by their missionary crew. The warriors were decorated with powdered lime and carried axes and shields, while the missionaries appeared dressed in long clerical robes. The first (Catholic) missionary group was vociferously attacked and their leader, Bishop Epalle, killed. As mentioned in chapter 7, Epalle met an even more ignoble end in the skit than that dictated by history. Not only was he "killed," but he was cooked and eaten as well, giving the actors the opportunity to play upon the regional joke of heathens finding that their victim's shoes do not make for easy eating.

The more fortunate Anglican Bishop George Selwyn, who followed Epalle in the next scene, succeeded in overcoming initial hostility (with mana) to gain acceptance and pave the way for second bishop (John) Selwyn and the eventual conversion of Soga in the final scene. Given that Soga personifies the heroic history of conversion for the entire island (in both the mission's own record of its progress, and in many local histories), the story of his conversion focuses and condenses many elements seen in regional narratives of Christianization. The Sepi skit dramatized an account of Soga's conversion that centers upon his miraculous recovery from a serious illness after being treated by Bishop John Selwyn. The skit portrays events that have also been a focal episode in mission chronicles of church progress on Santa Isabel. As documented by a mission historian of the era,

[Soga] was wretchedly ill and weak . . . The Bishop wished him to try a mixture of quinine and brandy, which had acted as a charm on his patients at Tega. He was quite willing, so it was solemnly mixed before them all. "Taste it," said Hugo [the catechist], and the Bishop did so . . . This was meant to show that there were no occult influences. Then the Bishop told Soga that with God alone are the issues of life and death, and he prayed Him to bless the medicine. This done it was taken readily . . . Within a week Soga was about again; and from that time his gratitude, and, better still, his trust, were unbounded. He at once sent the Bishop a canoe full of presents, allowed a school to be started in his village, and sent boys that two might be chosen for Norfolk Island [catechist training]. Soga's history is fully dwelt on, for he was the most exceptional native the Mission has had to deal with, a born king and ruler of men. The Bishop's words about strength showing itself in mercy, spoken to one who only a month before had attacked and massacred a whole village, went home to him; and followed by what seemed to him a miraculous cure, had a great effect on the fortunes of the Mission in Ysabel.   (*Armstrong 1900: 251–2*)

As with the mission's historiography, the story of Soga is also "fully dwelt on" among local historians of the church, oral and written. As noted previously, even those concerned to inscribe localized chiefly genealogy may feel compelled to address the legend of Soga and its significance for customary forms of leadership (Naramana 1987). As a narrative of the historic origins of the paramount chief and, indeed, of the spread of Christianity throughout Santa Isabel, the story of Soga's conversion is fairly well known around the island, and is recounted prominently in one of the few publications on Santa Isabel by an indigenous writer, Dr. Ben Zeva, a former medical practitioner from the Kia area (Zeva 1983). Perhaps even shaped to some degree by written mission histories that educated islanders would encounter in church-run schools, the local versions have distilled historical detail into a more compact drama of miraculous cure and sudden conversion that turned Soga's mind and chiefly powers toward the work of evangelism.

In Zeva's account, Bishop Selwyn had been trying to convert Soga for a month when the chief became seriously ill, an affliction that could be ascribed to angry spirits or, as stated by Ben Zeva, the medical officer, "possibly malaria." After talking with Soga, Selwyn went back to his ship and returned the next day with some drugs ("possibly quinine"):

The feverish man agreed to drink the tablets, and the Bishop looked up to heaven, blessed the tablets and gave them to him. Three hours later the fever left him and Soga decided to return to Sepi. The following day the Bishop led his party to Sepi village and Soga sent out three warriors to inform him that Soga had decided to become a Christian.   (*Zeva 1983: 134*)

For Zeva, like the Sepi play, the element of Godly mana is inescapable, producing an instantaneous effect that led ultimately to total Christianization. The scenario sketched above relies upon some of the same assumptions about spirit power and causality that appear in the regional conversion narratives (chapter 7). It is specifically through the agency of spiritual intercession, mediated by the bishop's blessing, that Soga comes to experience the effectiveness of Christian practice and turns his own powers toward church work. Similarly, the climactic moment in the play came with Soga's sudden transformation at the moment of miraculous healing enacted by Bishop Selwyn blessing and administering the tablets of quinine. Even though the mission had been working extensively in several Bughotu villages prior to Soga's treatment in 1886, and even though Soga was not baptized until three years later, both the play and the published account imply a greater immediacy. Continuing from above, Zeva writes: "Soga demanded from the Bishop that his whole family be converted to Christianity, so the Bishop baptised the paramount chief and his wife, son and two other brothers" (1983: 134). This sort of condensation produces an historiography that is at once heroic and episodic. The origins of the church may now be dated: "Ninety-six per cent of the people on Isabel today belong to the Anglican community, which was started by Bishop Selwyn at Sepi village in 1886" (*ibid.*: 135). Indeed, the ceremonial installation to follow the next day would reproduce a similar version of episodic history.

As the play was going on in the middle of the expansive village ground, rehearsal of another drama, the installation of Tuti as paramount chief, was underway by lamplight only yards away in front of the church where the ceremony would take place the next day. The principal actors in that drama, Bishop Tuti, Archbishop Palmer and others, traced their parts as set out in a program prepared by Willie Betu. Betu had scripted the church service with key passages in the installation ceremony written out in some detail. This had then been printed in booklet form by the Church's Provincial Press in both Bughotu and English under the title *Na Book Bali Vatabuagna Ma Na Siuviagna Na Paramount Chief* (The Book For Blessing and Anointing the Paramount Chief).

The following day, Tuesday, July 8, was a full day of celebrations and ceremony. The day began with an elaborate outdoor church service lasting about two hours with numerous prayers, hymns and speeches. The centerpiece of the service was the "blessing and anointing" of Tuti as paramount chief. Following the service, Tuti, the paramount chief, was the recipient of a ritual presentation of turtle and other foodstuffs by people from his home region of Kia. This was followed by the distribution of food by the hosts so that people could eat as they watched the first of an entire afternoon of dances and dramatic performances. Every region had prepared some kind of performance for the occasion, and group after group of performers regaled the audience with dances and skits until late into the afternoon when most had to begin making their way back home.

The day began with a sunrise Communion service under clear skies in the open air of Sepi village. An altar had been set up next to the church in order to accommodate the large number of people. Those who presided later estimated that sacraments were served to 700 people on this occasion. The service was conducted by the two bishops (Tuti and Leonard) and the archbishop, flanked by all the clergy of the diocese seated in rows to each side of the altar. After Communion had been celebrated, Tuti the bishop re-emerged as Tuti the chief and was ritually installed as paramount chief. This portion of the ceremony consisted of speeches, prayers and gift-presentations that unfolded over the next forty-five minutes or so. The climax of the installation was the "anointment" of Tuti by the archbishop. The act of anointing Tuti as paramount chief not only ritually validated his passage to a new status, it in fact *recreated* the status (as ritual often does) as part of present social reality. After the anointment, Tuti re-emerged in full chiefly regalia and was ritually bestowed with the full range of roles and "powers" befitting the paramount chief through a series of gift presentations.

With Communion complete, a priest introduced the installation portion of the ceremony by reading a prefatory passage from the program. This introduction, read in the Bughotu language, framed the meaning of the event as a reinstantiation of principles first established with the conversion of Soga, the first paramount chief. An English version of the introductory remarks was also given in the printed program (Church of Melanesia 1975: 1):

Soga, before he converted to the Christian religion offered a human sacrifice to his god, by cutting off a child's head, and with his warriors drank the blood of the child to make his conversion to Christianity and renounce his allegiance to his god.

Soga turned his warlike spirit to win men and women for Christ. He made treaty of peace [*sic*] with all other chiefs to end warfare, and asked them to follow his religion.

Soga became the first Paramount Chief. On his death bed, he summoned some of his chiefs and subjects, and asked them to keep the Church teaching and the school; and to live in peace, and to care for the land and the sea.

Isabel has now realized their great leader's faith and aspirations. All our people are Christians, all our children have gone to schools, the island is being developed, and above all our people live in harmony and peacefully.

Here the meaning and authenticity of the paramount chief idea is found in the moment of Christian conversion, particularly in the conversion of the legendary Soga, portrayed just the preceding evening in the *thukma* play. That moment draws its significance from both sides of the transformation: from heathen violence and Christian peace. Like many of the stories of pre-Christian violence that circulate in Maringe communities, the contrast between heathen and Christian practices is drawn in stark and even grotesque imagery – that of decapitating a child. And, similar to local narratives of conversion such as those of the Knabu and Khakatio descendants, an episode of violence precedes the emergence of Christian peace. At the same time that a contrast between heathen violence and Christian peace is drawn, a fundamental continuity is also established. The violent acts of Soga and "his warriors" call attention to the transformative power of Christianity. Soga may have "renounced" "his god," but his "warlike spirit" is "turned" to the task of converting others to Christianity and, ironically, "ending warfare." The strength and vitality inherent in pre-Christian violence fuels the Christian transformation.

By installing a new paramount chief, the Sepi ceremony reproduces a mythic history that combines culturally salient themes of person, power and identity. Recalling the conversion of Soga derives the Christian present from the past and restates the church's saga as an accomplishment rather than a hope. Soga's aspirations for knowledge, peace and prosperity are now found in the fact that all Isabel people are Christian, living in peace, with children in schools and development underway.

The priest reading the introductory statement from the program continued:

It is our duty to perform the ninety-year-old ceremony handed down from Soga to his successors; and today our Chief Dudley Tuti will be blessed and anointed as his predecessors, and he will keep promises made by Soga:

1. That he will teach God's people through the Bible and His Church.
2. That he will maintain Law and Order for the Government of his people.
3. That he will take care of his people's land and sea.

Here the historical origins of the paramount chief are spelled out more explicitly. The institution is said to have its origins with Soga, ninety years ago, so that the Sepi ceremony is defined as replicating events and promises "handed down" through Soga's successors to the person of "Chief Dudley Tuti." The promises are enumerated as three leadership roles in church, government and local community (as caretaker of "people's land and sea"). This trilogy, reflecting conceptual dimensions that underlie contemporary images of leadership (chapter 9), was the major motif for the ritual installation to follow, combining disparate elements of sociopolitical structure in the person of the paramount chief. The above preamble and the ritual enactment that followed sought to create understandings of the paramount chief based on a model of chiefly leadership that could incorporate and mediate the opposed spheres of church and government.

While the introductory statement was being read, Tuti had retired out of sight to change from his bishop's cape and mitre to ordinary dress for the next phase of the ceremony. With the preamble complete, he was then ushered in for the anointment by a group of ten chiefs from all around the island. Like Tuti, all were dressed simply in shorts and shirts. In this manner, Tuti's identity as a "chief" among other chiefs was highlighted just at the moment of ritual transition that would see his status elevated to a position of paramountcy. With Tuti in the lead, the group of chiefs entered the altar area from the side and walked to "center stage" where they stood, with backs to the audience, facing Archbishop Palmer and Bishop Leonard, both dressed in colorful flowing robes.

Tuti then stepped forward and knelt with bowed head in front of the archbishop. The climactic moment of the ceremony, the elevation of Tuti to

Plate 14 Archbishop Norman Palmer and Bishop Leonard Alufurai anoint Dudley Tuti Paramount Chief, Sepi village (July 8, 1975)

the status of paramount chief, was about to occur, validated in the Christian idiom of "anointment" or "blessing." With Bishop Leonard standing to one side, the archbishop, reading in English, then led Tuti through a series of questions and answers pertaining to each of the "promises" outlined above. As the archbishop read each question, Tuti, answering in the Bughotu language, vowed to perform each role in the trilogy. Following the taking of vows, the archbishop read a prayer followed by everyone joining in saying the Lord's Prayer. With this scene complete, the status transition of Tuti from "chief" to "paramount chief" was effectively accomplished. What followed was a series of ritual transactions in which the meaning of the position was further elaborated, especially in terms of the church/government/tradition triumvirate.

After having been anointed, Tuti left the altar area as the audience sang a hymn together, marking the close of that portion of the ceremony. A few minutes later Tuti the paramount chief, dressed in the traditional regalia of an important chief, reappeared seated in a covered divan chair carried aloft by four "warriors." The warriors, walking to the accompaniment of rhythmic drumming, carried Tuti to center stage where they placed the chair on the ground, facing the audience. Here the producers of the event had crafted a marvelous visual realization of the image of the *kastom* chief, and an important chief at that. All the accoutrements of the scene – Tuti's physical appearance, the paramount chief's chair and the two rather fierce looking armed warriors standing on either side – combined to project a portrait of the traditional chief, the culmination of the process of recreating a "ninety-year-old tradition."

As the paramount chief, Tuti wore a tapa cloth waistcloth and exceptionally fine body decorations made of shell and porpoise teeth. A porpoise teeth belt and strands of shell-money criss-crossed his upper body, a circular clamshell ornament hung on his chest and shell armlets graced both arms. Apparently, no shell-disc could be found to wear on his forehead, so one had been woven with dyed fibre for the occasion. The warriors stood poised with axes and shields on both sides of Tuti's divan chair. With their bodies daubed with powdered lime and wearing only loincloths, these *kastom* guards personified the image of stereotypic "strong men." The chair, made of wood and woven bamboo, was typical of those that have been used in Isabel (at least through the colonial period) to carry prestigious guests aloft upon their arrival at a feast or celebration. In this case, it was an apt symbol for the act of installation – an act referred to metaphorically by some as "seating," *fagnohgnokro.*

With Tuti seated facing the audience, holding his glasses and a copy of the program so that he could read his part, the next phase of the ceremony unfolded as a sequence of gift presentations. Each gift, a metonym of power in a particular sphere of activity, was presented by someone identified with that sphere. The sequence of three gifts spanned areas of social activity framed in the introductory statement: church, government and indigenous locale. Bishop Leonard made the first presentation, followed by the president of the Isabel council, and finally a woman offering tokens of identification with "the land and sea." The presentations by leaders in church and government were particularly significant since they symbolically legitimized the paramount chief's titular involvement in both institutional spheres. And it was here that the potential for controversy lay just beneath the surface. Some of the young councilors who had decided not to recognize the paramount chief formally were "boycotting" the ceremony and disagreed particularly with the act of ritual deference in which the council president was called upon to make one of the gift presentations.[3] But given that all the senior Isabel big-men in domains of both church and government were lined up behind the installation, his participation was never seriously in doubt.

Invented ritual tends toward self-conscious sophistication, leaving little to the interpretive imagination. In the gift-giving sequence, each presentation framed its own significance with an accompanying utterance to the effect: "Take this symbol of activity X." The gifts of government and indigenous leadership were even labeled "symbols" in the written program.

The gift-giving began with Bishop Leonard of Malaita standing before the seated paramount chief and handing him a Bible. As he did so, the bishop said in English: "Take this Bible and teach your people with God's holy words through his church." The bishop's directive restated the proposition implicit in the anointment that had just taken place: the paramount chief derives knowledge, power and moral authority from the church. (The fact that the paramount chief was also bishop obviated questions about how this role would be constituted in practice.)

The second (and potentially more controversial) presentation was made without incident by the president of the council. The items written into the script as tokens of government involvement were an axe and shield. Following the same procedure as the bishop before him, with the added touch of kneeling instead of standing, the president offered up the axe and shield with the words: "Take these as a symbol of peace, that you maintain law and order for the good government of our people." In an apparent inversion of their usual meaning in legend and song, the "axe and shield" presented to the paramount chief on this occasion were said to be a "symbol of peace" – but nonetheless signifying the sort of activity that would "maintain law and order."

The third and final presentation was made by a woman who knelt before the paramount chief and offered him several locally produced items identified with the productive activities of gardening and fishing. These gifts consisted of a net bag and pandanus mat (commonly used to carry garden produce) and a fishing net. As objects of indigenous manufacture, these symbolized customary knowledge (*kastom*) and, specifically, the value-laden symbol of land with its important connotations of descent and locale. Through the woman's words to the paramount chief, the scripted exegesis itself stated: "Take these. They are a symbol of your authority to rule your people's land and sea." Here the core of indigenous leadership is identified with power over productive resources – increasingly the source of local conflict in the age of commercial development.

Although not part of the written script, a final presentation was made by a representative of the chief minister of the Solomon Islands, Solomon Mamaloni (first chief minister of the self-governing country just prior to independence). David Kausimae, a prominent politician from Malaita and member of the national governing council, had made the trip to Sepi from Honiara with Willie Betu and other dignitaries. He took his turn in the gift-giving sequence by standing before Tuti and presenting him with a decorated walking stick – a token of chiefly authority and priestly mana. In making his presentation, Kausimae read from a letter sent by the chief minister recognizing Tuti as paramount chief of Santa Isabel. In line with Willie Betu's key role in the entire paramount chief episode, Mamaloni's gift here signaled strong rhetorical support among national politicians for the emergent discourse of *kastom*. The Kausimae/Mamaloni contribution to the ceremony neatly validated the inter-island role for the paramount chief as a representative for Santa Isabel as a whole in the evolving area of national politics. Presenting the walking stick as a gift created the necessary external context in which the paramount chief could be seen as the totem for an emergent island-wide identity constructed in relations with "significant others" from other islands and nations.

The church service, with its climactic events of anointing and celebrating the paramount chief, concluded at this point with a brief sermon, prayers and a hymn. The sermon was given in Solomons Pidgin by a priest from the Russell Islands, after which the paramount chief led the Lord's Prayer in the Bughotu language. This was followed by Bishop Leonard saying a concluding prayer in English. The installation ceremony was then brought to a close with nearly everyone joining in a Bughotu hymn.

Following the closing hymn, the scene of activity shifted to the shoreline where men from Tuti's home region of Kia put on their own ritual acknowledgement of Tuti's status as paramount chief. Adopting the format traditionally used to mark the return of a turtle-hunting expedition, two canoes full of warriors and food offerings came ashore to present Tuti with several live turtle and baskets of food. As the canoes could be seen approaching from seaward, Tuti was carried in the divan chair to await their arrival nearer to shore. As the large crowd of people looked on, the two "war canoes" filled with men dressed as warriors paddled to shore as another Kia warrior performed a ritual welcome by prancing up and down the shoreline, gesticulating with his spear and shield, and calling out in the Kia language. Once the canoes had landed, the warriors, bearing axes, shields and spears, began carrying the large turtles up the beach in single file. Each offering was placed in front of the seated paramount chief, and then followed by a loud display of bravado in which the warrior would let out a yell and take a wild swipe with his axe at a banana tree implanted in the sand for the occasion. This type of posturing is said by Kia people to be the traditional manner in which returning warriors (or turtle-hunters) would demonstratively present the spoils of a good hunt. (It did not take many swipes before the banana tree was reduced to a short stump.)

The performance of ritual practices associated with the pre-Christian past effectively located the paramount chief in the domain of *kastom*. Turtle-hunting, once associated with headhunting expeditions, for example, carries particularly potent connotations of customary power and (male) strength. As people from other regions took turns during the remainder of the day putting on the dances and skits that they had prepared for the occasion, the theme of indigenous, customary practice emerged repeatedly. In the case of several performances, this consisted of "*kastom* dances" such as men's war dances in which two lines of men holding axes and shields move their way across the dance ground with slow up-and-down swaying movements accompanied by rhythmic chanting. Two *thukma* skits also recreated visual portraits of the ways of the past. In one of them, people from Togasalo and surrounding villages enacted the primordial scenario of human sacrifice that had been described for me by Forest and Josepa during my walk through the Knabu forest. And here was Josepa acting the part of the custom priest, complete with sharpened bamboo knives! This skit replayed an entire sequence of events depicting the significance of ancestral (human) sacrifice as a way of dealing with crisis in the past. The play began with a narrator informing the crowd that people of this group were getting sick, so the custom priest (Josepa) would use a divination device to consult with his ancestor spirits about what to do. Having done this and discovered that a human victim sacrificed at the shrine was required to dispel people's misfortunes, a party then enacted a raid and capture of a victim who was summarily brought back and subjected to the priest's knife for sacrifice. The other notable skit offered as part of the afternoon's entertainment was the conversion drama performed by the Nggela people described in chapter 7. As noted earlier, in this skit the performers re-enacted the first missionary encounter and subsequent conversion of their ancestors. While the Sepi celebration was overtly an occasion for celebrating Christian (and Isabel island) identity, this was accomplished through performances that displayed localized identities through the distinctive practices and histories of particular regions.

Many of the social meanings to emerge from the Sepi ceremony appear to be both transparent and self-conscious. Certainly the scripted anointment with its printed commentary about "symbols" of chiefly roles tells a story of reintegration that resonates with many of the historical and cultural processes discussed throughout this book. But, beyond the melding of church mana, government strength and local legitimacy that emerges from the ceremony as text, the ritual process yields an additional reading centered upon Tuti the person and bishop. Overtly, the ceremony was a rite of passage in which Tuti passed from the status of chief to that of paramount chief. When Tuti was anointed, he stepped forward from among the ranks of *chiefs*. However, as everyone present well understood, and as was vividly dramatized during the prior Communion service, it was not simply Tuti the chief, but Tuti the *bishop* who was installed as paramount chief. If one looks at the church service as a whole, Tuti may be seen to have undergone two status transitions signified by his dress and role performance that marked passages from bishop to chief and then chief to paramount chief. He began the service as a bishop, wearing a striking tapa cloth robe and mitre, presiding over Communion. It was after that, in the middle phase of the ceremony, that Tuti reappeared as a traditional chief standing among other chiefs, dressed in shorts and shirt, so that he could be elevated from their ranks to the position of paramount chief.

Even though the installation was conducted as if *any* chief could have been anointed paramount chief, the fact that it was Tuti the bishop makes for a considerably more powerful story of transformation. It is, in particular, a transformation that may be read as an inversion of the elements of *kastom* and Christianity that underlie the Soga myth and, indeed, the entire genre of conversion narratives discussed in chapters 7 and 8. In the Soga story, the chief's conversion represents the transition from chief to Christian chief. But for Tuti the bishop, the paramount chief rite constitutes a passage from Christian leader (bishop) to chief. Whereas the story of the conversion of Monilaws Soga offers a mythic resolution of the opposition of *kastom* and Christianity in a narrative of original transformation, the Sepi ceremony uses that story to create a new narrative of revitalization appropriate to the contemporary situation. In and of itself, the social meanings encoded in the Soga myth would not be sufficient to rationalize and compel its reproduction in such grand form in contemporary Santa Isabel. However, the presence of Dudley Tuti with his unique combination of personal history and bishop's status permitted an innovative recombination of elements of self and history that work in the contemporary context – a context in which talk of *kastom* by national politicians preparing for independence created an opportunity for the rhetorical melding of church, government and "tradition" in a single ceremony.

"... in our own culture"

Just as the discussions and plans leading up to the Sepi ceremony revealed multiple points of view, so subsequent interpretations of the significance of the paramount chief were quite varied. While some entertained notions that the ceremony might signal real change in the current government setup, others saw it as a symbolic act, a way of dramatizing Tuti's status as a traditional leader and elevating him and Santa Isabel to greater prominence throughout the Solomons. In either case, the ceremony expressed themes that run long and deep in Isabel social history. Subsequent events indicate that the implications of this most recent instantiation of paramount chieftainship for the local political economy have yet to unfold fully.

People in the Maringe area showed considerable enthusiasm for the new paramount chief idea during the months following the Sepi ceremony. One moment of expression of this came just a few days after the Sepi ceremony, when the people of Buala organized a surprise welcome for Tuti as he returned to his house at Jejevo near Buala. The local clergy took the lead in organizing the welcome as Fr. Hugo Kmudu (the narrator of the *bina boli* skit in chapter 7) convened a village meeting to work out plans for a ceremonial greeting. Fr. Kmudu laid out a "script" for a ritual welcome that, like the Sepi ceremony itself, retraced the transition from heathen violence to Christian love by first challenging Tuti at beachside in the manner of armed warriors, and then leading him through various welcoming activities until arriving at his house where he would be regaled with Christian hymns. As Fr. Kmudu explained the rationale for the ceremony, he was quite explicit about the symbolism of all this as representing the move from "heathens who used to kill people and fight" (*bongihehe, mae te fa'aknu naikno, te magra*) to the "peaceful ways" (*puhi blakno*) of "Christian persons."

Prior to Tuti's return to Jejevo, nearly one hundred people from Buala gathered at the shoreline for the occasion. It was about 7.30 o'clock at night and dark when he finally arrived on the church ship *Ebb Tide*. As Tuti was paddled in from the ship anchored in the lagoon, he was met by the shouts of several warriors dancing on the beach dressed in loincloths and brandishing shields and spears, yelling out rhetorical challenges like "Who dares to come to our land?", punctuated by the trumpeting of a conch shell. As the paramount chief stepped out of the canoe that had carried him ashore, one of the warriors took him by the hand and led him to a decorated divan chair that was waiting to carry him aloft to his house. He was first carried to the second stage of the welcome midway between the shore and his house where a festive group was performing a *gleghi* dance and song. A spokesman for this group welcomed Tuti with a gift of betel nut, similar to the scene in the Buala *thukma* where the returning Christians were welcomed by friendly heathens with gifts of food.

As the ritual event progressed from beach to bishop's house, from heathen to Christian, Tuti was finally carried to his own house where he was greeted by the practiced voices of the Buala choir singing Christian hymns. Next, as he settled in a chair on his porch, the choir sang a special greeting song that had been composed by Hugo Kmudu, followed by the ritual presentation of a series of three gifts, again symbolizing the various leadership roles of the paramount chief. The welcoming song, although quite simple, concludes with a stanza that underscores the meaning of the event as welcoming Tuti *as paramount chief*, using the English language terminology to refer to this new status:

Cheke fakeli ni God	Give thanks to God
Eigna noda funei ulu	For our leading chief
Te thoke mei gognaro	Who has now arrived
Tahati gle'a rahngi ni	We all are happy for him
Ka mei gna gognaro gne	Because of his return now
Noda funei nafnakno na	Our renowned chief
Ka iagho u baubatu re	With you there is leadership
Ka iagho u nahma re	With you there is love
Mala di u thumu gre	For these children of yours [us]
God te togho nigho na	It is God who helps you
God te fablahi nigho na	It is God who blesses you
Mala di u nou gloku re	So that you may do your work
Welcome nigho paramount chief	Welcome you, paramount chief
Ka narane gognaro gne	On this day today
Hoe, hoe paramount chief	Hoe, hoe paramount chief

With the song completed, Fr. Kmudu then gave a short welcoming speech to Tuti as both bishop and paramount chief, followed by gift presentations given by three different men in sequence. The first to walk up on the porch was a man dressed in a loincloth, that ubiquitous index of *kastom* identity.

He presented Tuti with a conch shell and proceeded to explain that it represented the power of the chief to call people together and organize collective activities like hunting and fishing expeditions. The second gift offered by the next presenter was a (steering) paddle, said to represent the leader's role in guiding people in the proper direction. Finally, the last presentation was a broom, indicating Tuti's moral leadership in keeping persons and the church free of "dirt" (usually taken to mean sexual transgressions). With the gift presentations complete, the welcome concluded itself, as so many honorific events do, with a custom borrowed from more distant shores – a hearty "three cheers."

With the ceremonies at an end, Tuti, visibly moved by the unexpected welcome, addressed the people assembled in front of his house. Seated in the lamplight on his porch, he spoke in English about his view of the paramount chief status that had just been bestowed upon him. His words, given in slightly edited form below, were translated into Cheke Holo by Fr. Kmudu.

Last week we enthroned the paramount chief. And it fell on me. But I want you to remember there are two sides to any position. One is only the high position. And human beings, they're always looking for a high rank, a high position . . . The other side is "What is the result of that position?" If it is only the high position, I will refuse to take it. But, "what will be the result of this position?" And this is why I accept it. "What is the result of this position?" Well, finding out about our tradition, our custom, our culture. Well, that is one of the things. Because I know very well if we only base our thinking, our progress in our own culture, we will go forward. But not what our grandfathers used to do. But whatever we do in the future, base it in our own culture. Then we must make progress. The other thing is unity. Maybe in all our chiefs before, there were different kinds of paramount chief. Maybe there was hatred in them. And there were people who grab people's property . . . And now we are in the Christianity . . . And this is probably one of the jobs of the paramount chief, to unite the people. What separates people? And what sort of things separate us from other people? Many many times it is about land. Many many times about other things which are very bad in our way . . . So now I'm going to use these gifts not to call people for war, not to call people so we can raid other people. But we have got to call people together for unity, and also for peace, and for things to make progress.

As Tuti stated it on this occasion, the paramount chief is part of a discourse of "culture" or "tradition." He talks about "our tradition, our custom, our culture" – of basing future plans "in our own culture." But his talk on the subject of tradition is multifaceted, evoking images of negation ("things which are very bad in our way") as much as continuity and authenticity. The tradition to be utilized by the paramount chief is "not what our grandfathers used to do" but something to be found in post-Christian society, where unity and peace are seen to have emerged in opposition to conditions of divisiveness and hostility. So the paramount chief is at once an exemplar of tradition and a guardian of Christian moral ideals – someone who is an active and creative synthesizer of past and present. Tuti here draws with apparent ease from concepts of both *kastom* and Christianity to construct images of shared identity, with the "new way" providing a kind of tempering or countervailing influence on *kastom*, selectively implementing desired aspects of tradition in the moral ideals of the day. The possibility of reconciling these often oppositional facets of identity is, I suggest, an important basis for the socioemotional appeal of the paramount chief idea today.

During the year following the Sepi ceremony, the revival of the paramount chief status in the person of Dudley Tuti also served to direct attention and interest to the role of chiefs in island affairs. As a sign of his new status, Tuti would occasionally wear a clam-shell pendant along with his bishop's cross when appearing on public occasions. A 1979 article in the *Pacific Islands Monthly* magazine reporting on an historic visit of the Archbishop of Canterbury to the Solomon Islands referred to Tuti as "paramount chief" of Santa Isabel and pictured him wearing both his bishop's cross and chiefly pendant.

As Tuti pursued his usual activities as bishop, he frequently addressed the role of chiefs in the ubiquitous meetings and speeches that were already his lot as an influential leader accustomed to speaking to all manner of social, political and economic issues. Village leaders, for their part, continued to talk about familiar problems of "recognition." For example, at one meeting chaired by Tuti following the dedication of a new church in the western end of the island, several speakers said they desired some way of acknowledging chiefs so they would be "recognized outside" their villages. By the end of the year, Tuti was referring to the paramount chief position as "not yet complete" and talking of the need to formalize some arrangement for the participation of chiefs in government. Chapter 4 described the large Christmas feast at which Tuti was the guest of honour as both bishop and paramount chief. After he had been suitably welcomed with warrior challenges, gift-giving, singing and speechmaking, Tuti gave his own speech in reply. At the end of those remarks (speaking in English, with translation) he alluded briefly to his view of the future of the paramount chiefship and its significance as part of a general move to revise the status of local chiefs in local political life:

Then, last of all, people ask me, "what is your job as a paramount chief?" Not only our people, but other people, including Europeans. But my answer is this. [The] paramount chief is not yet completed. What we have done this year at Sepi is only a beginning. There are other people in every area, in every village who are chiefs in their right. People look up to them . . . So those [chiefs] got to be recognized first. They are still here. But because we are misled by the new election of members in the council, head people in the districts. But you know them. In the village you know them. In the district you know them. So those people got to be brought back. And let us recognize them. Then the paramount chief and those chiefs in the area, chiefs in the village, they will work together to help their people.

As mentioned before, ideas about instituting a "system of chiefs" were circulating in some quarters prior to the Sepi ceremony. Willie Betu, for one, had sketched such a plan in his document. When I talked with him at Sepi village the day before the installation ceremony, he indicated that he could foresee the possibility of the paramount chief setting a precedent for new forms of provincial government that might emerge after independence. In his view, the position could be a prototype for a kind of provincial governor. Tuti had voiced a similar view before the Sepi ceremony. He had envisioned the paramount chief as part of an island-wide body of traditional chiefs representing each "district." He had also speculated about the possibility of these chiefs, with the paramount chief, forming the government council. Once Tuti was recognized as paramount chief, he began thinking somewhat more concretely, saying to me, for example, that he wanted to convene a meeting of chiefs from each "district," possibly seven in number, who would meet to discuss matters of *kastom* and "development." In 1980 Tuti announced his retirement as bishop (set for 1982) and gave as one of his reasons his interest in devoting more time to the work of the paramount chief. Events since that time have seen these visions gradually take shape, although the gap between the activities of chiefs and the institutions of government remains a continuing source of contradiction.

Just at the time that Tuti was retiring as Bishop of Santa Isabel, he began a collaboration that proved to be important in enabling a new discourse of chiefs and *kastom*. In each manifestation of the paramount chief, alliance between the aspiring chief and one or more persons who occupy positions of influence in colonial institutions has been an important ingredient in supporting the position and linking it with encapsulating structures of power. In this case, in the post-independence Solomon Islands, that person has been Dennis Lulei who served as one of the island's two members of parliament from 1980 to 1988. Lulei was one of the first Isabel people to receive a university degree and, after he was elected, sought out Tuti to jointly formulate plans for developing a "system of chiefs" under the aegis of the paramount chief.

During the 1980s Tuti and Lulei led efforts to create a "Council of Chiefs" that would offer a modern style quasi-bureaucratic structure for involving chiefs in the management of island affairs. Much of the interest in formalizing political roles for "traditional chiefs" during this period, and continuing to the present, is connected with the formidable problems and conflicts surrounding land ownership. With new possibilities for commercial development in the form of mining, forestry and even fisheries fueling divisive disputes about land, local political leaders have sought ways of resolving land conflicts. Since the chief is above all else a spokesman for land-owning descent groups, talk of somehow formalizing the chief's status in government aims at producing a codified or legalized discourse of chiefly pronouncements that will carry weight in the contexts of national law. Space does not allow a close accounting of the process by which the idea of a Council of Chiefs has taken shape as a political reality in Santa Isabel. However, a brief sketch will indicate the level of interest and activity that has been sustained during recent years. The picture that emerges is one of a continually evolving discussion about how to go about instituting the new structure. Even now, years after a 1984 meeting billed as the "first meeting of the Council of Chiefs," details of its composition and responsibilities are in flux.

A large "meeting of chiefs" attended by the premier of the provincial assembly and the new Bishop of Santa Isabel (among others) convened near Tuti's house in Jejevo in April 1983. That meeting discussed a plan to form a Council of Chiefs by having each of five areas or "districts" select a representative chief. Within a year, the first meeting of the Council of Chiefs was held at Jejevo in March of 1984, a meeting also attended by the provincial premier and secretary. This time the number of districts was expanded to six and the selection was left up to the paramount chief.

The relation of this nascent Council of Chiefs to the existing institutions of government remains open to numerous interpretations and possibilities. Even before the Council of Chiefs had been constituted, the central body of provincial government, the Isabel provincial assembly made up of fifteen elected members, passed a resolution in 1984 allowing for the "Council of Chiefs" to select six persons, one from each of six districts, to participate in assembly meetings as "appointed members." In the next assembly meeting in June 1984, just a few months after the first Council of Chiefs meeting, the assembly passed a "Council of Chiefs" resolution that began, "BE IT RESOLVED that the Isabel provincial assembly recognize the existence and traditional role of the council of chiefs, their powers with respect to matters of tradition and custom . . ." This document went on to enumerate areas where chiefs exercise power in local life, focusing mainly on land and genealogy. Beyond that, the document spelled out the role of the Council of Chiefs as essentially "promoting traditions and customs" and "making recommendations" to the various bodies of local government.

Although the provincial premier and others indicated at an early stage that a portion of the provincial budget was earmarked for support of travel by the chiefs, so far financial support has not materialized through bureaucratic channels. And the extent to which new powers may in fact devolve to chiefs through this current process remains uncertain. But, to examine this resurgence of talk about chiefs and *kastom* only in the context of post-colonial political institutions would miss the more fundamental point that the *process* of meeting, discussing, planning and creating does itself constitute a new discourse, or reconfigured set of truths, of the type envisioned by those who talk of a role for chiefs in island affairs.

Once plans had been laid in the arena of provincial government in 1984, Tuti and Lulei began traveling to every district to convene meetings for the selection of "district chiefs" who would constitute district-level councils analogous to the provincial government's "area councils." In a manner much like Fallowes' campaign to institute church chiefs in the 1930s, these selections were then ritually validated in a church service in which Tuti, the retired bishop, would bless the chiefs and give them certificates signed by him as paramount chief. But these meetings did more than select chiefs. They also provided a new set of contexts for local-level discussions of sociopolitical issues that have always taken place, but are now shaped by the global rhetoric of economic "development." These latest meetings or "conferences" convene in situations defined self-consciously as a congregation of chiefs led by a paramount chief and a parliamentarian. Meetings and festivities organized under the aegis of the "Council of Chiefs" externalize idealized understandings of person, community and leadership that resonate more closely with local models than the more bureaucratic discourse of a modern nation state. But their inventive, hybrid form, incorporating much from national institutions and the idioms of modernity, is by no means fixed or uncontested. When I participated in one of the meetings led by Lulei and Tuti in 1987 to bless chiefs from one of the districts and, at the same time, convene a "development seminar," one of the participants grumbled to me that he was confused by much of the talk on this occasion (much of it from "experts" invited from various government ministries speaking on development issues), and felt that many others in the host village were as well.

During recent years talk of *kastom* is common in major ceremonial occasions attended by national and foreign dignitaries. For example, the day chosen to mark the provincial government's anniversary is now also designated as a "chiefs' day." And, in March of 1987, the Prime Minister of the Solomon Islands, Ezekiel Alebua, was invited along with other national dignitaries to the "annual convention of chiefs" held at the Bughotu village of Nagolau. The attendance of the Prime Minister at the 1987 chiefs' day mirrored the presence of a representative of the chief minister at the paramount chief ceremony in 1975 who ceremonially presented the new paramount chief with a walking stick as a gift from the chief minister. In both cases, national politicians act to recognize and affirm the importance of "traditional chiefs" and Santa Isabel's new paramount chief in particular. On these occasions, talk of *kastom* conjoins national and local political discourse.

As previous chapters have shown, attempts to formulate a more satisfying set of relations between local communities and surrounding structures of power have been continuing at least from the time of the first Soga, especially during the period of Fallowes and the church chiefs. Just as strong sentiments about Christianity and *kastom* fueled attempts at revitalization in the 1930s, so they continue to be articulated today in efforts to recreate the paramount chiefship and re-examine relations between chiefs and government. As this chapter has made clear, a distinctive feature of the Santa Isabel paramount chiefship (in the person of Dudley Tuti and in previous incarnations) is its ability to encompass elements of both indigenous *kastom* and Christianity, providing a somewhat unique set of political possibilities for leaders who combine the authority of church and tradition. However, as Loiskandl (1988: 126) notes for Melanesian Christianity in general, sentiments about the importance of indigenous tradition, and about church leaders as guardians of tradition, are widespread in the region. As seen not only elsewhere in Melanesia but in the priest-politicians of Latin America and Africa as well, there is considerable political potential in the role of those who represent and promote a unified cultural identity in an otherwise fragmented field of meaning and power.

11

Conclusion

The separate paths often taken by cultural histories and ethnographies of the self tend to produce either semiotic interpretations devoid of experience or psychological accounts removed from social and political process. This book has suggested avenues of rapprochement. The approach taken here to the Santa Isabel paramount chief ceremony, as well as to quieter forms of historical discourse, suggests that narratives of the past do pragmatic work as cultural tools building both self-understanding and sociopolitical realities.

A common criticism of structuralist analyses is that the search for coherence and pattern in cultural forms leaves them ungrounded in the varied particulars of either individual cognition or social practice. The tenuous connection between structural model and social or psychological reality has on occasion evoked skeptical criticism from the uninitiated. For example, a recent book dealer's catalogue commented that a new volume of Polynesian studies "in the structuralist mode" has "much to ponder, little to accept as not a reflection of each author's mind rather than of Polynesian social ways present or past" (*Cellar Book Shop* 422: 8, cited in Marcus 1988: 111). Whereas the poststructuralist response to this and other critiques is to subsume problems of mind or subjectivity within broader historically based discourses of power, the tack taken in this book has been to locate subjectivity in discourse by examining directly the practices that produce collective self-understanding. In pursuing this tack, I have argued that narrative constructions of the past are a central, probably universal, mode of self-representation that is also constitutive of social relations. Where such recollection is enacted in collective, even ritualized practices of remembrance, past events become history as they are enshrined in socially produced narratives. In considering the diverse practices of self-representation in Santa Isabel, the salience of narratives of conversion to Christianity emerges again and again. Asking what these stories are about, and why they are told and retold in a variety of contexts and genres, leads to readings that are at once socioemotional and sociopolitical.

Noting that conversion narratives focus upon heroic ancestors who first incorporated Christian knowledge, mana and peace reveals their multiple meanings in reproducing both localized identities and generalized conceptions of Christian identity. The portraits of chiefly strength and Christian mana that emerge in moments of first contact between violent heathen and peaceful missionaries crystallize concepts of person and power that also have relevance in relation to contemporary concerns with vulnerability and conflict in everyday life. Identity constructs such as the "Christian person" or the "good chief" have moral force because they build upon more basic understandings of experience at the same time as they work to define collective realities. In the case of the paramount chief, the overtly syncretic quality of the category opens up possibilities for reconfiguring relations between localized identities and the institutions of church and state.

As the status has been reconstituted in each historical epoch, its meaning has been refracted somewhat differently by shifting institutional forces. In the era of conversion the emergence of Christian chiefs provided the conceptual and political bridge necessary to institutionalize Christianity through the established power and authority of chiefs. Since the new religion challenged the traditional premises of their moral authority and personal power, Christian status offered new sources of legitimacy. In this context, the first paramount chief, Soga, became an agent of Christianity who personified the heathen-to-Christian transformation. But, once the mission society was well established, Christian chiefs receded in prominence, entering into positions of co-leadership with mission catechists and priests who gradually replaced them as new sources of knowledge, power and moral authority. In this context, with the expansion of the colonial regime in the 1920s and 1930s, the notion of Christian chiefs was renewed with the invention of "church chiefs," again through alliance with mission leaders, only this time seeking to bolster the influence of the church vis-à-vis the government. Here the paramount chief emerged in quasi-bureaucratic guise as a counterpart to the district government headman, and ultimately became part of the parliament movement challenging the colonial regime.

In the most recent instance, coming at a point when indigenous leaders were rising to positions of power in colonial institutions on the eve of national independence, the status is instantiated more overtly in terms of its integrative functions through the person of Dudley Tuti. This time the politically and ceremonially orchestrated revival of the paramount chief highlighted elements of tradition or *kastom* by seeking connections between chiefship and the institutions of church and state. At this juncture in history, one hundred years after Soga was baptized, the facet of the paramount chief status that is foregrounded is not that of Christian identity (the recipient was *already* bishop), but a reinvigorated traditionalism. Installing such a powerful figure as Bishop Tuti as a *chief* signaled the opening round of another era of efforts to reconstrue the place of traditional practices in contemporary life, and refigure the relations among key dimensions of identity and experience.

Tuti's installation must be seen in the context of regional efforts to find paramount chiefs in many of the islands that make up the newly independent Solomon Islands. During the year following the Sepi ceremony, parallel events were unfolding in the Kwara'ae area of neighboring Malaita. Three paramount chiefs were selected in West Kwara'ae (David Gegeo, personal communication) and numerous others in the eastern district. These activities led to a major meeting at Auki on Malaita in 1978 at which some 180 men were designated as "chiefs" to act as upholders of *kastom* (Burt 1982: 393–4). These activities continue today in other areas where attempts are being made to reconstruct positions of chiefly leadership. In June of 1988 about 4,000 people from Guadalcanal attended a ceremony to install the outgoing Governor General of the Solomon Islands, Sir Baddeley Devesi, as paramount chief of the Tasimboko area of that island. And in that same year local leaders on Nggela, seeking to model their efforts on the experience of Santa Isabel, invited paramount chief Dudley Tuti to speak to them at a meeting devoted to discussing plans for "chiefs" and "paramount chiefs" in their society. And, extending the scope of regional influences even further, Tuti and member of parliament Lulei were planning a trip to Fiji to learn about their Council of Chiefs when the military coup in that country in 1987, backed by the Council of Chiefs, led them to abort their plans.

As previously noted, these various regional efforts to revitalize "traditional chiefs" are legitimated in national politics by periodic statements by elected officials affirming their importance for local government. Beginning with the governing council before independence, and recorded in a constitutional provision acknowledging "the role of traditional chiefs" (Section 114[2]), the topic of chiefly leadership was recently given further attention by a national committee established to review the structure of provincial government. This committee devoted a chapter of its report to "The desire to involve Chiefs and Traditional Leaders more fully in the process of Government at both Provincial and rural levels of Solomon Islands Community" (*Report of the Provincial Government Review Committee, 1986–1987*, pp. 63–7). In this part of their report, the authors attempted to address the inherently contradictory problem of formalizing relations between the highly personal, variable and informal roles of village leaders – "chiefs" – within the formal and legal apparatus of a modern

bureaucracy. Terms such as *kastom* and "chief" are abstract and polysemous (Keesing and Tonkinson 1982). Their multiple meanings allow these
constructs to be used rhetorically by national politicians and still be applied
in a great variety of ways at the local level. The Santa Isabel paramount
chief presents a case in point. Although Tuti himself invoked the national
agenda of promoting traditional chiefs as a rationale for the Sepi ceremony,
the meaning of the installation ritual for most participants derived from a
complex array of understandings of person and history specific to local
cultures and histories.

In the Sepi ceremony, it was not so much Tuti who acquired power from
the status as the status that was revived by Tuti. The category is reinvented
by installing *it* in a person who combines most of the key facets of the
mythic history of the Santa Isabel paramount chief. In cognitive terms, his
instantiation of the category is *prototypic*, encompassing all of its major
features in a single instance. As a "chief," he combines both the personal
reputation and the genealogical criteria of chiefly status. As a Christian he is
the pre-eminent spiritual and moral leader for the island, occupying the
status of bishop at the time of his installation. And in his own personal
history of involvement in island-wide development activities, Tuti more
than anyone during previous decades extended the person-centered style of
community leadership to the island as a whole. Although Tuti and others
talk as if any prominent chief could become paramount chief, his presence
is a necessary ingredient in the current manifestation, especially as manifested in a single person.

The impression of cultural homogeneity given by global social descriptions (or individuated psychological ones) tends to obscure elements of
dissonance, ambivalence or contention that are central to the pragmatics of
identity constructs (Wallace 1967). The events surrounding the Sepi
ceremony not only revealed considerable diversity in understandings of the
paramount chief status, they showed that it is an object of self-conscious
debate about identity and power – debates that are "argued" through
differing readings of history. The sources of variation and dissension range
from the young councilors who rejected the idea and even "boycotted" the
ceremony, to innumerable conversations among villagers who wondered
about the validity of a status that claims power extending throughout the
entire island.

Despite the nearly universal popularity of Tuti as a leader, voices of
ambivalence may still be heard regarding efforts to "revive the system of
chiefs" by the paramount chief and others. During recent fieldwork in 1988
I participated in two conversations with people from inland villages who
expressed skepticism about the meaning and purpose of the revival. As one
man put it, he felt some of the activities, such as a recent *kastom* festival,
were "without foundation" (*the'o nafugna*). Why, he wondered, should he

mobilize people from his village to contribute a pig for an activity which, as far as he could see, had little connection with the ongoing activities and concerns of his area? Another Cheke Holo person spoke in somewhat fearful tones about the motives of individuals associated with Tuti whom he saw as working to create positions of personal power.

These ambivalences, the "dilemma of dominance" discussed in chapter 4, are central to the emotional significance of chiefly leadership. As argued there (and in the classic "big-man" model), it is in the person of the chief or leader that ambivalence is resolved by framing postures of dominance as desirable or acceptable within the contexts of community goals and personal reputation. The challenge to the paramount chief status, and to other chiefly positions created in the bureaucratic idiom of "districts" and "councils," is to extend existing models of community to novel contexts in the contemporary milieu. Although such constructions are fragile and open to subversion from both within and without, their relative success in Santa Isabel is underwritten by the many regional histories of Christian conversion that valorize emergent island-wide identities in localized contexts.

In light of the potentials for dominance, conflict and suspicion in cultural models of chiefly leadership, we may now return to the question posed in the introductory chapter. How is it that the paramount chief ceremony, a novel and largely symbolic event, was able to generate such widespread interest and enthusiasm? Put somewhat differently: "How does the paramount chief constitute understandings of identity that resonate with the experience of people living in localized communities while still working in the arenas of national and international relations?"

It is here that the focus upon representational practices illuminates the processes that variously internalize and externalize models of identity. Theories of ritual (e.g., Turner 1969) have often noted the ability of ritual activities to link categories of identity with powerful emotions, but often focus on events defined as separate from more ordinary forms of discourse (cf. Connerton 1989). The range of practices surveyed in this volume allow no such boundary between ritualized and mundane practices, and much of the interpretation has drawn upon data from ordinary language and metaphor as well as specialized performances. Modern-day big-men and local ancestral heroes alike are objects of both conversational and ceremonial discourse articulating shared concerns with problems of interpersonal conflict and well-being.

The theme of personal vulnerability that frequently emerges in Cheke Holo talk finds a community parallel in narratives of victimization during the pre-Christian past. The mythic histories of conversion that circulate in Isabel villages tell a story that is simultaneously about the vulnerable self and the victimized community. Retelling accounts of past violence transformed by Christian mana and peace do not only recall an earlier time; they also reproduce models of and for lived experience. The Soga story draws upon those same models to give meaning to the novel event of installing a paramount chief, enlivening an emergent sense of island identity with emotions engendered in ancestral locales. The analogy between these historical narratives and mythology is suggested by the writings of both Malinowski (1954) and Leenhardt (1979) who well recognized the experiential dimensions of myth in the Melanesian world (cf. Young 1983).

Narrating historic moments of missionary contact and conversion renews cultural oppositions of *kastom* and Christianity in scenarios that replay the original incorporation of Christian knowledge and mana. Whereas European missionaries saw Cheke Holo heathens "coming out" (of darkness), Cheke Holo history tells a story of Christianity "coming in." The symbolic portrait of transformation represented in conversion histories is in fact reported as *experience* by many older Santa Isabel people who, in casual conversations, comment on a perceived shift in ethos during their own lives such that the constant vigilance which was once maintained against sorcery and tabu violation may now be somewhat relaxed. For example, a Kia man with whom I was talking in Buala village one day commented on this change in attitude when he observed my four-year-old son go off unattended. He remarked that when he was a young man people would not allow their children to wander alone in places other than their home village, lest bits of clothing or excrement be obtained by sorcerers wishing to harm them. But despite this man's optimistic assessment of present progress, the appearance of the *meomekro* ("crazy") revival movement in 1984 concerned with eradicating sorcery testifies to the continuing reality of dangerous spirit forces within the enchanted universe inhabited by most Cheke Holo speakers.

Conversion narratives also speak to a dilemma that the missionary experience poses for people who remain embedded within localized traditions of ancestry and place. The origin of Christian teaching in institutions dominated at first by Europeans holds the potential to subvert local discourses of knowledge and power. Consider, for example, the attitude of European missionaries who sought to destroy ancestral shrines, whereas the indigenous approach has been rather to bless or "baptize" them. In a different way, the various local histories of conversion offer parallel attempts to incorporate or mediate Christian knowledge through stories of transformation that recenter the process of change within localized histories of person and place. Not only do indigenous catechists become culture heroes, but "good chiefs" such as Matasi Iho are portrayed as catalysts for conversion or as *already* personifying Christian traits. An analog to these messages may now be found in the writings of some Cheke Holo students of Christian theology who are interpreting certain traditional practices as precursors of Christian faith. For example: "Even though we worshipped the ancestral spirits, the Christian Holy Spirit is part of the true God and we believe that behind those spirits was, as St. Paul puts it, 'the unknown God.' Indeed he was unknown simply because he was not yet to be known until the right time came and that was when Christianity arrived in the Pacific world" (Vilasa 1986: 65).

Such rhetorical strategies for finding Christianity in or "behind" the indigenous is analogous to attempts elsewhere in the Solomons and Melanesia to produce local cosmologies that replant the roots of religious knowledge and power in indigenous soil. Among the Kwara'ae of Malaita, for example, some people subscribe to the view that their first ancestor, Bilitigao, arrived on a raft called "Ark" about twenty generations ago and worshipped the Christian God, after which time subsequent generations lost the practice (Burt 1982: 385). A somewhat different but related strategy for recentering or reappropriating Christianity may be found in the movements begun by Silas Eto of New Georgia (Tuza 1977) and Moro of the Guadalcanal weather coast (Davenport and Coker 1967). Both of these men, charismatic leaders who established religious movements that have persisted over decades, had personal visionary experiences that subsumed elements of Christian knowledge within the framework of their ancestral religions. Each of their cosmologies, routinized in different ways over time, is concerned in some way with the problems of fragmentation and decentering posed by the challenge of "imported" Western or Christian knowledge to the legitimacy of local knowledge bound up in microtraditions of land, descent and chiefly leadership (cf. Lindstrom 1990).

The cosmological solutions of new religious movements in the Solomon Islands are similar in effect to the themes of deception that have been widely noted in "cargo cult" doctrines postulating that ancestral power and wealth have been co-opted by Europeans (see, e.g., Lawrence 1964; Schwartz 1973, among others). Like the rhetorical moves found in Isabel narratives that localize the origins of the church or find the Christian in the heathen, these doctrines constitute attempts to deal with the contradictions of imported ideology by making the "outside" "inside." Noting similarities between the historiography of Isabel conversion narratives and the doctrines of new religions or "cargo cults" suggests that this book's discussion of identity processes in Santa Isabel has much wider relevance, not only for other Pacific Island societies, but everywhere that people are engaged in reproducing ethnic and cultural identities through narratives of history, especially histories of colonial encounter. To move beyond reductions of either "cargo" or "resistance" and better understand the global resurgence of movements for cultural distinctiveness, we could do worse than to listen more carefully to the stories that people tell about their pasts, making identity through history.

Notes

2. First encounters

1. I decided to work with Ehamana's language group for the eminently practical reason that, of four major languages spoken on the island, his (Cheke Holo) is spoken by more than half of the total population (see White et al. 1988).
2. 1986 census statistics put the Isabel population at 14,616. With an estimated growth rate of 3.2 percent per annum, rapid increases in population density imply dramatic change in island demography in the not-so-distant future (Solomon Islands Statistics Office, Bulletin No. 3/88).
3. The only other church presence are the Seventh Day Adventists, limited primarily to two villages in the Bughotu region.

3. Portraits of the past

1. Based on a census I compiled in 1975, Togasalo is typical of eight villages surveyed. With a resident population of 648 people in those eight villages, I counted just 101 in twenty-four households in the largest village and 47 in eight households in the smallest.
2. Many people today hold the view that the ideal arrangement is for just *two* clans to inhabit the same region, forming an intermarrying pair. Whatever the extent of this type of dual organization in the past, it has long since been overtaken by events of migratory circulation. More often today one finds at least three clans present in any given region. The dominant view in Santa Isabel today is much the same as that stated by George Bogesi, an educated Bughotu man who wrote: "Nearly the whole island of Santa Isabel has only three clans" (1948: 213, cf. Rivers 1914: 245). But just which clans make up this trinity varies as one moves from one region to another throughout Maringe and Bughotu. In the area surrounding Vavarenitu and Togasalo, the three major clans are Nakmerufunei, Posamogo and Thauvia.

   The appropriateness of the traditional ideal of two intermarrying clans continues to surface in comments that, somehow, one of the three clans in a certain area is bogus or illegitimate, that it was "made up" at the whim of a chief, or in order to cover up an endogamous marriage. Even though strong feelings about the inappropriateness of endogamous marriage (*khabi*) remain, several cases cropped up in my census data. It is said that in the past anyone having sexual relations with someone of the same clan was subject to death at the command of chiefs.

3. Except for marrying outside one's clan, contemporary marriages do not adhere closely to narrow prescriptive rules. People I asked about marriage patterns in the past, when marriages were typically arranged by parents and elders, indicated that cross-cousin marriage was the ideal.

4. In anthropological parlance, Cheke Holo kinship terminology conforms to an Iroquois pattern.

5. The fact that Gebe begins his statement by contrasting the local ideology of matrilineality with biblical patriarchy reflects the way in which the encounter with Western ideas has evoked self-conscious commentaries about customary practices in Santa Isabel. There is, in fact, a considerable tradition of collective self-reflection about matters of descent and marriage in Santa Isabel, with topics such as clan identity and marriage rules taken up repeatedly in meetings of various sorts to examine their relevance in the context of contemporary society.

6. There are indications that myths of origin associated with the major Isabel clans partake in regionally distributed forms. I recorded an account of the beginning of the Posamogo clan from a Maringe man that closely mirrors a narrative recorded by Harold Scheffler on Choiseul (1965: 241).

7. It is not just anthropologists who evoke reconstructions of ritual sacrifice on the Knabu altars. Just ten years after Hudson Lagusu helped to re-enact the sacrificial scenario for me, he wrote a paper on the topic for his work at Pacific Theological College, a paper subsequently published under the title "Smoke and ashes for the Knabu gods" (Lagusu 1986).

8. The generic term for "spirit" (*na'itu*) in Cheke Holo takes numerous modifiers used to distinguish distinct types of spirit, including "forest spirits" (*na'itu mata*), "live spirits" (*na'itu kahra*) or "sea spirits" (*na'itu thongna*). Ancestor spirits were the focal, unmarked spirit beings, referred to simply as *na'itu*. However, at least since conversion to Christianity, the Bughotu word *tharunga* has been used extensively to refer to a person's spirit after death, as well as to the "holy spirit" (*tharunga te blahi*).

9. The intense ambivalence that marks relations between the living and the dead is coded in various traditional religious practices, particularly rites surrounding birth and death. At birth when newborn babies are felt to be most vulnerable to spirit attack, they would be hurriedly moved from the birthing hut to their home in the village, with lime powder thrown into the air by a priest to "cover the scent" of the baby so that spirits could not follow the baby back and cause illness. At the other end of the life-cycle, when a person died, relatives were said to "trick" the spirit into leaving the village, so that the living would not be endangered. I was told that one way of doing this was for someone to carry a sack of newly cooked food out into the forest and then heave it away in a remote area so that the spirit would follow it and not find its way back to the village.

10. However, when I did get a malaria-like illness just two days after returning to Vavarenitu, this was one explanation that was later offered. During the height of the sickness, Josepa (one of the shrine owners) was one of several healers who visited to offer a cure using *kastom* medicine.

11. Missionaries and early colonial representatives were often greeted and honored with gifts of shell valuables such as armlets, pendants, and porpoise teeth belts and bracelets, resulting in the removal of these icons of chiefly status from circulation – a practical reminder of the asymmetries that had intruded into the reciprocal pattern of *diklo* feasting.

12. I use the term "heathen" because it is often used locally when speaking in Pidgin or even Cheke Holo to refer to pre-Christian persons and practices. Despite its pejorative connotations (which may be more harsh among English speakers than among islanders who use the English terminology), the meanings of the English term are more in line with local usage than the alternative "pagan" preferred in many anthropological writings. Since much of this chapter is concerned with interpreting the social meanings of Christian and pre-Christian identities, it is hoped that a fuller picture than that communicated in a single label will emerge in the text.

13. Since the first Christian settlements were along the coast, much of the missionary work was aimed both "up" and "in" to high, interior regions. However, the verb used in the Knabu narrative and others like it to describe "going in" is that used to express entering a dwelling (*jugru* or *rumu*) rather than the directional verb "going toward the interior."

14. Among Cheke Holo speakers, metaphors of OPEN and CLOSED have felicitous ethnopsychological connotations pertaining to the social and emotional conditions associated with personal well-being. An "open" person is one free of internal conflicts or hidden bad feelings, as opposed to one who keeps moral conflict hidden inside, as a closed container (see White 1985a, 1989). The conceptual links between Christian metaphor and models of the person and experience infuse figurative speech with moral significance that goes well beyond their surface meanings.

15. I cannot say whether Gagai may in fact have been related, through marriage, to Knabu people. Since the Knabu had taken refuge for years near Gagai's home region of Bughotu, some intermarriage is possible.

4. Chiefs, persons and power

1. Many anthropological writers have disavowed talk of "chiefs" in favor of the big-man – Melanesia's contribution to the study of comparative political systems (Sahlins 1963; and see Lindstrom 1982a for a brief terminological history). Initially attractive as a way of dislodging unwanted connotations of inherited rank or ascribed title, the usefulness of the "big-man" as a regional type has declined as the diversity of Melanesian societies becomes more apparent.

    In Santa Isabel, both inherited (ascribed) and achieved criteria affect political fortunes. Status within a matrilineage, as a senior spokesman for a descent group, is a necessary but not sufficient condition for achieving recognition as a major chief. As Michael Allen has argued, "authority legitimation" in Melanesian political systems is likely to depend more upon cultural models of achievement, however that might be defined, than upon either ascriptive criteria or the extraction of resources from followers (1984: 35–6). If descent criteria were a sufficient condition for leadership status, we would expect to find that regional leaders are replaced by their sisters' sons, according to the matrilineal principle. But few people seem to expect that any such principle operates automatically. To the contrary, where ideas about succession emerge, they often pertain to the "replacement" of chiefly fathers by their sons, as in the case given at the end of this chapter.

2. There are legends in the Bughotu and Kia areas about the heroic actions of early ancestress-chiefs, such as Sumana of Zabana who is said to have led her people in a historic migration between those areas. These legends are seemingly

incongruous with the male-centered ideology of shrines and spirit powers. There are, however, also a small number of contemporary instances in which women have laid claim to chiefly status. It is my suspicion (and this is a topic deserving of careful research) that such claims remain an unrealized cultural potential; that there are no absolute barriers to women emerging as chiefs. But the elements of reputation, knowledge and social support that are required have traditionally been the province of male activity and knowledge. To a large extent, the institutions and practices of chiefly leadership described in this chapter, combined with the greater ability of men to circulate outside the island, reproduce the dominance of men in present-day political arenas. Additionally, local gender ideologies seem to draw distinctions between the procreative and nurturative powers of women such as those articulated in Jon Gebe's metaphors of matrilineality and the powers appropriated by men by virtue of their former roles in managing defense and ritual transactions.

3. The first Spanish explorers refer to a number of these forms in their description of a local chief who boarded their ship dressed in full ceremonial regalia: ". . . with many bracelets of bone [probably shell] upon his arms, and a plate of the same round his neck, and bracelets of very small stag's teeth [porpoise teeth?], and very small stones resembling coral [shell money]" (Amherst and Thomson 1901: 125). The chief described in this passage then proceeded to enact a ceremonial recognition of the Spanish leader's status by hanging a shell-disc around his neck and putting shell armlets on his arm (*ibid.*: 126). These actions seem to represent an attempt to establish relations with the newcomers according to local models of chiefly alliance.

4. One particular practice said to have been reserved for influential chiefs was that of calling for gifts or payments from others upon recovery from serious illness. This was done by sending a messenger with the chief's decorated walking stick to visit the settlements of his supporters (see also Naramana 1987: 46). Upon seeing the walking stick, it was expected that each group would offer up some gift in the form of food or valuables as a token of sympathy and support. This practice (called "sending a walking stick," *fatali phaki*) is indicative of the influence and even intimidation attributed to regional chiefs.

5. This finding is based on a lexical study using thirty-seven Cheke Holo terms (see White 1978 for details). By analyzing people's judgments about which terms are similar in meaning, it is possible to produce a picture of oppositional clusters of terms that reflect broad conceptual themes or dimensions. The resulting matrix of terms shows two major, cross-cutting themes: a dimension of "dominance/submission" formed by two opposed clusters ("strong"–"commanding"–"brave" versus "fearful"–"quiet"–"obedient") and a dimension of "solidarity/conflict" formed by another opposition ("sympathetic"–"kind" versus "recalcitrant"–"greedy" and the like).

5. Crisis and Christianity

1. It is difficult to estimate the extent of raiding prior to the period when documentary evidence is available, since the era of early contact was marked by a dramatic increase in the scale and frequency of raids. That increase is registered by local historians who assert that the headhunting upsurge represented a deviation from the mostly peaceful society that preceded it. Yet we know from the accounts of the first Spanish explorers that an extensive military capacity existed on Santa Isabel in 1568 (Amherst and Thomson 1901).

2. There is no indigenous name for the entire island, although the name of the peninsula at the southeastern tip, Bughotu, came into use when missionary work was begun there in the 1870s.
3. I am indebted to Michael Meeker for this insight into the strategic significance of canoes and their resulting association with wealth and power, having noted an analogy between the symbolism of war canoes in the Solomons and the camel in the Near East where camel-herding tribes tend to be regarded as the most fierce and inveterate raiders.
4. Information cited here from the Woodford Papers is derived from notes generously shared by Kim Jackson.
5. Following World War II the Seventh Day Adventist Mission made inroads on Santa Isabel with the conversion of a few Melanesian Mission adherents. The work of the S.D.A. church has over the years converted only two villages on the island.

6. Conversion and consolidation

1. This period was standardized by the mission at two years in 1911 (Melanesian Mission 1911: 172). For many people in the Maringe area, the texts of the new religion were not comprehended, since prayers, hymns and biblical passages were all learned in the language of Bughotu, the medium of mission instruction throughout the island. Since many did not know Bughotu, there were even fewer contradictions in assimilating the "new" ritual practices to established patterns. The Bible has not yet been fully translated into Cheke Holo; and it was not until 1973 that prayers were printed in Cheke Holo, and 1975 that the first hymnal (*Khoje Blahi ka Cheke Maringe*, literally, "Sacred Songs in the Maringe Language") was published.
2. Hebala here draws upon a fundamental image in local understandings of emotion. Sorcery wishes, in many ways the epitome of heathen practices, are lodged "inside" the person, "hidden in their hearts." To eradicate the sorcery threat, the person must "confess" (literally, "talk out") or reveal what has been kept inside (White 1985a, 1990). Note the homology between the *community* which must be "brought out into the open" and the *person* who must "confess" or expose hidden wishes. In both cases the relation of "heathen" and Christian is expressed in the metaphorical opposition of inside/outside (and hidden/visible).
3. One example given by Whiteman (1983: 352) is the case of two brothers and a sister accused of practicing sorcery. They are said to have all died within three months of kissing the Bible in one of Fr. Gnhokro's ceremonies.
4. Similar social processes associated with missionization were described by Hogbin for the neighboring island of Malaita. He observed that Christianity "... provided for broadening the concept of brotherhood until it embraces not only the inhabitants of neighboring settlements but also strangers" (1958: 182). However, he also noted that these were ideal conceptions which existed alongside notions of morality that remain locally contextualized.
5. Following Welchman, George Andrews took up residence on Mara na Tabu but died of "fever and dysentery' in 1912 (Melanesian Mission 1912: 205). Brother Edmond Bourne who had assisted Welchman then worked intermittently on the island along with Andrew Thomson who was based on Mara-na-Tabu from 1914 to 1917. Thomson was followed in 1919 by Rudolph Sprott and his wife, Emily. Sprott became the third priest of the Melanesian Mission to

die and be buried on the island in 1924. Emily Sprott, however, remained a prominent resident for the next twenty-five years, living on the mission-owned island of Tasia in the Maringe Lagoon during the 1930s and 1940s (see Fox 1958: 200).

6. The European priests spent a great deal of their time treating disease. Indeed, Henry Welchman was a trained physician. During his time on the island in the 1930s Richard Fallowes routinely listed in his diary the number of injections he administered as well as the number of people who received Communion. In one tour of the island in 1932, he visited seventeen villages, gave 300 injections and held Communion service for 1,600 (Diary: August 29, 1932). The demands of his doctoring were such that he lamented in a letter to his sister: "I fear that in the attempt to be both priest and doctor to the people I shall end in being an indifferent priest and an indifferent doctor" (Letter: May 1, 1931). Nonetheless, his medical healing must have had an inestimable confirming effect upon perceptions of his personal, spiritual power.

8. Missionary encounters: narrating the self

1. No doubt Hageria's own training as a priest contributed to the prominence of Christian prayer and priestly mana in his account of these events. Once inside the fort, Welchman's evening prayer is described as attracting attention and awe, particularly at the sight of his robe and eyeglasses. This scene is quite similar to the native amazement at Western clothing and other accoutrements mentioned in the discussion of comedy skits.

2. According to Welchman's diary as well as the local legends, Figrima presented his visitors with a pig and numerous baskets of food. Here, as in the Buala *bina boli*, Christianity is introduced in the context of a reciprocal exchange, particularly with the chief who acts as the host or sponsor. As such, the chief presents his guests with offerings of food in exchange for the "gift" of Christianity and its promise of peace.

3. Descendants of Figrima recall a large feast which he sponsored for Soga in about 1895, offering five pigs, food and shell valuables. The rationale was to form a defensive alliance such that Soga would "protect" (*fofotho*, from *fotho* "shut") against enemies approaching from the sea or from the west, while Figrima and others would defend Soga from attacks from the inland "side" (Naramana 1987).

4. I am indebted to Sherry Cox for listening to several *thautaru* songs and offering comments on their musical features.

5. Richard Naramana, nephew of the composer of this *thautaru*, kindly offered corrections and expansions on my initial translation.

6. For many Isabel communities such as the Knabu, the first moment of Christian encounter was not with a European, but with an indigenous missionary.

9. Collisions and convergence

1. Plant and others in the Melanesian Mission also referred to the Nggela parliament simply as the "Vaukolu," from the Nggela word for "meeting."

2. Presenting a sum of money to Woodford was in line with local expectations about the manner in which alliances are formed through gift exchange between chiefs. In particular, an ally who provides protection or other services would be given gifts of shell money or other valuables to signify the relationship. In later years, Lonsdale Soga organized a presentation of 200 pounds to their new ally's

war effort in World War I. This money was ultimately donated to the British Red Cross Fund (WPHC 4/II/10 1674: 1917).

3. The establishment of a government post on Santa Isabel coincided with the growing number of Europeans residing on the island. By 1915 there were twenty-five men, three women and one child on eighteen plantations. This compares with only three resident Europeans in 1975 (including the two of us).

4. Speakers of Cheke Holo were somewhat slow to participate in economic dealings with Westerners. But, with the introduction of the head tax in 1920, extensive plantings of coconut trees were begun. As reported by a district officer in 1925: "Native coconut plantations are being formed everywhere, and for natives extensive ones of 5 and 6 acres each, the trees being planted in regular order" (District officer, Santa Isabel to Resident Commissioner: WPHC 937/ 1925). Despite decline in the world economy, the 1930s saw a dramatic increase in local efforts to participate in the cash economy. By 1934, thirty village stores had been licensed to operate; and five years later the number had increased to fifty-three. And by 1937 there were fifty-seven launches registered to native owners (Isabel District Reports, 1935 and 1939: BSIP F14/7).

5. A list of the duties of church chiefs was compiled by the headman Walter Notere in his attempt to protest these developments. The "orders given by Fallowes" to the church chiefs were said to be (BSIP 479/33):

    (1) To help the teachers and to fix up any business reported to them by the teachers (catechists).
    (2) To see that the Church, School and Missionary's houses are kept clean.
    (3) To see that all children go to school and go to Church.
    (4) To tell all the people that they must work all Saturday cleaning around the Church.
    (5) To report any adultery or other business to Rado [Gado] who will in turn report to Fallowes.
    (6) If they find a man who is not "strong along mission" to report him.
    (7) To fix up anything which is not good along mission and to work hard in this respect.
    (8) To fix up all sins named in the Bible.

6. The certificate which served as a "license" for church chiefs was written as follows (Acting Commandant Armed Constabulary to Resident Commissioner, March 5, 1933: BSIP 479/33):

Melanesian Mission
This license authorises _____ to act as Church
Headman ... in the Village or DISTRICT of _____
X MERIVALE MELANESIA Date Dec 2nd 1931
Signed R. P. Fallowes District Priest

7. Fallowes saw adultery as "the great sin of Bugotu." Since there was, indeed, plenty of church work to be done in this area, sexuality became a disputed subject of mission and government authority. Fallowes insisted that sexual transgressions fell within the purview of the church. To demonstrate this, he introduced a new form of corporal punishment for adultery – whipping with a lawyer cane. Cases of adultery were reported by church chiefs and catechists to Fallowes who offered offenders the choice of receiving a public whipping or being suspended from attending church. It is vivid testimony to the seriousness

of church suspension that most offenders chose whipping as their punishment. In a few cases, Fallowes whipped people for offenses other than adultery, such as fighting. One young man was whipped for "speaking ill of the teacher in his village" (Fallowes, Diary: August 24, 1932).

Fallowes' use of physical punishment angered the government headman Notere who saw such coercive sanctions as the sole province of government. His complaints ultimately led to a legal trial for Fallowes. His whippings were investigated by the government in 1933, with the result that he was charged with fourteen counts of assault. After statements had been considered from several recipients of beatings, most of whom did not wish to give testimony against Fallowes, he was found guilty on three counts where it was ruled that consent had been induced by threat. He was fined 10 shillings for each (Legal advisor to Resident Commissioner, June, 1933: BSIP F43/14).

8. Fallowes also worried that Notere had a hostile attitude toward the mission. He discussed Notere's position with district officer Wilfred Fowler and argued: "He has undoubtedly usurped powers which do not belong to him" ("Diary": November 2, 1931). He also confronted Notere directly, warning him "about his conduct toward the Church" ("Diary": July 16, 1932); and he publicly urged people on at least two occasions to ignore tabus which Notere had placed on betel palms and reef waters ("Diary": June 20 and September 20, 1932).

9. This task was done with the same twenty-nine people asked to characterize the "Christian person" (chapter 4). I asked them to describe a "Christian person" after they had characterized the different types of big-men.

10. The matrix of derived similarity measures among all pairs of status categories was analyzed with multidimensional scaling and hierarchical clustering techniques (Kruskal, Young and Seery 1973; D'Andrade 1978). Scaling depicts similarity among the statuses in terms of spatial distance, such that similar categories are positioned closer together. The clustering technique operates by successively grouping the most similar statuses in a hierarchical arrangement of nested sets (indicated in figure 2 by lines drawn around the most similar items).

11. Another apparent exception to the government/church dichotomy is the "teacher." Although informants were asked to interpret this category as the contemporary school teachers who often play important roles in community life, the term is also still used to refer to catechists who, after all, were the first teachers in the early village church schools.

12. Because the clustering technique is unable to draw overlapping circles (i.e., nonhierarchical clusters), it masks this cross-cutting pattern due to the overriding pull from associations with church-type and government-type big-men in the two large clusters. The clustering process begins with the most similar statuses, and then encircles successively larger groupings at somewhat weaker levels of similarity. At the highest level, the hierarchical structure may be unable to represent similarities that cross-cut clusters already formed.

13. Grouping together the status types in each of the two opposed clusters, it is possible to assess the degree to which each descriptive term is associated significantly more with one set of leaders than the other, thus differentiating the two sets. Since there are five categories in each cluster, an informant could use any given trait up to five times in characterizing the statuses in each cluster. The average frequency (across all informants) with which each trait was used to characterize the church statuses can be compared with the average frequency with which it was attributed to the government statuses by using a paired t-test

of means (ranging between 0 and 5). Computing the same measure for the three statuses that are strictly church statuses (bishop, priest and catechist) in comparison with the three statuses that are strictly government statuses (headman, councilor and committee) produces the same result, with even stronger contrasts (see White 1980b).

10. The paramount chief: rites of renewal

1. Fallowes' particular interest in strengthening the mission on this occasion was connected with the arrival of a Seventh Day Adventist teacher (a man named Tutua from the neighboring island of Choiseul) to gain converts in Kia. He had in fact gained adherents among one family who, when queried by Fallowes, said they were interested in learning to read and write English – something offered by the S.D.A. teacher. Fallowes, with support from the government district officer, Wilfred Fowler, held an inquiry into the matter and convinced the family in question to return to the Anglican fold.

2. A close reading of this genealogy may pose the question: "How is it that Lonsdale Gado and Monilaws Soga, two men identified with Sepi village in Bughotu, are related to two prominent men in Kia village at the extreme opposite end of the island?" A large segment of this lineage migrated from Kia to Bughotu in the mid-nineteenth century. Because its descendants are recognized as the last representatives of a major, chiefly lineage, several members, including Tuti's mother and great-uncle, Edmund Bako, were "spirited away" back to Kia where they married back into the community there.

3. Led by the younger members of the Isabel council, all the councilors except the president and one other absented themselves from participation in the installation portion of the Sepi ceremony. However, a number of organizers of the ceremony hurriedly found the president so that he could make the necessary offerings on this occasion. He was later asked to apologize to the council for his actions.

References

Alasia, Sam 1989. Politics, in *Ples Blong Iumi: Solomon Islands, The Past Four Thousand Years*, H. Laracy, ed. Suva: Institute of Pacific Studies.

Allen, Michael 1984. Elders, chiefs, and big men: authority legitimation and political evolution in Melanesia, *American Ethnologist* 11: 20–41.

Amherst of Hackney, Lord, and B. Thomson, eds. 1901. *The Discovery of the Solomon Islands*. London: The Hakluyt Society.

Armstrong, E.S. 1900. *The History of the Melanesian Mission*. London: Isbister and Co., Ltd.

Babadzan, A. 1988. *Kastom* and nation-building in the South Pacific, in *Ethnicities and Nations: Processes of Interethnic Relations in Latin America, Southeast Asia, and the Pacific*. Houston, TX: Rothko Chapel and University of Texas Press.

Basso, Keith H. 1979. *Portraits of "the Whiteman": Linguistic Play and Cultural Symbols Among the Western Apache*. Cambridge University Press.

Bauman, Richard 1986. *Story, Performance and Event. Contextual Studies of Oral Narrative*. Cambridge University Press.

Bellah, R.N., R. Madsen, W. Sullivan, A. Swidler and S. Tipton 1985. *Habits of the Heart: Individualism and Commitment in American Life*. Berkeley: University of California Press.

Belshaw, Cyril S. 1950. The significance of modern cults in Melanesian development, *Australian Outlook* 4: 116–25.

Bennett, Judith 1987. *Wealth of the Solomons: A History of a Pacific Archipelago, 1800–1978*. Honolulu: University of Hawaii Press.

Berger, Peter L. and Thomas Luckmann 1967. *The Social Construction of Reality*. New York: Doubleday.

Biersack, Aleta, ed. 1991. *Clio in Oceania: Toward a Historical Anthropology*. Washington, DC: Smithsonian Institution Press.

Blu, Karen 1980. *The Lumbee Problem: The Making of an American Indian People*. Cambridge University Press.

Bogesi, George 1948. Santa Ysabel, Solomon Islands, *Oceania* 18: 208–32, 327–57.

Borofsky, Robert 1987. *Making History: Pukapukan and Anthropological Constructions of Knowledge*. Cambridge University Press.

Bourdieu, Pierre 1977. *Outline of a Theory of Practice*. Cambridge University Press.

Brenchley, Julius L. 1873. *Jottings during the Cruise of the H.M.S. Curaçoa among the South Sea Islands in 1865.* London: Longmans, Green and Co.

Bruner, E.M. 1986. Ethnography as narrative, in *The Anthropology of Experience*, V.W. Turner and E.M. Bruner, eds. Urbana: University of Illinois Press.

BSIP (British Solomon Islands Protectorate) 1921–42. Annual and Quarterly Reports of the Santa Isabel District Office. Honiara: Solomon Islands National Archives.

BSIP 1907–42. General Correspondence of the Office of the Resident Commissioner. Honiara: Solomon Islands National Archives.

Burt, Ben 1982. Kastom, Christianity and the first ancestor of the Kwara'ae of Malaita, in *Reinventing Traditional Culture: The Politics of Kastom in Island Melanesia*, R. Keesing and R. Tonkinson, eds. *Mankind* 13: 374–99.

Carrier, James, ed. n.d. *Tradition and History in Melanesian Anthropology*. Berkeley: University of California Press (in press).

Chapman, Murray and Peter Pirie 1974. *Tasi Mauri: A Report on Population and Resources of the Guadalcanal Weather Coast*. Honolulu: East–West Center.

Clifford, James 1988. *The Predicament of Culture: Twentieth-Century Ethnography, Literature, and Art.* Harvard University Press.

Clifford, James and George Marcus, eds. 1986. *Writing Culture: The Poetics and Politics of Ethnography*. Berkeley: University of California Press.

Codrington, R.H. 1891. *The Melanesians: Studies in Their Anthropology and Folklore.* Oxford: Clarendon Press.

Connerton, Paul 1989. *How Societies Remember*. Cambridge University Press.

Coote, Walter 1883. *The Western Pacific*. London: Sampson Low, Marsten, Searle and Rivingston.

Crapanzano, Vincent 1990. On self characterization, in *Cultural Psychology: Essays on Comparative Human Development*, J. Stigler, R. Shweder and G. Herdt, eds. Cambridge University Press.

D'Andrade, Roy G. 1978. U-statistic hierarchical clustering, *Psychometrika* 43: 59–67.

Davenport, W. and G. Coker 1967. The Moro movement of Guadalcanal, British Solomon Islands Protectorate, *Journal of the Polynesian Society* 76: 123–75.

Dening, Greg 1980. *Islands and Beaches: Discourse on a Silent Land. Marquesas 1774–1880.* Honolulu: University of Hawaii Press.

Douglas, Bronwen 1979. Rank, power, authority: a reassessment of traditional leadership in South Pacific societies, *Journal of Pacific History* 14(1): 2–27.

   1982. "Written on the ground": spatial symbolism, cultural categories and historical process in New Caledonia, *Journal of the Polynesian Society* 91: 383–415.

Dumont, Louis 1970. *Homo Hierarchicus*, Mark Sainsbury, trans. University of Chicago Press (original French edition, 1966).

Errington, Fred 1974. Indigenous ideas of order, time, and transition in a New Guinea cargo movement, *American Ethnologist* 1: 255–67.

Fallowes, Richard 1929–34. Letters to his sister. Canberra: National Library of Australia, ms. 2478.

   1931–4. Diary. Canberra: National Library of Australia, ms. 2478.

   1975–6. Correspondence with the author.

Fiji Agent of General Immigration 1876–1914. *Journals of Government Agents*, 67 vols. Suva: Central Archives of Fiji.

Fleurieu, M.L.C. de 1791. *Discoveries of the French in 1768 and 1769 to the Southeast of New Guinea*. London. Printed for John Stockdale.

Fowler, Wilfred 1959. *This Island's Mine*. London: The Adventurers Club.

Fox, Charles E. 1958. *Lord of the Southern Isles: Being the Story of the Anglican Mission in Melanesia 1849–1949*. London: A.R. Mowbray.

Fox, James J. 1980. Retelling the past: the communicative structure of a Rotinese historical narrative, *Canberra Anthropology* 3(1): 56–66.

Geertz, Clifford 1984. "From the native's point of view": on the nature of anthropological understanding, in *Culture Theory: Essays on Mind, Self and Emotion*, R. Shweder and R. LeVine, eds. (originally published 1974).

Gergen, Kenneth 1990. Social understanding and the inscription of self, in *Cultural Psychology: Essays on Comparative Human Development*, J. Stigler, R. Shweder and G. Herdt, eds. Cambridge University Press.

Gewertz, Deborah 1983. *Sepik River Societies: A Historical Ethnography of the Chambri and Their Neighbors*. New Haven: Yale University Press.

Goldie, J. 1914. The Solomon Islands, in *A Century of the Pacific*, J. Colwell, ed. Sydney: Beale.

Guiart, Jean 1970. The millennarian aspect of conversion to Christianity in the South Pacific, in *Millennial Dreams in Action*, S.L. Thrupp, ed. New York: Schocken Books.

Hallowell, A.I. 1967. The self and its behavioral environment, in *Culture and Experience*. New York: Schocken Books (originally published in 1954).

Handelman, D. 1981. The ritual clown: attributes and affinities, *Anthropos* 76: 321–70.

Handler, Richard and Jocelyn Linnekin 1983. Tradition, genuine or spurious, *Journal of American Folklore* 97: 273–90.

Hanlon, David 1988. *Upon a Stone Altar: A History of the Island of Pohnpei to 1890*. Honolulu: University of Hawaii Press.

Hanson, Alan 1989. The making of the Maori: culture invention and its logic, *American Anthropologist* 91: 890–902.

Hau'ofa, Epeli 1975. Anthropology and Pacific Islanders, *Oceania* 45: 283–9.

Hereniko, Vilsoni 1991. Polynesian clowns and satirical comedies. Unpublished Ph.D. dissertation. University of the South Pacific.

Hezel, Francis X. 1988. New directions in Pacific history: a practitioner's critical view, *Pacific Studies* 11(3): 101–10.

Hill, Jane n.d. The cultural (?) context of narrative involvement. Unpublished manuscript.

Hilliard, David 1974. Colonialism and Christianity: the Melanesian Mission in the Solomon Islands, *Journal of Pacific History* 9: 93–116.

   1978. *God's Gentleman: A History of the Melanesian Mission 1849–1942*. St. Lucia: University of Queensland Press.

Hocart, A. M. 1922. Cult of the dead on Eddystone, *Journal of the Royal Anthropological Institute* 61: 301–24.

   1931. Warfare in Eddystone of the Solomons, *Journal of the Royal Anthropological Institute* 61: 301–24.

Hogbin, H. Ian 1958. *Social Change*. London: Watts.

   1964. *Guadalcanal Society: The Kaoka Speakers*. New York: Holt, Rinehart and Winston.

1970. *Experiments in Civilization.* New York: Schocken Books (originally published 1939).

Holland, Dorothy and Naomi Quinn, eds. 1987. *Cultural Models in Language and Thought.* Cambridge University Press.

Hopkins, A.I. 1928. *In the Isles of King Solomon: An Account of Twenty-Five Years Spent Amongst the Primitive Solomon Islanders.* Philadelphia: J.B. Lippincott Company.

Jack-Hinton, C. 1969. *The Search for the Islands of Solomon, 1567–1838.* Oxford: Clarendon.

Jackson, Kim B. 1975. Head-hunting and the Christianization of Bugotu, 1861–1900, *Journal of Pacific History* 10: 65–78.

Jameson, Frederic 1981. *The Political Unconscious: Narrative as a Socially Symbolic Act.* Cornell University Press.

Jolly, Margaret 1990. Custom and the way of the land: the politics of tradition in Vanuatu and Fiji. Paper read at meetings of the Association for Social Anthropology in Oceania, Kauai, HI.

Jules-Rosette, Bennetta 1975. The conversion experience: the apostles of John Maranke, *Journal of Religion in Africa* 7: 132–64.

Keesing, Roger M. 1978. Politico-religious movements and anticolonialism on Malaita: Maasina Rule in historical perspective, *Oceania* 48: 241–61; 49: 46–73.

1980. Antecedents of Maasina Rule: some further notes, *Journal of Pacific History* 13(2): 1–6.

1982. *Kwaio Religion: The Living and the Dead in a Solomon Island Society.* New York: Columbia University Press.

1985. Killers, big-men, and priests on Malaita: reflections on a Melanesian troika system, *Ethnology* 24: 237–52.

1989. Creating the past: custom and identity in the Pacific, *The Contemporary Pacific* 1–2: 16–35.

Keesing, Roger M. and Peter Corris 1980. *Lightning Meets the East Wind: The Malaita Massacre.* Oxford University Press.

Keesing, Roger M. and Robert Tonkinson, eds. 1982. *Reinventing Traditional Culture: The Politics of Kastom in Island Melanesia. Mankind* (Special Issue) vol. 13, no. 4.

Kirkpatrick, John 1981. Appeals for "unity" in Marquesan local politics, *Journal of the Polynesian Society* 90: 439–64.

1983. *The Marquesan Notion of the Person.* Ann Arbor: UMI Research Press.

Kirkpatrick, John and Geoffrey M. White 1985. Exploring ethnopsychologies, in *Person, Self and Experience: Exploring Pacific Ethnopsychologies,* G.M. White and J. Kirkpatrick, eds. Berkeley: University of California Press.

Kondo, Dorinne K. 1990. *Crafting Selves: Power, Gender and Discourses of Identity in a Japanese Workplace.* University of Chicago Press.

Kruskal, J.B., F.W. Young and J.B. Seery 1973. *How to Use KYST, a Very Flexible Program to do Multidimensional Scaling and Unfolding.* Murray Hill, NJ: Bell Laboratories.

Lagusu, Hudson 1986. Smoke and ashes for the Knabu gods, in *Pacific Rituals: Living or Dying.* Suva: Institute of Pacific Studies.

Laracy, Hugh M. 1976. *Marists and Melanesians: A History of Catholic Missions in the Solomon Islands.* Canberra: Australian National University Press.

1983. *Pacific Protest: Maasina Rule Movement, Solomon Islands, 1944–1952.* Suva, Fiji: Institute of Pacific Studies.

Lawrence, Peter 1964. *Road Belong Cargo.* Manchester University Press.

Lederman, Rena 1986. Changing times in Mendi: notes towards writing Highland New Guinea history, *Ethnohistory* 33(1): 1–30.

Leenhardt, Maurice 1979. *Do Kamo: Person and Myth in the Melanesian World.* University of Chicago Press (original French edition, 1947).

Levy, Robert 1973. *The Tahitians: Mind and Experience in the Society Islands.* University of Chicago Press.

Lindstrom, Lamont 1982a. Bigman: a short terminological history, *American Anthropologist* 83: 900–5.

1982b. Leftamap kastom: the political history of tradition on Tanna (Vanuatu), in *Reinventing Traditional Culture: The Politics of Kastom in Island Melanesia,* R. Keesing and R. Tonkinson, eds. *Mankind* 13(4): 316–29.

1990. *Knowledge and Power in a South Pacific Society.* Washington, D.C.: Smithsonian Institution Press.

Linnekin, Jocelyn 1990. The politics of culture in the Pacific, in *Cultural Identity and Ethnicity in the Pacific.* Honolulu: University of Hawaii Press.

Linnekin, Jocelyn and Lin Poyer, eds. 1990. *Cultural Identity and Ethnicity in the Pacific.* Honolulu: University of Hawaii Press.

Loiskandl, Helmut H. 1988. Melanesian identity in the making: competing ideologies in a Melanesian elite, *Man and Culture in Oceania* 4: 111–28.

Lutz, Catherine 1988. *Unnatural Emotions: Everyday Sentiments on a Micronesian Atoll and Their Challenge to Western Theory.* University of Chicago Press.

MacQuarrie, Hector 1946. *Vouza and the Solomon Islands.* Sydney: Angus and Robertson.

Malinowski, Bronislaw 1954. Myth in primitive psychology, in *Magic, Science and Religion and other Essays.* New York: Doubleday (originally published 1926).

Marcus, George E. 1988. Review of *Transformations of Polynesian Culture,* A. Hooper and J. Huntsman, eds. Auckland: The Polynesian Society (1985), *Pacific Studies* 11: 111–23.

Mauss, M. 1938. Une catégorie de l'esprit humain: la notion de personne, celle de moi, *Journal of the Royal Anthropological Institute* 68: 263–81.

McDowell, Nancy 1985. Past and future: the nature of episodic time in Bun, in *History and Ethnohistory in Papua New Guinea.* Oceania Monograph No. 28. Sydney: Oceania Publications.

McKinnon, J. 1975. Tomahawks, turtles and traders, *Oceania* 45: 290–307.

Mead, George Herbert 1934. *Mind, Self, and Society.* University of Chicago Press.

Melanesian Mission 1895–1946. *Southern Cross Log.* Auckland, Australia and New Zealand edition.

1900–1947. *Southern Cross Log.* London: English edition.

Meleisea, Malama 1987. Ideology in Pacific studies: a personal view, in *Class and Culture in the South Pacific,* A. Hooper et al., eds. Suva: Institute of Pacific Studies.

Miller, J., R. Potts, H. Fung, L. Hoogstra and J. Mintz 1990. Narrative practices and the social construction of self in childhood, *American Ethnologist* 17: 292–311.

Monberg, Torben 1962. Crisis and mass conversion on Rennell Island in 1938, *Journal of the Polynesian Society* 71(2): 145–50.

Morrell, W.P. 1960. *Britain in the Pacific Islands*. Oxford: Clarendon Press.

Naramana, Richard Basil 1987. Elements of culture in Hograno/Maringe, Santa Ysabel, *'O'O: Journal of Solomon Islands Studies* 1(3): 41–57.

Oliver, Douglas L. 1955. *A Solomon Island Society: Kinship and Leadership Among the Siuai of Bougainville*. Boston: Beacon Press.

Parmentier, Richard J. 1987. *The Sacred Remains: Myth, History, and Polity in Belau*. University of Chicago Press.

Penny, Arthur 1876–88. Diary. 11 volumes. Sydney: Mitchell Library, B807–17.

1888. *Ten Years in Melanesia*. London: Wells Gardner, Darton and Co.

Peterson, Nicolas 1965–6. The church council of South Mala: a legitimized form of Masinga Rule, *Oceania* 36: 214–30.

Quinn, Naomi and Dorothy Holland 1987. Culture and cognition, in *Cultural Models in Language and Thought*. Cambridge University Press.

Read, Kenneth E. 1955. Morality and the concept of the person among the Gahuku-Gama, *Oceania* 25: 233–82.

1959. Leadership and consensus in a New Guinea society, *American Anthropologist* 61: 425–36.

Riesenfeld, Alphonse 1950. *The Megalithic Culture of Melanesia*. Leiden: E.J. Brill.

Rivers, W.H.R. 1914. *The History of Melanesian Society*, Vol. I. Cambridge University Press.

Rosaldo, Michelle Z. 1980. *Knowledge and Passion: Ilongot Notions of Self and Social Life*. Cambridge University Press.

Rosaldo, Renato 1980. *Ilongot Headhunting 1883–1974: A Study in Society and History*. Stanford University Press.

Sahlins, Marshall 1963. Poor man, rich man, big man, chief: Political types in Melanesia and Polynesia, *Comparative Studies in Society and History* 5: 285–303.

1985. *Islands of History*. University of Chicago Press.

Scheffler, Harold W. 1965. *Choiseul Island Social Structure*. Berkeley: University of California Press.

Schwartz, Theodore 1973. Cult and context: the paranoid ethos in Melanesia, *Ethos* 1: 153–74.

Sherzer, Joel 1988. A discourse-centered approach to language and culture, *American Anthropologist* 89: 295–309.

Shineberg, Dorothy, ed. 1971. *The Trading Voyages of Andrew Cheyne, 1841–44*. Canberra: Australian National University Press.

Shore, Bradd 1982. *Sala'ilua: A Samoan Mystery*. New York: Columbia University Press.

1991. Twice-born, once conceived: meaning-construction and cultural cognition, *American Anthropologist* 93: 9–27.

Shweder, Richard and Robert LeVine, eds. 1984 *Culture Theory: Essays on Mind, Self and Emotion*. Cambridge University Press.

Sinavaiana, Caroline n.d. Where the spirits laugh last: comic theater in Samoa, in *Clowning as Critical Practice: Performance Humor in the South Pacific*, W. Mitchell, ed. (forthcoming).

Somerville, H.T. 1897. Ethnographical notes in New Georgia, Solomon Islands, *Journal of the Royal Anthropological Institute* 26: 357–412.

Strathern, Marilyn 1988. *The Gender of the Gift: Problems With Women and Problems With Society in Melanesia*. Berkeley: University of California Press.

Stromberg, Peter 1990. Ideological language in the transformation of identity, *American Anthropologist* 92: 42–56.

Taylor, Charles 1979. Interpretation and the sciences of man, in *Interpretive Social Science*, P. Rabinow and W. Sullivan, eds. Berkeley: University of California Press (originally published 1971).

Thomas, Nicholas 1991. Alejandro Mayta in Fiji: narratives about millenarianism, colonialism and post-colonial politics, in *Clio in Oceania: Toward a Historical Anthropology*, A. Biersack, ed. Washington, DC: Smithsonian Institution Press.

Thomson, Andrew 1914–17. Unpublished diary. Jejevo, Santa Isabel: Bishop's House.

Tippett, Alan R. 1967. *Solomon Islands Christianity*. London: Lutterworth Press.

Toren, Christina 1989. Making the present, revealing the past: the mutability and continuity of tradition as process, *Man* 23: 696–717.

Turner, Victor 1969. Forms of symbolic action: introduction, in *Forms of Symbolic Action*, R.F. Spencer, ed. Seattle and London: American Ethnological Society, pp. 3–25.

Tuza, Esau 1977. Silas Eto of New Georgia, in *Prophets of Melanesia*, G. Trompf, ed., pp. 65–88. Port Moresby: Institute of Papua New Guinea Studies.

Valentine, D.A. 1963. Men of anger and men of shame: Lakalai ethnopsychology and its implications for sociopsychological theory, *Ethnology* 1: 441–77.

Vilasa, Ezekiel 1986. The fafara ritual of Santa Ysabel, in *Pacific Rituals: Living or Dying*. Suva: Institute of Pacific Studies.

Wagner, Roy 1975. *The Invention of Culture*. University of Chicago Press.

Wallace, Anthony F.C. 1956. Revitalization movements, *American Anthropologist* 58: 264–81.

    1967. Identity processes in personality and in culture, in *Cognition, Personality and Clinical Psychology*, R. Jessor and S. Feshbach, eds., pp. 62–89. San Francisco: Jossey-Bass, Inc.

Watson, James B. 1967. Tairora: the politics of despotism in a small society, *Anthropological Forum* 2: 53–104.

Wawn, William T. 1893. *The South Sea Islanders and the Queensland Labour Trade*. London: Swan Sonnenschein & Co.

Welchman, Henry 1889–1908. Diary, Missionary Life in the Melanesian Islands. 12 volumes. Canberra: National Library of Australia microfilm m728, 805–6.

Wendt, Albert 1987. Novelists and historians and the art of remembering, in *Class and Culture in the South Pacific*, A. Hooper et al., eds. Suva: Institute of Pacific Studies.

Wertsch, James, ed. 1985. *Culture, Communication and Cognition: Vygotskian Perspectives*. Cambridge University Press.

WPHC (Western Pacific High Commission) 1875–1941. Inward correspondence, general. Honiara: Solomon Islands National Archives

    1942–54. General correspondence, F. series. Honiara: Solomon Islands National Archives

White, Geoffrey M. 1978. Ambiguity and ambivalence in A'ara personality descriptors, *American Ethnologist* 5: 334–60.

    1979. War, peace and piety in Santa Isabel, Solomon Islands, in *The Pacification of Melanesia*, M. Rodman and M. Cooper, eds. Ann Arbor: University of Michigan Press.

1980a. Conceptual universals in interpersonal language, *American Anthropologist* 82: 759–81.

1980b. Social images and social change in a Melanesian society, *American Ethnologist* 7: 352–70.

1985a. Premises and purposes in a Solomon Islands ethnopsychology, in *Person, Self and Experience: Exploring Pacific Ethnopsychologies*, G. White and J. Kirkpatrick, eds. Berkeley: University of California Press.

1985b. "Bad ways" and "bad talk": interpretations of interpersonal conflict in a Melanesian society, in *Directions in Cognitive Anthropology*, J. Dougherty, ed. Urbana: University of Illinois Press.

1988. Symbols of solidarity in the Christianization of Santa Isabel, Solomon Islands, in *Culture and Christianity: The Dialectics of Transformation*, G. Saunders, ed. Wesport, CT: Greenwood Press.

1989. Narrating history, constructing selves: wartime encounters in Santa Isabel, in *The Pacific Theater: Island Representations of World War II*, G. White and L. Lindstrom, eds. Honolulu: University of Hawaii Press.

1990. Emotion talk and social inference: disentangling in Santa Isabel, Solomon Islands, in *Disentangling: Conflict Discourse in Pacific Societies*, K. Watson-Gegeo and G. White, eds. Stanford University Press.

White, Geoffrey M. and John Kirkpatrick, eds. 1985. *Person, Self and Experience: Exploring Pacific Ethnopsychologies*. Berkeley: University of California Press.

White, Geoffrey M., Francis Kokhonigita and Hugo Pulomana 1988. *Cheke Holo Dictionary*. Canberra: Pacific Linguistics, Series C. No. 97.

White, Hayden 1990. *The Content of the Form: Narrative Discourse and Historical Representation*. Baltimore, MD: Johns Hopkins University Press.

Whiteman, Darrell L. 1983. *Melanesians and Missionaries: An Ethnohistorical Study of Socio-Religious Change in the Southwest Pacific*. Pasadena: William Carey Library.

Wilson, Ellen 1935. *Welchman of Bugotu*. London: Society for Promoting Christian Knowledge.

Woodford, Charles M. n.d. Papers. Canberra: Department of Pacific and Southeast Asian History, Australian National University.

1890. *A Naturalist Among the Headhunters*. London: G. Philip.

1909. The canoes of the British Solomon Islands Protectorate, *Journal of the Royal Anthropological Institute* 39: 506–16.

Worsley, Peter 1968. *The Trumpet Shall Sound: A Study of "Cargo Cults" in Melanesia*. New York: Schocken Books.

Young, Michael W. 1977. Doctor Bromilow and the Bwaidoka wars, *Journal of Pacific History* 12: 130–53.

1983. *Magicians of Manumanua: Living Myth in Kalauna*. Berkeley: University of California Press.

Zelenietz, Martin 1979. The end of headhunting in New Georgia, in *The Pacification of Melanesia*, M. Rodman and M. Cooper, eds. Ann Arbor: University of Michigan Press.

Zeva, Ben 1983. Church and state on Isabel, in *Solomon Islands Politics*. Suva: Institute of Pacific Studies.

Index

Cambridge Studies in
Social and Cultural Anthropology

Editors: ERNEST GELLNER, JACK GOODY, STEPHEN GUDEMAN, MICHAEL HERZFELD, JONATHAN PARRY